A CONCISE HISTORY OF THE MODERN WORLD

A Concise History of the Modern World

1500 to the Present

William Woodruff

Graduate Research Professor in Economic History
University of Florida, Gainesville

First edition 1991
Second edition 1993

 Published by
MACMILLAN PRESS LTD
Houndmills, Basingstoke, Hampshire RG21 6XS
and London
Companies and representatives
throughout the world

ISBN 0–333–54727–6 hardcover
ISBN 0–333–60412–1 paperback

A catalogue record for this book is available
from the British Library.

10   9   8   7   6   5   4   3
03   02   01   00   99   98   97   96

Printed in Great Britain by
Ipswich Book Company Ltd
        Ipswich, Suffolk

 Published in the United States of America 1991 by
ST MARTIN'S PRESS, INC.,
Scholarly and Reference Division
175 Fifth Avenue, New York, N. Y. 10010

ISBN 0–312–09962–2

In memory of
Hedwig and Richard
and
Anne and William

Contents

List of Maps

Preface

This overview of world history since AD 1500, with its underlying theme of shifting global power, is the result of a lifetime's work. It tells in short compass how the modern world has come to be what it is. That is why I have placed special emphasis on the period since 1914. To sharpen the focus of this ecumenical study, I have adopted a topical as well as a chronological approach.

In our present dramatic phase of world history – marked as it is by the revolutionary movements taking place throughout Europe and the Soviet Union, and with war in the Middle East – there is an urgent need to see events in the broader setting of world change.

In emphasizing the study of humanity as a whole, this volume continues the work that I began in *Impact of Western Man* in 1966. It was then that the words of the poet John Donne came to have special significance for me: "No man is an island entire of itself, every man is part of the main." Every nation, like every man, has become part of the main. While not denying the uniqueness of national or regional history, or the indisputable contribution made by historical minutae, I felt, as I feel now, that the growing communality and interdependence of nations justifies taking the wider view.

To provide insights into five hundred years of world history and put them into compact form has not been easy; making sense of great masses of material never is. No matter how much one tries to avoid it, some items will invariably be given more, some less attention than they deserve; the tendency will be to present history as much more uni-directional and continuous than events in the real world confirm. Of necessity, the historian's desire to elaborate runs contrary to the need for brevity. In sifting the wheat from the chaff, I have followed the maxim of Voltaire. "Les détails qui ne mènent à rien sont dans l'histoire ce que sont les bagages dans une

armée, *impedimenta;* il faut voir les choses en grand."
[Meaningless details in history are like the baggage
of an army: *impedimenta;* one must take the wider
view.] Details are not ends in themselves.

In placing history in a global setting, I have been helped
by scholars in many parts of the world. My debt in knowledge and inspiration (as the acknowledgements in previous volumes and the footnotes and bibliography of this
book make abundantly clear) is considerable. I especially
wish to thank Professors David Carneiro, Tsuyoshi Hara,
G.S. Maddala, Neill Macaulay, David Niddrie, Yoshitaka
Komatsu, Takashi Kotono, and Hernan Vera for reading
and criticizing parts of the present work. None of them, of
course, bear any responsibility for the use I have made or
failed to make of their specialized knowledge.

I should also like to thank my research assistants John
Philips and Michael Gamble for their untiring help and
diligence.

My debt to Helga, as always, is immeasurable.

William Woodruff
University of Florida at Gainesville
February 1991

1

Origin of our Times: An Asian-dominated World

The purpose of this book is to provide an overview of world history from AD 1500 to the present. In a global age the need for historical understanding is both vital and pressing. Only by using the past to cast light on the present[1] can we hope to know how the world has come to be what it is and where it might be headed.

In investigating the course of world affairs since roughly 1500, special emphasis has been placed upon the struggle for power – by which is meant the use of organized force of one sovereign state to impose its will upon another. Perhaps the greatest difficulty in this task is the illusive nature of power itself. There is no clear-cut line which enables us to separate one kind of power from another. On the evidence of the past 500 years, it is chiefly military force which has prevailed. "War," said Heraclitus, "is the father of all." Certainly, war has been the midwife of the modern age.

The perpetual aggressiveness of both individuals and states underlies all history. It is the underlying theme of Thucydides, the father of history, who wrote about the Peloponnesian Wars, as it is of Herodotus who dealt with the Greek-Persian Wars. The nineteenth century German historian Leopold von Ranke (1795–1886) in his *Weltgeschichte*[2] viewed world history as the history of power. Power is essentially what Darwin and Marx are talking about – one in biology, the other in economics. The former spoke of the "struggle for survival", the latter of "class conflict". It is not love or morals, or international law, that determine the outcome of world affairs, but the changing distribution of organized force. Power and expediency (one is tempted to add hypocrisy) remain the language of international relations. At this point of history, universal love is an illusion. Weak states invite aggression.

The realities of power have, in fact, seeped into and controlled every institution devised to regulate international life. The declaration of principle has always been of secondary importance. This was true of the Holy League, founded in 1495 by Pope Alexander VI, of the Holy Alliance, founded by the Czar of Russia in 1815, and of the League of Nations and the United Nations established after the First and Second World Wars. Forums established for rational discussion quickly give way to a struggle for power (horse-trading and lobbying) by the interested parties. Power dictates the course taken by any political institution. Until a code of international law evolves – and is enforced – power politics will continue to determine our lot. Paradoxically, it is the awesome power of nuclear deterrence that until now has ensured our security.

While arbitrary power, and coercion (even terrorism) continue to govern the relations between sovereign states, there have been times when economic power has been all important.[3] Crucial to the prolonged European wars of the seventeenth and eighteenth centuries was the creditworthiness of the combatants. The ability to raise funds is one of the reasons why the British and the Dutch were able to fight as long as they did. The most recent example of the use of economic power is the embargo imposed in 1990 by the United Nations against Iraq.

At other times, intangible power – intellectual, philosophical, and religious – has swayed world events. Christ, Mohammed, Luther, and Marx led no armies, yet the power of their word proved mightier than the sword. The "soul force" of non-violence practiced by Gandhi against British rule in South Africa, and later in India, is a classical example of the power of the spirit[4] defeating the power of the sword. As yet, the materialists do not have all the answers.

Anyone who undertakes to investigate the role of power politics in history must run the risk of being linked with the amoral practices of the Florentine political theorist and statesman Niccolò Machiavelli whose principal work *Il Principe*, *The Prince*, was published in 1513. Yet Machiavelli did not originate power politics. "The lust for power", wrote the ancient Roman historian Tacitus, "is the most flagrant of all the passions." We are all its victims. It is not power itself that calls up its own nemesis; it is human nature. Every age has known the dangers accompanying the use of power. "Power", said the nineteenth century English historian, Lord Acton, "tends to corrupt and absolute power corrupts absolutely." Henry Adams said power was poison.

However condemned, power remains as valid a concept in international political life as it ever was. Power is to politics what energy is to the physical world. It is what politics is all about. Far from being the malevolent force it is made out to be, power is an inherent feature of the relations between sovereign states. The struggle for power is not the only key to the course of world affairs – the past is also a story of sacrifice, love, and mutual aid[5] – but it is the master key. No society, national or international, is possible in which power and compulsion are absent. Without authority, anarchy reigns. While love and trust make our personal worlds go round, we delude ourselves in thinking that the same is true of the relations between states.

In the present century, especially since 1945, our ability to create military power has far outstripped our mental and moral faculties to direct its use. Worse, we are increasingly using power devoid of principle. In the international sphere, material might continues to triumph over moral right. While the United Nations and the Hague Court proclaim what is right and proper, the nations continue to enforce their will.

One cannot commence an inquiry into the role of power in world affairs without taking a world view. Modern history only makes sense in a global context. As the nineteenth-century Swiss historian Jacob Burckhardt put it, "Nur das Ganze spricht" – "Only the whole has meaning." There is hardly an important problem that faces the world today – whether it is nuclear arms, pollution, or AIDS – that is not a world problem.[6] Although much of our lives is controlled by international forces, we still think in national terms. Modern history is an ever-growing struggle for power not so much within but between states. Increasingly, the problem of our survival lies more in the foreign than in the domestic sphere. Indeed, in the global age in which we live, some nations can no longer control their own physical or economic destiny. Think of the worldwide activities of the international corporation, or the manner in which finance has become globalized. Not that the decline of national power will lead to our taking a world view.[7] Yet we cannot hope to understand the world around us – which increasingly determines our destiny – unless we do take a wider view.

Equally important is the need to take a historical view. Without some knowledge of the past the present is unintelligible, and whether in the political or economic sphere, much more hazardous than it need be. We cannot see the present except through the past. It is not only language that divides the human race, but also history. People not only have a history, they are history. "The past is never dead", wrote William Faulkner, "it's not even past."

The alternative to experience and accumulated knowledge – which we call history – is a sickness called amnesia. We can no more shed the past than we can shed our shadows (except by blundering about in the dark). Truly, those who ignore history will be forced to relive it. Meanwhile, history remains the ignored dimension in world affairs.

Not that history is the source of ready answers. Nor is it a science. The role of chance, the way in which history is overtaken by events, the difficulty of predicting human action, invalidates such a claim. As the collapse of communist power in eastern Europe and the reunification of Germany in 1990 make abundantly clear, history is not so much the outcome of a step-by-step process as of storm and tumult. Unlike an experiment in chemistry, geometry, and physics, which can be repeated, in human affairs nothing is constant, all is flux. There is no way that we can anticipate the outcome of human behavior, especially in times of war.[8] There are no inflexible laws that determine our destiny. Laws can be imposed on historical events only *a posteriori*. There is no way that we can tell – with any degree of certainty – what the future will hold. Except for those who share the view of the Spanish scholar and mystic, Miguel de Unamuno (1864–1936), that "history is the word of God in the world of man", there is no finality or certainty in it. To see the past "wie es eigentlich war" – "as it actually was", as the German historian Leopold von Ranke (1795–1886) advocated, will never be completely possible. We never know the past. We know only someone's story of the past. Meaning is always shaped by writer and context.

One cannot spend one's life practicing the historian's craft without being struck by the fragility of the human lot and the indefiniteness of human affairs. The past reveals itself not in a linear fashion, but dialectically, by comparison. History is oblique. A Portuguese proverb puts the matter more succinctly: "God writes straight, with crooked lines." Crooked or straight, in providing us with an imaginative understanding of the origins and consequences of what we are doing, history provides us with perspective, with balance, with wisdom – not for the moment, or the day, but for the totality of our lives and the society in which we live.

Having stressed the role of power politics in world affairs, and the need to take both a world and a historical view, it remains to explain why I chose to begin this inquiry at 1500. I did so because it is about then that the European Middle Ages ended and the increasingly secular modern age (fostered by the Renaissance, the Reformation, and the growing rational spirit of capitalism) began. By the 1500s the *Reconquista* of the Iberian peninsula from the Arabs had become a Christian crusade which was about to carry the Portuguese and the Spaniards into the world. In

1519–1522 the Spaniard Juan Sebastián del Cano (following Ferdinand Magellan's (1480?–1521) death in the Philippines) completed the first circumnavigation of the globe. A tremendous impetus was given to European man's discovery and colonization of the world. Two years after Christopher Columbus (1451–1506) set out in search of Asia, the pope (under the Treaty of Tordesillas, 1494) divided the world between Spain and Portugal.[9] In 1498 the Portuguese navigator Vasco da Gama (1460?–1524) reached the Malabar Coast of India. By the early 1600s English, Dutch, French, and Danish trading companies all reached India, eager to exploit the riches of the East. Impelled by the desire to profit, by an extraordinary degree of megalomania, and the will to power,[10] the scales of fortune began to tip in Europe's favor. They would continue to do so for the next 500 years.

The period beginning at 1500 is also important because the sixteenth century witnessed the rise and spread of nationalism. The power to form a nation is difficult to define. Athens lacked it; Rome and Castile possessed it. It has been described as ". . . a gift, like a talent for art or religion". It is not simply a matter of crude force, otherwise Ghengis Khan would have founded a nation. However defined, it was the newly emerging national states of western Europe, such as Britain, France and Spain, that put an end to feudal particularism and Christian universalism. National consciousness had scarcely existed in Europe's Middle Ages. Under feudalism – which in time would be undermined not only by nationalism but by war[11] and a growing money economy – men's loyalties were concentrated on their immediate lord. Beyond that they were conscious of membership in the universal Christian Church. Between 1400 and 1700 the terms Western Christendom and Europe were used interchangeably.[12] While in 1498, John Cabot could explore far lands unknown "to Christians", in 1764, the Englishman John Byron looked for lands "unvisited by any European power". By that date the European secular states had come to overshadow Christendom.[13] Indeed, in 1520, more than two centuries earlier, when the kings of France and England met on the Field of the Cloth of Gold, close to Calais in France, the idea of a European Commonwealth – a Europe unified in *res publica Christiana* – was as good as dead. The Congress of Mantua in Italy (1459–1460) was the last international gathering presided over by the pope. By the time Henry VIII declared himself "supreme head" of the Church of England in 1534, the prestige of papal authority had been shattered by the Protestant Reformation. What mattered henceforth was not the church but the nation.

Finally, this study begins at 1500 because the sixteenth century was an age of great scientific and technological achievement in the West. Science and technology came to be used, not as they had always been used, to ensure stability in society, but to stimulate change. Although the idea of scientific progress is taken for granted in the West today, against the backcloth of time, it was an innovation of first importance. Before the sixteenth century, the West had depended upon the East for many developments in science and technology. Now the East became reliant upon the dynamic West.

Of course, in 1500 no one foresaw these things. No one predicted that Europe would eventually control most of the world. In 1500, Asia, not Europe, was pre-eminent. In the sixteenth century all the major empires in Eurasia were Asian (see Map I). Whatever aspect of power we consider, whether it is military, economic, or spiritual, it is to Asia, not the West, that we must first turn.

In 1500 Europe's closest Asian neighbors were the Muslim Ottoman Turks. Having migrated from central Asia, in 1453 they captured Constantinople, the capital of the Greek Orthodox Byzantine Empire which had been founded as a second Rome by Constantine the Great a thousand years before. Unable to obtain much help from the Christian West; too poor to buy European cannon similar to those which the Turks used for forty days to batter down its walls; without the funds to bribe the attackers to go elsewhere – Constantinople and the Byzantine Empire went down to defeat. Henceforth, the

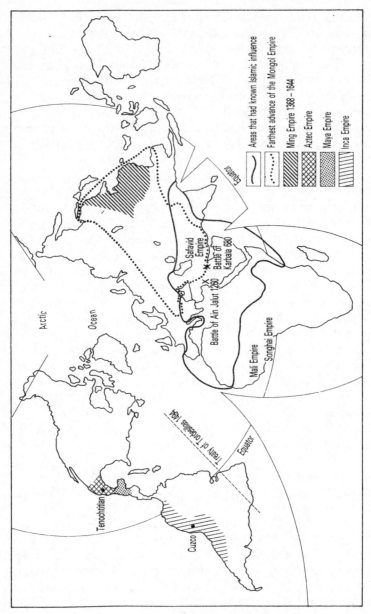

THE WORLD BEFORE 1500
Map I

Ottoman Turks, with a population far exceeding that of most other European powers,[14] ruled over one of the greatest empires the world has seen. They were indisputably the greatest Muslim power of the time. In 1500 they held much of south-west Asia, the North African plains, and part of the Balkans. Few empires flowered as brilliantly as theirs.

Although the collapse of the Byzantine Empire in 1453 opened the floodgates for the spread of the Islamic faith in Europe, Islam's[15] invasion of the West long predates the fifteenth century. Helped by the power of its prophesy, by the fire of its faith, by its call to brotherhood, as well as by its prowess in arms, by the eighth century the Arabs, spurred by their Islamic faith, had built an empire that stretched from Mecca and Medina westward to the Atlantic and eastward to the China Sea. No faith spread so quickly.[16] The Muslim general, Tarik ibn Ziyad, having crossed from Ceuta in Morocco to Gibraltar in AD 711, began a Muslim occupation of Spain that was to last almost 800 years. His successors were only halted and turned back in AD 732 by the Franks (a description applied by Asians to most western Europeans) under Charles Martel (the hammer) at Tours, a thousand miles north of Gibraltar.[17] Temporarily, at least, Islam's challenge to Christian Europe had been met. Not until 1492, when the last outpost of Moorish rule was crushed in Granada by the armies of Ferdinand of Aragon and Isabella of Castile, was Islam's occupation of Spain ended.

While the Christian victory over the Marinids (Muslim Berbers from Fez in Morocco) at Salado in 1340 had brought to an end the long history of the invasion of the Spanish peninsula, the fall of Constantinople in 1453 prompted the strongly militarily inclined Islamic Turks to extend their rule to the whole of western Europe.[18] In the 1520s, under Suleiman the Magnificent (1520–1566), Hungary was overrun, Vienna (center of Habsburg rule) was threatened. In the 1680s, the Ottomans reached Vienna again. They were turned back by Austria, and its too often disunited Christian allies, only in the nick of time.[19] In 1687, at the second battle of Mohács, Turkish power in

Hungary was broken. Within a century the Ottomans passed from the offensive to the defensive. A humiliating peace with the Holy League (Austria, Poland, Venice, and Russia) followed in 1699 (the Treaty of Karlowitz) whereby the Turks surrendered most of Hungary. This was the turning point in Ottoman fortunes. By providing a constant military challenge to the West, as well as by barring the land routes to the East, the Turks (like the Arabs before them) played a pivotal role in the unfolding of Western history.

Matching the glory of the Ottoman empire in the 1500s was that of Persia (Iran). The Safavid dynasty, the first national dynasty in many centuries, was founded there in 1501 by Shah Ismail Safavi (c.1487–1524) who proclaimed himself the legitimate leader of Islam, the rightful successor of the prophet. (Persia had been under Muslim control since the Arab invasions of the seventh century). This led to intermittent warfare between the Persians and their Muslim neighbors throughout the sixteenth and early seventeenth centuries. The charge of heresy so intensified the discord between Muslim Persians and Muslim Turks that it led to a series of battles beginning with the Turkish victory at Chaldiran in north-west Persia in 1514.

If the Afghans, Turks, and Persians seemed to display an unusual degree of ferocity in their battles, it was because heresy was at stake. Whereas Constantinople was the center of the Sunni sect, Persia was the home of the Shi'a (the party of Ali), the chief minority sect. The feud between them dates from Mohammed's death in AD 632. The Shi'a differs from the orthodox Sunni sect in its belief that succession to the prophet should have remained in Mohammed's family. Whereas the Sunnis believe that they have a direct relationship with God (the principal role of the Sunni immans is to lead the prayers of the congregation), the Shi'ites accord great importance to their religious leaders (as they did more recently to the Ayatollah Khomeini) who are responsible for interpreting Islam. Following the example set by the martyred Hussein,[20] they also stress martyrdom.

Persia's fortunes improved under the strong leadership of Shah Abbas I (1587–1629). Between 1603 and 1619 Abbas recovered Tabriz from the Ottomans, recaptured all of north-west Persia, took Erivan, and won a decisive victory against the Turks near Lake Urmia. In 1622 he seized the strategic Gulf island of Ormuz from the Portuguese. His conquest of Azerbaijan and Kurdistan was followed in 1623 by the seizure of Baghdad.

Alas, the reign of Abbas the Great was followed by that of Shah Safi the Weak. Helped by Safi's neglect, the Turks soon reconquered large parts of Persian territory. Azerbaijan fell to them in 1635. The final blow to the Safavids, however, came from the Afghans in the East. In 1722 the Muslim Afghan ruler Mir Mahmud overcame the Persian army at Gulnabad. The last of the Safavids was deposed in 1736.

The Afghan victory was the signal for Persia's other neighbors, Russia and Turkey, to seize whatever Persian territory they could. They were prevented from dismembering Persia only by the appearance of the powerful Persian leader Nadir Shah (1736–1747). He succeeded in holding Persia's predators in check. In a series of battles he routed Afghans, Turks, and Russians. In 1739 he carried his wars of conquest across Afghanistan into Mogul India where he sacked and looted Delhi. In 1747 Nadir Shah was assassinated. His rule was followed by political divisions and civil war. Only in 1750, with the establishment of the Zand dynasty, was an element of stability restored. In 1794 Persia was again thrown into disruption by an internal struggle for power. Henceforth, for much of the nineteenth century, Persia became a pawn of Russian-British rivalry in central and eastern Asia.

A third great Asian Muslim empire – the Mogul[21] Empire of India – was founded in 1526 by Babur the Tiger who invaded India from Afghanistan. Babur's victory over the sultan of Delhi at Panipat in 1526 was for the eastern wing of Muslim power what the victory at Mohács on the Danube (also in 1526) was for the Ottomans. With these victories Islam reached from Morocco in the west and

Austria in the north, through the Safavids of Persia, to the center of India.

Babur laid the foundations of a dynasty which lasted over three centuries. Within four years he had conquered the greater part of Hindustan. Thenceforth, his followers extended their power and their religion across most of the subcontinent. The reign of his grandson Akbar the Great (1556–1605), who renewed and consolidated Mogul rule, is considered a golden age in India's past. A benevolent despot, Akbar is remembered for the synthesis he achieved between Hindu and Islamic cultures. Following the death of Akbar's successor Jahangir (1605–1627), further extensions of Mogul rule were made by Shah Jahan (1628–1657) and Aurangzeb (1658–1707).

The turning point in Islam's fortunes came with the death of Aurangzeb whose attempts to consolidate power were undone by rebellions and wars. His efforts to forcibly convert Hindus to Islam had also aroused widespread hostility. Henceforth, harried by the Marathas, the Sikhs, and the British (who had established their first trade factory near Bombay in 1612, and who are said to have conquered India "in a fit of absence of mind"), there was a steady decline in Mogul power – a decline accelerated by its own internal weaknesses and the rigid and unchanging outlook of the Mogul elite.

The purely commercial attitude of European traders in India ceased to be tenable when the Mogul Empire began to collapse in the eighteenth century. British victories over both Indians and Europeans in India culminated with British supremacy. In 1786 the first British Governor-General of India was appointed. British control of most of the sub-continent, however, had to wait upon the final defeat of the Marathas in 1817. Following the Mutiny and uprisings of 1857, Britain banished the last Mogul Emperor, Bahadur Shah II. Only after the Mutiny had been suppressed and the private East India Company had been taken over by the British government in 1858, did England feel safe to turn from commerce and conquest to the more civilizing contributions begun under Lord William Bentinck, Governor General of British India (1828–1835).[22]

The most populous empire in Asia in the 1500s was the Ming Empire (1368–1644) of China,[23] which in 1368 had replaced the Mongol (Yuan) dynasty (1260–1368).[24] If Mongol rule sat ill with the Chinese, it was not only because the Mongols had laid waste to much of China, but also because the Chinese considered themselves a superior people. The world, seen from the Chinese bell tower, was always subservient; mankind was one family, of whom they were the head.

China's basic strength in the 1500s lay not in its age (the Chinese empire had been founded in 221 BC), its numbers, or the richness of its land, but in its ancient culture and civilization. Europeans visiting China at this time idealized the Chinese way. China, then as now, was a non-acquisitive, non-hereditary, secular, centralized society in which men of humble origin could rise to the summit of power.

China's wealth impressed foreign observers as much as its culture. Yet China has never been a commercial civilization. The Chinese mandarinate system and the agrarian self-subsistence of the Chinese people inhibited the rise of a merchant class, which, for most of Chinese history, was regarded as parasitical. Although the merchant's lot improved during the Sung dynasty (AD 960–1279), the market has not played the pivotal role in Chinese history that it came to play in the West. Trade – foreign and domestic – was not allowed to change the empire's economic, cultural, and intellectual institutions. The goal of Confucian[25] harmony, based as it was on the land, the family, and the scholar-gentry meritocracy, was preferred.

China's official attitude toward the merchant class does not seem to have hindered China's technological development. Until the nineteenth century China's agrarian standards were probably unmatched. In the first fourteen centuries of Christian Europe, many Chinese inventions were adopted by the Europeans without their knowing where they came from. Three of the most important inventions: printing, gunpowder, and the maritime compass are of Chinese origin. While certain early travelers, such as the Jesuit scholar, Matteo Ricci, played an important role in transferring Western scientific thought to the East, it is doubtful if the West had much to teach China before the eighteenth century.

In particular, the Chinese in earlier centuries excelled in shipbuilding technology. They passed to the Arabs (who subsequently brought the ideas to Europe) the techniques of watertight bulkheads, stern-post rudders, and navigational aids such as the compass. Continuing the policy of maritime expansion of the Sung dynasty, between 1405 and 1433, in an attempt to show their flag and impress distant lands with Chinese supremacy,[26] seven great naval expeditions were sent by the Mings from China into the Indian Ocean as far as Arabia and Africa. The first voyage began in 1405 with more than sixty large vessels (up to 440 feet long), 255 smaller vessels and a crew of about 28,000 men.[27] Contrast this with Columbus' three ships and crew of ninety. Columbus' flagship, the "Santa Maria" measured 117 feet long. Roughly seventy years before Vasco da Gama rounded the Cape of South Africa, the Chinese (having collected giraffes and other exotic things) returned home to continue their traditional policy of isolation. They had sought neither conquest nor trade. No overseas territories were acquired; no colonies established. The naval expeditions were never resumed. Having satisfied their curiosity they returned to China and – in contrast to the Sung and Yuan dynasties – shut their door. The Chinese door remained closed until it was forced open by the West in the nineteenth century. One can only speculate what might have happened had the Chinese been in the Indian Ocean when Vasco da Gama rounded the Cape.

The decision of the Ming dynasty (1368–1644) to revert to a defensive strategy did not save it from attacks. In the sixteenth century Japanese pirates invaded the Chinese coast with impunity. In 1592 when the Japanese invaded Korea, the Chinese crossed the Yalu River and successfully intervened – as they would do several hundred years later against the American General Douglas MacArthur. In the seventeenth century they were beset by the Manchus. The fall of Peking in 1644 to a rebel force (rebellions had swept much of China from the 1620s onward), provided the Manchus with the ideal conditions for invasion.

Having crushed all resistance to their new Ch'ing dynasty (1644–1912), the Manchus followed a policy of expansion in inner Asia, including the Amur Valley, Mongolia, and Tibet. Their invasions of Burma in the 1760s, like their later eighteenth century invasions of Nepal and Vietnam, proved abortive. Meanwhile, a new threat had appeared from the West. In 1515 Portuguese traders and buccaneers had appeared off the southern China coast. In 1565 the Spaniards arrived from the Philippines, bringing with them not only a new religion and superior arms, but also the products from their recently discovered New World (among them maize, sweet potatoes, and tobacco). With the arrival of the Spaniards, the colonization of China by the West (which would continue until the Second World War) had begun.

Of all these Asian empires (see Map II), none were to have greater world-wide effect than those of the Arabs and the Turks. Wherever they spread, the Muslim Arabs and Turks stamped the unity of Islamic life upon the areas they conquered. Almost all the languages of the Muslim world have borrowed heavily from Arabic, which (as Greek had done earlier and Latin would do later) provided a bridge between East and West for every field of endeavor. Not least, the Islamic empire helped to transfer superior Chinese technology to the West. Muslim cities, such as Baghdad, Iraq (immortalized in *The Thousand and One Nights*), or Córdoba in Spain, became centers of scientific and philosophical learning. The Arab philosophers, Ibn Hazm and Ibn Rushd, and the leading Jewish scholar of the Middle Ages, Maimonides, were all sons of Córdoba. Under Abd-al Rahman (who in AD 732 crossed the Pyrenees and captured Bordeaux) and his successors, Córdoba, boasting 500 mosques, 300 public baths, 70 libraries, and lamplighted streets, became one of the great cultural centers of Europe.

Arab contributions to the sciences and the arts were crucial to later Western developments. The Arab world was the conduit through which passed the ideas of the

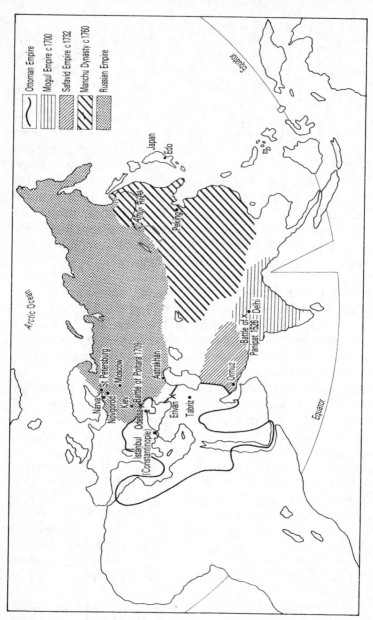

ASIAN EMPIRES *c.1763*
Map II

East. Before 1500 many of the classical Greek and Arabic scientific works had been translated into Latin, increasingly the language of Christendom. In translating and diffusing the learning of the Greeks, the Romans, the Jews, the Persians, and the Hindus, Islam made available to the West the heritage of antiquity. Muslim Spain, as well as Italy, was the cradle of Europe's Renaissance during the fourteenth and fifteenth centuries. While the Arabs and other Muslims in Spain were creating buildings of breathtaking beauty and establishing libraries that far surpassed anything the Europeans possessed, the leaders of Christian Europe were only just learning to write their names.

Yet the day came (at the end of the fifteenth century) when the Arabs, and their semitic cousins, the Jews, were driven from Spain. The grandeur of the Arabs' last stronghold, Granada, died. For the next several centuries the Arabs of North Africa and Arabia were ruled by the Ottoman Turks. The fact that both Ottomans and Arabs belonged to the Sunni sect of Islam made Ottoman rule no easier to bear.

Although Ottoman power probably reached its zenith before 1700, it was not until the continuous and exhausting defensive wars of the seventeenth and eighteenth centuries against Venice, Austria, Poland, Russia, and Persia had reduced the Ottomans' possessions in Europe by half, that the Islamic tide in Europe was turned.[28] So great were the Ottoman Turks' military reverses in the last half of the eighteenth century that Turkey was called the "sick man of Europe". By then the military prowess, the pragmatic creativity, the vitality, and the remarkable leadership of earlier times had all declined. The rigidity of Muslim thought, coupled with an incompetent, despotic, centralized rule, had also stifled the earlier interest in the human and physical world. The fact that after 1566, Suleiman the Magnificent (1520–1566), under whose rule the Ottoman Empire reached its height, should have been followed by Selim the Sot (1566–1574), and Selim was only one of the thirteen incompetent leaders who followed Suleiman, demonstrates the decline of Ottoman leadership.

The wonder is that the conglomeration of people that the Ottomans ruled should have been held together for as long as they were. So weak had the empire become by the mid-eighteenth century that even the scattered tribes of Arabia were encouraged to try to rid themselves of Ottoman rule. They did not succeed until the First Great War (1914–1918) broke the Turkish grip.

2

The Rise of the West

Whatever the importance of Asia before 1500, the modern world was created not in the East but in the West. Christopher Columbus' journey to the New World and Vasco da Gama's rounding of the Cape were the forerunners of a movement which culminated in the triumph of Europe's power in the world. How such a relatively undistinguished group of Europeans ever came to lay claim to the entire world is one of the riddles of the past.

Europe's rise to world supremacy cannot be understood without acknowledging the importance of the European Renaissance from the twelfth to the seventeenth centuries. The Renaissance[29] is important because it helped to change the course of European art, music, literature, architecture, politics, commerce, science and technology. It was one of those wide-spread, deep cultural changes that take place every now and again (such as the spread of Christianity and Islam in earlier times, or the imposition of Communist rule and its eventual unraveling in the present century) about which it is difficult to be precise. The Germans call it Zeitgeist – the spirit of the times. The focus of that change, whether we are dealing with the art forms of Leonardo da Vinci or Michelangelo, or the political writings of Niccolò Machiavelli, or the scholarly works of Erasmus in Holland, or the writings of Shakespeare in England, or Rabelais in France, was on the human and the secular. With the Renaissance, in contrast to the static past, a new emphasis was placed on the dynamic. It is not surprising that the sixteenth century religious upheaval, which we call the Protestant Reformation, came when it did. The Protestant Reformation provided a tremendous spur to action and change. It is also understandable that the astronomers Nicolaus Copernicus (1473–1543) and Galileo Galilei (1564–1642) should have clashed with church authorities when they did. They not only undermined Ptolemy's theory, formulated at Alexandria 1,400 years earlier, which held that the earth was the center of the universe, and was motionless; they also disputed Aristotelian and church doctrine, which had gone unquestioned for a much longer period. Their challenge was worldly, Luther's challenge was spiritual. All of them challenged existing authority.

The importance of Copernicus and Galileo is that they offered a new view of the universe, a view which in time (in so far as it altered our perception of the earth's relation to the universe, and man's relation to the cosmos) altered the appearance of everything. Thus were sown the seeds of modern science – of what later was called the Scientific Revolution. By the late sixteenth century, pragmatic, creative scientists coming from all over Europe had turned Padua, Ferrara, Florence, and Bologna – heirs to the much earlier Greek heritage of rational thought – into the foremost institutions of science and technology of their day. These cities were free of the constricting feudalism of other parts of Europe, and in Bologna's case, free also of papal influence. In the 1500s the Polish astronomer Copernicus was only one of many highly talented Europeans studying at Bologna, Europe's first university.[30] Improvements in Portuguese navigational aids (which enabled the Portuguese to plot their positions on the high seas, and to forge their way down the African coast), were one of the many fruits of this scientific ferment. From it emerged a new rational spirit based on mathematics and logic, which sought reasoned truth in contrast to revealed truth: "I believe because I know", rather than "I know because I believe", without which there would have been no modern science, no capitalist spirit of enterprise, no Industrial Revolution, and no Western idea of progress.[31] The idea that man could independently improve his lot, that he (not God) was the originator and the measure of all things (something which many westerners never stop to question), was perhaps the most profound revolution that Western thought has undergone. Increasingly, the concern became not for man to adjust himself to the inherently incalculable vicissitudes of life, but to control life.

The new stress placed upon man, rather than God, the new emphasis placed upon the individual,[32] rather than the family, tribe or state, the new insistence placed upon the growing freedom to make individual choice and individual decisions, all helped to release a veritable torrent of explosive energy upon society. The "timeless, perpetual present", as portrayed in the work of fifteenth-century artists like Fra Angelico gave way to linear, goal-oriented progress. There was a shift from the perfection of the spirit to the perfection of matter. Like his contemporaries, Fra Angelico was primarily concerned with redemption, which was not linked to time, and for which goal-oriented "time", as we know it, had no meaning. "Watch therefore: for ye know not what hour your Lord doth come" (Matt.24:42). Henceforth, especially after the Protestant Reformation, emphasis was placed not on timeless redemption, but on progressive, worldly, tempestuous, volcanic, demoniac action. Time, purposive time, came to play a new role in the West. With the growth of a money economy, time became money; the market became supreme. Increasingly, nothing was permanent, fixed, stable, or immutable.

This shift in emphasis during the Renaissance toward the secular, toward science, toward the individual, toward action, toward constant change, toward the quest, expresses the genius of European civilization of that time. It also helps to explain the source of Europe's supremacy in the world. The Asian empires that preceded the rise of the West were probably more glorious than anything that Europe subsequently achieved. China in the thirteenth century was undoubtedly the most technically advanced and economically powerful state in the world. Yet, being more despotic, these states provided less scope for individual action, and hence were less dynamic.

The growing role of secularism in the Renaissance – the ever-growing competitiveness among Europeans in commerce, technology, and arms – should not lead us to underestimate the role of the spiritual factor in the rise and expansion of Europe.[33] The Christian Cross bore the sign "In Hoc Signe Vinces" – "In this sign (i.e. the sign of the

Cross) shall we conquer". In post-Reformation Europe (Martin Luther [1483–1546] nailed his Ninety-Five Theses to the door of the ducal chapel at Wittenberg on 31 October 1517) it is often difficult to separate the political from the religious factors at work. Not until the end of the Thirty Years War in 1648 does national rivalry (especially between Spain and France) take precedence over religious disputes. Portugal's Henry the Navigator (1394–1460) was not only a man of worldly activity, he was also a religious ascetic. Leonhard Euler (1707–1783) was not only the leading mathematician of eighteenth century Europe, he was also the leader for the revival of piety in the Lutheran church. Christianity's spiritual dynamism invaded the temporal sphere and helped to provide the basis underlying the rise of the West. It was Christianity's certainty,[34] righteousness and messianic outlook, coupled with its domination complex, which compelled it, like Islam, to go out into the world in search of souls. Unlike Daoism, Confucianism, and Hinduism, Christianity was a missionary religion. Without the messianic and evangelizing aspects of its beliefs (not to say its aggressiveness and Pauline intolerance of other religions) it is doubtful if Christian Europe could have come to dominate the world.

No other European country demonstrates the importance of the spiritual factor in history so well as Spain.[35] Its *Reconquista* and its spilling into the world are not to be understood outside the crusade-like religious fervor and missionary zeal of Spanish Catholicism. Sheltered from the rest of Europe by the Pyrenees, the Spaniards never really accepted the secularism of the Renaissance, or the pluralism of the Reformation.[36] The great commercial, scientific and industrial revolutions taking root in sixteenth century Europe also left Spain largely undisturbed. The Spaniards took little part in the expansion of commerce from the seventeenth century onward. Money and the values of the marketplace – however stimulating to the development of the nation state – were never allowed to play a dominant role. Unlike its commercial rivals Britain and the Netherlands, Spain did not develop a middle class. Spain's spurning of commerce meant that much of the wealth of its majestic empire ended up in British and Dutch hands. Wealth to the British and Dutch Protestants was a sign of God's providence as well as a reward for their own industry.

Heeding the warning of the Spanish philosopher Seneca, "From the time money came to be regarded with honor, the real value of things was forgotten",[37] the Spaniards seem to have disregarded the loss of money as they disregarded the loss of blood. Like Don Quixote, they pointed and fought in all directions at once. Well might Philip II's emblem be *Nec Pluribus Impar* – A Match for Many. Between 1500 and 1659 they fought in every dynastic and religious struggle they could find. With brief interludes, they fought France for fifty and the Dutch for eighty years. Endlessly, they fought the Turks. They remained deaf to the warnings of contemporaries that endless war – with its staggering costs and its run-away inflation (1500–1630) – would undo them. For a hundred years, in a great and prolonged drama, Spain also fought those who were trying to tear its empire apart.[38]

Nor did the Spaniards show much enthusiasm for the patient, organized work that modern science and industry demanded. Their wealth came from other sources. In addition to its windfall gains in precious metals from South America, it was able to draw upon the income obtained from Castile taxes, and the growing mercantile wealth of Italy and the Lowlands. It also had a virtual monopoly of the slave, spice (mainly pepper, cinnamon, cloves, and nutmeg), and sugar trades. Yet, although nominally the richest state in Europe, it became bankrupt with astonishing regularity. Charles V, whose revenues were consumed by interest payments on past debts, had insufficient funds to bury his mother, Joan the Mad. In 1556, his successor, Philip II, inherited an empty treasury and a bankrupt state. When Philip died in 1598, the official debt of 20 million ducats, which he had inherited, had risen to 100 million. The bulk of his revenues were being consumed by debt payments.

Some scholars, such as Werner Sombart,[39] ascribe

Spain's penury to the persecution of the Jews. The Inquisition (a chilling example of the dreadful extremes to which religious bigotry will go),[40] Sombart argued, drove from Spain the best Jewish financial talent. Others, such as Max Weber (1864–1920)[41] and R.H. Tawney (1880–1962),[42] place greater stress on the Protestant spirit which enabled both Britain and Holland to outstrip Spain.[43]

The trouble with these arguments is that they evaluate Spanish success or failure in French, British, or Dutch terms. Understandably, the Spaniards preferred their own values and their own goals. The fact is that after the defeat of the Armada by Britain in 1588, Spain, its crusading spirit spent, its earlier vigor and vitality lost, preferred to withdraw from the center of the European stage and sleep. In the material realm it passed from "wanting to be too much, to too much wanting not to be".[44]

In terms of territorial aggrandizement, Spain achieved what it did not only because of the material and spiritual elements of Christianity but also because it exercised the power of a nation.[45] It is difficult to exaggerate the significance to Europe and the world of the appearance in western Europe, during and after the Renaissance, of national territorial states, including Portugal, Spain, France, Britain, and the Netherlands.[46] Despite the present trend toward globalism, the decisive force in the organization of the economic and political institutions of our time remains the gospel of nationalism. The rise of nations such as Spain – which marked the end of feudal particularism and Christian universalism (in 1555 at Augsburg Charles V was obliged to let each member state of the Holy Roman Empire follow the religion of its own choice: "Cuius regio elus religio" – "the rulers determine the religion"), and their continual struggle for power, heightened Western energies and provided an immeasurable impetus to Western expansion. Political diversity and political fragmentation stimulated the expansion of European states. For a period – perhaps until 1914 – European national states and European nationalism were the engine of change in the world. The so-called "Discoveries"[47] – which were preceded by long rivalries between Spain and

Portugal in the Atlantic – stemmed directly from the growth of central government in these newly founded rival nations.

An all-important factor in Europe's rise to greatness was Europe's supremacy in weapons.[48] "They have found out Artillery", wrote the Englishman John Donne in 1621, "by which warres come to quicker ends than heretofore, and the great expense of bloud is avoyded." Donne, of course, was proved wrong. In the development of superior weapons,[49] on land and sea, these improvements in artillery (which the West had gleaned from the East) were only the beginning. The improvement of arms since the sixteenth century is a field of activity in which the West has excelled – not least because developments were too widespread, and too competitive, for any one European country to be able to establish a monopoly (as the government did in China) or a lasting superiority in armaments manufacture. Underpinning all European efforts from the seventeenth century onward was Europe's overwhelming military and naval power.[50] The exceptional progress made by Europeans in the science and technology of navigation, weapons, and military organization ensured their superiority.

Among the many other elements helping to explain the rise of the West is that of geography. The West was divided physically as well as politically. It was one thing for the Mongols to sweep across the Russian and Polish plains, and another thing for them to pierce the more varied western terrain. Geography also provided a stimulus to the maritime nations of Europe. Once the trade monopoly of the Italians and the Arabs in the Levant was broken (by the opening of new sea routes around Africa[51] to the East), the shift from the Mediterranean to the Atlantic provided a spur to the maritime nations, first to Spain and Portugal, and later to France, Britain, and the Netherlands.

These changes stimulated the development of mercantilist regulations of trade which became a system of power in themselves. World-wide commerce became the source of much of Europe's strength. Superior business organizations, such as the joint stock company, were devised to exploit the growing trade. Shares could be bought and sold on the newly-founded stock exchange of Amsterdam. Marine, life, and fire insurance reduced the risks of trade. Private property rights were protected under a rule of law.

The western Europeans enjoyed a degree of personal security which sprang not only from important legal documents, such as the *Magna Carta* (AD 1215), and the gradual acceptance of the rule of law, but also from the fact that the West was safe from the incursions of Mongols and Turks. Had the Byzantines (before the fall of Constantinople in 1453), the Poles, and the Russians not provided a bulwark which kept the Mongols and later the Turks at bay, western Europe might not have experienced the Renaissance or the Scientific and Industrial Revolutions. In 1238 the Russian city of Vladimir (between Moscow and Gorky) was razed by the Mongols. Today the city commemorates the heroic people of Vladimir who ". . . by their self-sacrifice . . . saved western Europe from suffering the same fate, and saved European civilization from extinction".

All in all, Europe faced less despoliation, fewer hindrances than Asia. Europeans were never beset to the same extent, as say India or China, by natural calamities. They never depended upon the coming of the monsoon, as did India, or the vagaries of the Yellow and the Yangtze Rivers, known as "China's sorrows".[52] The age-old need for social conformity in China cannot be separated from the control of water, both for irrigation as well as to prevent flooding. There also was a better relation in the West between human and material resources. No European country was as overwhelmed with numbers as China. One can understand why the idea of progress originated in the more stable West rather than in the more convulsive East.

Perhaps the explanations of Europe's rise were human qualities and human toil, coupled with Europe's resources. Perhaps the chief stimulus was human greed, or the search for glory. Not least important was the self-transformation that Europe underwent as a result of the discovery and colonization of the New World. Perhaps it was a matter of success breeding success. However we explain the rise of the West[53] – and we cannot account for it if we ignore the fortuitous conjunction of circumstances of the time such as the narrow margin by which the Christian armies triumphed over their Muslim opponents before Vienna in 1529 – we do know that Europe's success bred a sense of superiority, if not illusions of grandeur. Hence the megalomania and the will to power of the Europeans.

Europe's uniqueness lies in its willingness to accept change. "Im Anfang war die Tat", – "In the beginning was action", says Goethe[54] in explaining the genius of Western civilization. The maxims "What is not can be", and "Resources are not, they become", are purely Western. Compare these with the maxim of Chinese Daoism[55] which is "Do nothing so that it might be done." European man's desire to mold the world to his will is in contrast to the Buddhist's desire to escape from worldly strivings, or the Hindu's sense of illusion when speaking of the actual world and of individual man, or the stress placed by Confucius on the need for harmony and stability. The emphasis in the Orient in earlier centuries, if not today, was upon age-old tradition, upon conformity, upon letting things take their course. Fatalism predominated. Puritan rationalism which sought to exercise rational control over the world is in contrast to Confucian rationalism which is an attempt to accomodate the individual to the world in a rational manner. In contrast to the idea of a Western quest – to the idea of reaching out purposefully for some distant goal – the East, even allowing for the stress Confucius placed on self-cultivation, was relatively static. Conversely, Westerners like da Gama and Pizarro were restless in their desire for conquest.

Even greater contrast exists between the importance placed by the West upon the role of the individual (especially in the post-Protestant period of European history) and that placed by the East on the collective. It was the

West which first elevated man to a dominating position in nature. While Western Renaissance art delights in expressing the individual – think of Michelangelo's "David" or the portraits of Velázquez – eastern art[56] makes the individual part of the whole. While the Orient is conscious of individualism,[57] it tends to stress the idea of a common destiny, of harmony, and of a central authority. One of the great problems of the early Christian missionaries was to establish individual guilt. Family or tribal shame was understood, but not individual guilt. One of the important questions asked of any traveler in China is: "to which group do you belong?"[58] Finally, it was the West that developed and adhered to the rule of law. Legalism in China is as old as China's first emperor, the Emperor Ch'in (third century BC), but too often Chinese law has been used by its rulers as an instrument of convenience. Mao Zedong (Mao Tse-tung, 1893–1976) himself explicitly admitted this.

Whereas the stress in the Occident came to be placed upon action, tension, and change, upon increased social mobility, the emphasis in the Orient remained upon stability and continuity. The Orient has never separated itself from the past. It does not make such fine distinctions as we do between past, present, and future. Its world view was the antithesis of Western Cartesian rationality.[59]

3

The Impact of Western Man[60]

The importance of Christopher Columbus is not that he discovered America. America had been discovered long before 1492. Columbus' importance[61] lies in the fact that he began a process whereby Western man extended his influence across the entire earth. By the end of the eighteenth century most of the world's seas and coastlines had been explored by Europeans. The first stages of global integration had been completed (see Map III).

It was a process in which the claim of one European power was always being challenged by that of another. No sooner had Spain and Portugal divided the world between them (the one following a western or south-western route that would result in Spain's discovery of the Americas, the other a south-eastern route that would result in Portugal obtaining a sea passage to southern Asia) than their claims were contested. With the destruction of Spanish sea power by the British in 1588, Spain forfeited its leading position. In the seventeenth century English, Dutch, and French East-India companies were formed to wrest the monopoly of eastern trade from the Portuguese. Each harrowing the other, British and French efforts were concentrated on India, while the Dutch attacked the Portuguese in Indonesia. Failing to beat off the other Europeans, by 1700 all that was left of the Portuguese East-Indian empire was Timor in Indonesia, the forts Goa, Daman, and Diu in India, and Macao in China.

In the sixteenth, seventeenth, and eighteenth centuries, a similar threat to Spanish and Portuguese power was made by the British, the Dutch, the French, the Prussians, and the Scandinavians along the north and west coasts of Africa. In 1652 the Dutch (who had broken from Spanish

EUROPEAN EMPIRES c.1763
Map III

control and had established their own Republic in 1581) began their colonization of the Cape Province in South Africa. A similar challenge to the Iberians was made in the Americas. Because better pickings were to be had elsewhere, and also because the British, the French, and the Dutch were too busy fighting each other to concentrate their efforts on robbing the Iberians of their American possessions, Spanish and Portuguese power in the Americas remained intact until it was broken by the indigenous revolutionary movements of the early nineteenth century.

By then the world-wide struggle between the European powers had been settled in Britain's favor.[62] Clive's victory over the French-supported forces of the nawab Siraj-ud-Daulah at Plassey in India in 1757,[63] and Wolfe's victory over the French at Quebec in 1759, had laid the basis of British world supremacy. Secure in the overwhelming strength accruing from its commercial and industrial developments, Britain finally defeated France at sea at Trafalgar in 1805 and on land at Waterloo in 1815. For Britain there followed a glorious century of prosperity and peace. Far from undermining the British economy, the French and Napoleonic wars had stimulated British trade and industry. The remarkable overall increase in British wealth had, in fact, made the strains of war easier to bear.[64]

Britain's eighteenth century victories over the French in India (1757) and North America (1759) set the stage for British exploration in the southern hemisphere. To enhance its naval power Britain needed naval bases as well as access to naval stores. In particular Britain sought to confirm the existence of an island continent which since earliest times had appeared on European maps as Terra Australis Incognita. Tales about this continent must have been set abroad by the Arabs, the Malays, the Indonesians, and the Chinese who as great seafarers could hardly have sailed in the Indian Ocean without stumbling on a continent the size of Australia. Since the early seventeenth century Dutch ships had sailed along the west coast of what they called New Holland (where many of them were shipwrecked) on their way to Batavia on the island of Java.

In 1642 a Dutch expedition under Abel Tasman sailed around the continent without sighting it, making landfalls on the west coasts of Tasmania and New Zealand. Throughout the seventeenth century Dutch and Spanish ships caught glimpses of the continent's western and northern coasts. The British were convinced that if they did not claim this territory soon, France or the Netherlands would.

The first official British link with Australia was the visit of the pirate-adventurer William Dampier who explored part of the north-west Australian coast in 1699. Real exploration had to wait until after the middle of the eighteenth century when several scientific expeditions were sent into the Pacific. The greatest of these were the three voyages of James Cook (1728–1779) who in 1768–1769 charted the coasts of New Zealand and sailed north along the east coast of Australia. Although he gave positive geographical identity to Australia and New Zealand, he at first claimed for Britain only eastern Australia and the adjacent islands in the Pacific. His later voyages (1772 and 1776) added greatly to Europe's knowledge of the region.

Not until the arrival of 717 British convicts in 1788 (five years after Britain had lost its North American colonies where it had formerly dumped its felons and outcasts) did Britain consider claiming the entire continent of Australia. At that time, with the exception of several hundred convicts, and a score of British mutineers from the *Bounty*, who had reached Pitcairn Island in 1790, there were no other European settlers in the South Pacific. Nor would there be until well into the nineteenth century.

By the 1830s, with almost no bloodshed, the British had laid claim to the Australian continent, an area almost equal in size to the continental United States. Tasmania had become a British colony in 1803. New Zealand was claimed as British territory in 1814 and, to foil the French, as a British colony in 1840.

By 1850 (the shipment of convicts to eastern Australia had ceased in 1840) the British population of Australia had grown to 400,000. Stimulated by the gold discoveries of 1851, the immigrant population passed the million mark by 1860. The dominant stock was English, Scottish, Irish, and Welsh. The only non-British immigrants to reach Australia were German agricultural settlers, Americans, and Chinese, many of whom became "diggers" on the gold fields. Americans were also active in trade, transport, whaling, and sealing. Later in the century Kanaka laborers were brought in from the Solomons to work in the plantation industry of northern Australia.

With the improvement of sea transportation, both Australia and New Zealand became sources of wool, sugar, and wheat for Britain. The improvement of steamship communications in the 1870s, and the successful introduction of refrigeration in the 1880s, made possible the development of the great Australian and New Zealand meat and dairy industries for the British market. Politically, economically, and militarily, Australia and New Zealand remained tied to Britain twelve thousand miles away.

In 1901 the Commonwealth of Australia was formed – the only nation with a continent to itself. By then the British population of Australia had grown to four million. To guard itself from being inundated by Asians (the implications of Japan's defeat of China in 1895 and of Russia in 1904–1905 were not lost on Australia's leaders) in 1902 Australia introduced its Immigration Restriction (White Australia) Policy. By this time the number of aborigines had undergone a dramatic decline: victims of acute cultural shock, of European sicknesses and alcohol, ill-armed, and insufficiently aggressive to meet the Western intrusion, they were overwhelmed by the ever-growing tide of white immigrants.

In the First Great War Australian troops played a crucial role in defending the interests of the British Empire. It was from the crucible of war, especially out of the battle for Gallipoli in 1915, that Australia found its national identity.

The first Europeans to visit New Zealand were seal and whale hunters; the first permanent settlements were made by British missionaries. Pioneering British agricultural settlements were founded in the 1840s. For the British it proved a much more difficult task to subdue the war-like

aboriginal Maori, a race of Polynesian-Melanesian de-
scent. The British fought two long wars against the Maori
(1843–1848 and 1860–1870) without subjugating them. The
discovery of gold in the 1860s caused an enormous influx
of British immigrants. Non-European migrants were kept
out of New Zealand by restrictive policies. In 1907 New
Zealand became a dominion within the British Empire. In
1914, with a European population of approximately one
million, and a Maori population of about 50,000 (one fifth
their eighteenth century numbers), New Zealand identified itself with the British cause.

Meanwhile, throughout the eighteenth and nineteenth
centuries, the rivalry of the European powers in the Pacific
had never ceased. In 1828 the Dutch annexed western
New Guinea. Tahiti and the Marquesas became a French
protectorate in 1842. In 1853 the French acquired New
Caledonia; in 1864 they took the Loyalty Islands. To offset
French moves in the 1870s the British claimed Fiji. In the
1870s and 1880s the United States and Britain squabbled
over Samoa and New Guinea. In 1884 the British annexed
the south-eastern part of New Guinea, which was turned
over to Australia in 1906 and given the old Portuguese
name of Papua. The Germans had already annexed the
north-eastern part of New Guinea as well as the islands of
the Bismarck Archipelago. In 1885 they also laid claim to
the Marshall and the Solomon Islands. In 1887 Britain and
France forestalled Germany by establishing their rule in
the New Hebrides. Cook Island became a British protectorate in 1888. In 1900, in exchange for German possessions in the Solomons, Britain relinquished its rights in
the Samoan Islands. The United States retained Tutuila
(Pago Pago became its naval base). The last extension of
European rule in the Pacific area before the outbreak of
war in 1914 was Britain's action in 1900 in making the
Friendly and Savage Islands its protectorates. By then the
colonization of the world by European man had almost
run its course.

While the European powers would try to settle scores in
the First and Second World Wars, the influence of Euro-

pean ideas and beliefs upon the non-European world would continue to grow. In contrast to the general retreat of Western political dominance in the world today, the influence of European political ideas is still felt.[65] The French Revolution (1789) and the Russian Revolution (1917) have bequeathed ideas which have affected the world ever since. The French Revolution not only espoused "liberty, equality, and fraternity", but also self-determination and nationalism.

Many European ideas were deliberately transmitted. Ignoring the social and historical circumstances of the territory over which they came to rule, ignoring tradition and social customs, ignoring or suppressing native religions, the Europeans imposed their political, economic, religious, philosophical, and legal ideas on many parts of the world. Land, labor, and capital became factors of production to be bought and sold in a self-regulating world market. In the eighteenth and nineteenth centuries, Western concepts concerning saving, investment, and production were introduced to non-Western communities for the first time. Also introduced were new ideas concerning time, punctuality, personal responsibility, taxes, monetary rewards and punishments. Under European tutelage, change came to be looked upon as a virtue rather than a threat.

In divorcing economic motives from the social environment, in introducing an all-purpose money which could buy and sell anything, in emphasizing the role of the individual instead of that of the family or the tribe, in treating individual ownership as sacrosanct, in creating a world economy dependent upon the West – in all these ways Western man transfigured the world. As a result, the economies of the other continents became linked to the interests of a politically and technically superior Europe. For many people – especially the Europeans – it created a richer world; yet it was a world that was much more complicated, much more sensitive to the booms and busts of capitalist Europe. For European and non-European alike, it created a less stable world than had existed hitherto.

European spiritual and secular ideas were part of the baggage carried by an unparalleled number of Europeans migrating to the rest of the world. Using the more reliable figures of relatively recent times, from 1851 until 1960 about 60 million Europeans left their homelands for overseas or for Siberia. It was the greatest migration of all time. One of the major influences prompting this movement was rapid population growth coupled with the scarcity of European land. Until the First World War, European large-scale migration was essentially the transfer of agricultural workers from areas where land was scarce to areas where land was plentiful. By and large, the movement of Europeans was characterized by individual want, individual hope, individual decision, individual enterprise and individual suffering. The outcome was the establishment, in the Americas, Siberia, Australasia, and the temperate parts of Africa, of a new European world outside Europe. If Europe had not risen and expanded as it did, white Americans, Canadians, and Latin Americans, white Australians, white New Zealanders, white South Africans, and many white Russians would not be where they are today: nor would a lot of colored people. While the European powers have lost their colonial empires, their descendents remain in possession of great parts of the world. It was fortunate for Europe that at the time of its most rapid population growth a vast new world could be colonized.

This unparalleled migration was not achieved without great distress being inflicted upon the people of other continents. The white man's success often heralded the undoing of the red, the black, and the yellow. Western needs – sometimes expressed as Western greed – aided by superior weapons, alcohol, and devastating sicknesses (including measles, smallpox, typhus, and influenza[66]) accelerated the decline of many native Americans, Africans, Australians, and Asians. While there were Europeans (this is especially true of the Christian missionaries) whose professional pride and humanitarian instincts enabled them to set aside thoughts of personal gain, the springboard of Western colonization was overwhelmingly the quest for wealth and power.

Europeans not only wrought change in the world through the diffusion of ideas and the migration of people. Assisted by the relative peace prevailing among the Great Powers during the nineteenth century, they eventually developed a network of world finance upon which depended the growth of world transport, trade, and migration. Before they could do so, changes had to take place in the outlook of whole sections of static, self-subsisting African, Asian, and American societies toward wealth and economic progress. Where circumstances were favorable, as in the United States, the British Dominions, and certain Latin American countries – the areas which before 1914 received most financial assistance from Europe – the effect of Western investment was considerable. In the economically less-developed regions of the world, including China, India, most of Africa, and Latin America, its visible impact was limited to those export sectors of the economy in which European interests and influence were greatest. The bulk of these investments in the century before 1914 went into critically important public utilities – especially transport and communication – which provided the economic foundations of a Euro-centric world.[67]

Whereas many parts of the world have rejected European secular and religious ideas, or have proved unsuitable for large-scale European settlement, or for the investment of European wealth, few parts of the world have remained uninfluenced by the diffusion of European science and technology. It was Europe's growing productive efficiency in the nineteenth century which helped to tilt the scales of power in its favor.

Yet, even as late as the eighteenth century, the general level of applied science – of technical knowledge – in Europe was low. Until the fifteenth and sixteenth centuries, many branches of Chinese, Indian, and Arab science and technology were superior to those of Europe. Long before the Europeans appeared in the Indian Ocean, Arab fleets had been sailing from Arabia to China. It was an Arab pilot who led da Gama to Calicut. When Hernando Cortez (1485–1547) reached the Aztec city of

Tenochtitlán (Mexico City) in 1519 he was astonished at the artistic, industrial, and administrative achievements of its inhabitants. Da Gama and other Europeans were equally astonished by what they found in India.

Partly because of the general dynamic situation in Europe at the time, which caused a new emphasis to be placed on scientific and industrial developments, and partly because it was profitable to those concerned, Europe's relative backwardness in science and technology underwent considerable change from the sixteenth century onward. The subsequent diffusion by Europeans of new ideas and practices, as well as the redistribution in the world of existing plants and animals, transformed world agriculture. Vast areas in the temperate and tropical zones were opened up for primary production. Cereals such as maize,[68] wheat, rice, barley, rye, oats; fruits such as bananas, oranges, limes, peaches, grapes; fibers such as cotton; beverages such as tea and coffee; crops such as sugarcane; draft animals such as the horse, the mule, and the ox; and animals for food such as fowls, hogs, sheep, goats and cattle (many of which Europe had itself inherited from Asia) were carried by Europeans to every part of the world. In particular, Europe's colonization of the New World allowed it to transfer to other continents many native American plants, including corn, cacao, certain beans, yams, manioc, potatoes, peanuts, pineapples, tomatoes, and tobacco. From Peru came two important plants: cinchona, the source of quinine, and coca, the source of cocaine. South America was also the source of rubber-bearing plants which became the basis of the rubber plantation industry of the Far East. Accompanying these plants and animals were European agricultural tools and machinery. The distribution, under European guidance and skilled management, of the cinchona (quinine), sugar, tea, cotton, and potato plants was to change the course of world history.

Europeans did more than transfer plants, animals, and agricultural tools and machinery from one part of the world to another; they also diffused scientific knowledge concerning the breeding of plants and animals, soil bacteriology, the use of artificial fertilizers, and systems of cultivation. The most important single way in which European influence was felt in tropical agriculture was through the establishment overseas of botanical gardens, laboratories, experimental stations and departments of agriculture.

Europe's contribution to world agriculture was matched by its contribution to the industrial arts. From the seventeenth century onward, Europeans became inventors and innovators of scientific instruments and industrial machinery on a scale previously unequalled. These changes culminated in one of the major landmarks in history, the "Industrial Revolution". In the eighteenth and nineteenth centuries European technology became increasingly dependent on metals, machines, inventors, and trained engineers. All-important was Europe's development of steam power (linked with the name of James Watt) and electrical energy (associated with the work of Michael Faraday and others).

The earliest industrial techniques diffused from Europe to the world were the simple basic manufactures (for example, textiles) as well as those employed in food and raw material processing and refining (food refrigeration and mining technology). These were followed by techniques needed for manufacturing capital equipment (for example, steel). Techniques in all these fields had, of course, existed before the European Age began. Europe's contribution was to change the scale of industry. Mass production techniques and concentrated, steam-driven industry were the hallmarks of Britain's Industrial Revolution. As the Western industrialized countries became rich and powerful, industrialization came to be regarded as the key to worldly success. In its seeming ability to turn dross into gold, Western industry played the role that alchemy had tried to play in the Middle Ages.

These industrial techniques could never have been developed had the Europeans not also provided the technology to open and develop the great mining areas of the world. Although minerals have attracted the attention of mankind since the earliest times, it was not until the end of the eighteenth and the beginning of the nineteenth century (most mining activity has come into existence since then) that important advances in the science of mineralogy (especially in the improvement of certain mechanical and chemical processes) were made by Western man. The rapid growth of coal, copper, precious metals (such as gold), and oil mining in the world these past two hundred years were made possible by these developments.

None of the changes in science and technology discussed so far had such a dramatic effect upon the world as the changes brought about by the Europeans and North Americans in transport and communications. Between 1815 and 1914, under Western auspices, a veritable transportation revolution took place. The steam locomotive, steamship, steam turbine, automobile, submarine, airplane, radio, telegraph and telephone were all invented before 1914. In 1869 the Suez Canal was completed. At the beginning of the nineteenth century Napoleon could travel no faster than Caesar had done 2000 years earlier. Half a century later – thanks to Western developments – the situation had been transformed. The extraordinary progress made in aviation, space exploration, nuclear science, television, weaponry, and computer science in our own age, should not blind us to the equally significant changes that took place prior to the First Great War, including the domestic comforts which we now take for granted, such as heat for the home, safe drinking water, and gas and electric light.

While many techniques have originated in non-Western parts of the world (particularly Asia), and have sometimes spread without Western man's intervention, Western man's contribution to the raising of general technical levels in the world has probably no equal. While we do not know all the factors that explain the changes the world power struggle has undergone this past half millennium, we know enough to be able to conclude that the development and transfer of Western scientific and technological ideas and practices has changed the relations hitherto existing between different parts of the world.

One of the outcomes of the world-wide diffusion of Western science and technology was a vast increase in international commerce. From the early decades of the nineteenth century, a world economy emerged focused upon western Europe (in particular upon the leading trading nation of the time, Britain). The great traders of the modern age were Europeans. It is they who accepted an all-purpose money and an all-powerful market, without which it is difficult to explain Europe's ascendancy. It is they who developed international trade until it embraced not only the luxury items of commerce, but the indispensable things of daily life. The essential benefits accruing from the growth of world commerce were the enlargement and concentration of production in the areas of the world most suitable for particular items of trade, and the closer economic and commercial integration of mankind. For some countries, trade with the West was the indispensable forerunner of their economic development. Consider the early dependency of European settled parts of the world, such as the Americas or Australasia, upon the export to Europe of primary produce. For many countries the commercial needs of the West became vital to their existence. Consider the great dependence of Mauritius on sugar, Colombia on coffee, Ghana on cocoa, Sri Lanka on tea, Liberia on rubber, Egypt on cotton, Bolivia on tin, and Suriname on bauxite. More recently, many countries, including Kuwait, Saudi Arabia, and Brunei have become almost totally dependent on the sale of oil. Nor is the economic impact the end of the story. There could not be economic impact without cultural impact. Accompanying Western trade were the aims and objectives of Western civilization.

While one should not exaggerate the influence of Western man in the creation of the modern world – the modern world is in fact the result of an extremely complicated, interrelated process in which it is often impossible to distinguish the impact of one civilization or era from another – the colonization of the world by Western man left behind it a legacy of dependency between Europe and the world that had never existed before. There had been "world economies" before the sixteenth century, but they had always been transformed into empires. Only Europe embarked on the path of capitalistic development on a world scale. Without European expansion there would have been no international economy as we know it; certainly there would have been no global economy such as we are increasingly experiencing today.

Europe's colonization of the world (by 1914 only Japan in Asia and Liberia and Ethiopia in Africa were free of European tutelage[69]) should not blind us to its limitations. Europe's imprint on the world remains, but its empires have vanished; most of the political ties which bound the rest of the world to Europe have been broken. The only advanced civilizations to be swept away by the Europeans overnight were the Aztecs, the Incas, and the Mayas. Even here, elements of the linguistic and cultural unity remain. Nowhere else did Western intrusion have such dramatic results. The West went on to carve up China into spheres of influence, but China never ceased to be China, nor India, India. Until the eighteenth century, changes in India came more from religious revival than from Mogul or Western invasion. Hindus, rooted securely in their own culture, always treated Moguls and Europeans as what they were – aliens. Two hundred years after Columbus sailed, the great Asian empires were still expanding. Australia and Oceania were still to be "discovered" by the West. It is only in the second half of the nineteenth century that Europe truly extends its dominion over the world (see Map IV). Even then, with the exception of the North Americans, and the other groups of ex-Europeans abroad, Europe's rule was short-lived. In Africa, European political dominance disappeared in a couple of generations.

It is not only European hegemony that has ended. European ideas are also being assailed. Throughout the Muslim world the secular rationality which sprang from the Renaissance and the French Revolution, is today being challenged by religious fundamentalism. Irrational forces based on faith rather than reason are growing. Men speak

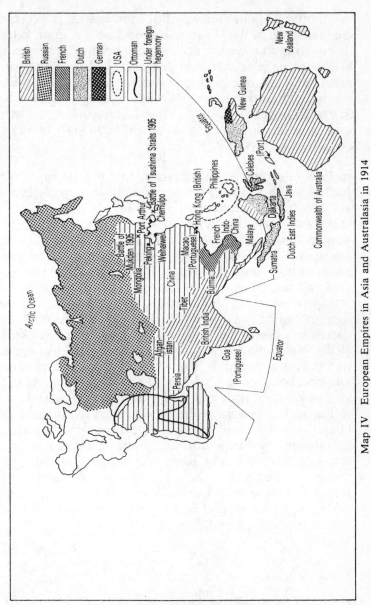

Map IV   European Empires in Asia and Australasia in 1914

EUROPEAN EMPIRES IN ASIA AND
AUSTRALASIA IN 1914
Map IV

of "the tyranny of reason". But then reason is peculiarly characteristic of the Western intellectual tradition. We are discovering that we are not only the heirs of Erasmus, but also of paleolithic man who has occupied the earth for all except the last one or two per cent of human time. Even the individual dynamic of Western society – upon which in explaining the Rise of the West I have placed such stress – is now being challenged by the dynamic of eastern collectivism.

In 1918 – despite the havoc caused by the First Great War – Europe was still a world civilization; European history was still the most important part of world history. European science and technology, European systems of administration and bureaucratization (such as that imposed by Britain upon India) and even European finance, continued to have an impact on the world. In 1918 much of the world was still dependent upon Europe. European ideas – not least the ideas of secular rationality, of progress, of self-determination, of nationalism, and of revolutionary socialism – were also very much alive. Even so, by the 1920s, the Euro-centric world of the nineteenth century had begun to crumble. There were Europeans, of course, who still believed in Christianity as a world religion; in the idea of Western progress for the human race; in their duty to lift up the people of the world; in individualism; in a liberal economic and political world order; in capitalism, rationalism, egalitarianism, and even revolutionary socialism – but by then they were becoming a minority. Even those who hung on to the idea of Europe's mission to the world no longer held that belief with the certainty, fervor, and compulsion – least of all with the megalomania and will to power – of earlier times.

4

The Expansion of the Russian Empire

The Soviet Union today occupies one-sixth of the earth's land surface. It is the largest political entity, the most extensive contiguous empire on earth (more than twice the size of the USA). In 1989 it had a population of 287 million people embracing one hundred different ethnic groups, speaking eighty different languages, writing in five different alphabets, and although (until 1990) officially atheist, practicing Islam, Judaism, Buddhism, and several versions of Christianity. While Russia is a wealthy country (it probably leads the world in mineral and fossil fuel resources and has an enormous industrial base and a skilled work force) it has many drawbacks. Much of its abundant land is uninhabitable (one third of it lies outside the temperate zone). Water transportation is limited. For much of the year the northern ports are frozen; the Siberian rivers flow northward into the Arctic Ocean; the warm water ports of the Black Sea are bottled up by the Bosphorus and the Turks. Militarily, Russia may still be considered a superpower; economically, the Soviet Union is at a considerable disadvantage.

Legend holds that Russia was founded by the Rus (Scandinavian Vikings) at Kiev in the Ukraine in the ninth century.[70] (Official Russian history holds that the first kingdom was founded by the Slavs). In AD 989–990, soon after Vladimir the Great embraced the Byzantine Orthodox Christian faith, centered on Constantinople, the Kievan Russian pagan state was forcibly converted to Christianity. Thenceforth, until the sacking of Russia by the Mongols in the thirteenth century, the infant Russian state continued to extend its power and foster its relations with Byzantium. When Ivan III came to the Russian throne in 1462, he emphasized Russia's connection with Byzantium by declaring himself the successor of the last of the Byzantine emperors. Constantinople (the "second Rome") having perished at the hands of the Turks, it was taken for granted that Moscow, which had grown in influence since the destruction of Kiev by the Mongols, would become the "third Rome" and the center of Russian authority. By then (1462) Moscow had already successfully repulsed western invasions by the Lithuanians, the Poles, the Germans, and the Swedes. In 1471, the principality of Novgorod (destroyed by Ivan IV in 1570) was subdued by Muscovy. In 1485 Tver suffered the same fate. Before Ivan III's death in 1505 the unification of modern Russia had taken place. By the time his son Vasili III died in 1533 a nation had been born; the Kievian tradition of a confederation of equal sovereign princes was giving way to the absolute rule of the Czar. The rival claims of other Russian principalities, such as Novgorod, had been successfully resisted by Muscovy.

From that time forward, during the reigns of Ivan III, the Great (1462–1505), and his grandson Ivan IV, the Terrible (1533–1584), Russia proceeded to expand (see Map V). Assisted by the use of gunpowder, which put an end to the eastern Tatar invasions, the Russians now struck fear into its neighbors. In 1492 Ivan III began Russia's westward expansion by invading Lithuania and reaching the coveted harbors of the Baltic Sea. In the Livonian War of 1557–1582, Ivan IV seized the port of Narva. However, in 1578, Russian moves were halted by the Swedes and the Poles. With the accession of Peter I, the Great, to the Russian throne (1682–1725), Russian fortunes changed dramatically. Peter was the first Russian sovereign to try to westernize his country. Symbolically, in 1703 he transferred Russia's capital from Moscow to St Petersburg (Leningrad) on the Gulf of Finland. His two great victories in the Great Northern War (1700–1721) over the Swedes at Poltava in 1709 and on the Baltic in 1721 ended Swedish supremacy and ensured Russian control over Estonia and Latvia. With the Peace of Nystad in 1721, Sweden became a second-class power; Russia's rise

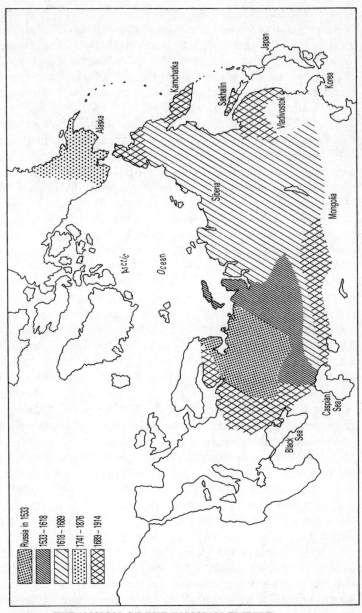

Russia in 1533
1533 – 1618
1618 – 1689
1741 – 1876
1689 – 1914

EXPANSION OF THE RUSSIAN EMPIRE
Map V

as a European power had begun.

Peter's objective – expansion at the expense of Sweden, Turkey, and Poland – was furthered by Catherine the Great (1762–1796). Under Catherine, Russia came to be feared by the Ottoman Turks on the Black Sea as well. Land-locked Russia has always sought access to the warm seas. Catherine's wars against the Turks (1768–1772 and 1787–1792) eventually brought the northern shores of the Black Sea under Russian control. Odessa was founded in 1795 on the Black Sea as an outlet for Russian exports. Two windows – one in the Baltic, the other in the Black Sea – had been opened by Russia on the world. In 1772, 1793, and 1795, Russia divided up the Polish-Lithuanian Commonwealth with Austria and Prussia. Poland was again partitioned (the lion's share going to Russia) by the same powers at the Congress of Vienna in 1815. It did not regain its freedom until the Treaty of Versailles, 1919.

Spurred by the desire for domination, by the search for furs, by the sense of adventure, as well as the desire to escape serfdom and an autocratic state, throughout the sixteenth and seventeenth centuries, the Russians also fought their way eastward against the Tatars and the Turks toward the Pacific. In 1552, during the reign of Ivan IV, they seized Kazan, a Muslim Tatar stronghold on the middle Volga. St Basil's Cathedral was built in the Red Square to celebrate the victory. Astrakhan was taken in 1554. For the remainder of the sixteenth and the whole of the seventeenth centuries,[71] they colonized the valleys of the Dnieper, the Don, and the Volga. With control of the entire Volga, Russian expansion to the south-west, as well as the east, was assured. Yet Russian expansion eastward had constantly to be defended from the rear. In 1571 Moscow was once more sacked by an invading force of Tatars.

In less than a century, by the late 1630s, Russia's eastward march had reached the Sea of Okhotsk. The Russians then swept southward to the banks of the Amur River, where for the next two centuries their expansion was held in check by the Manchus who had established their rule in China by 1644. The Treaty of Nerchinsk, concluded in 1689, which demarcated the Chinese-Russian border, was the first such treaty between East and West. Treaties with China would eventually extend Russia's southeastern frontier to Vladivostok. In 1707 the Kamchatka Peninsula, north of Japan, was annexed. By 1741 Russian traders had crossed the Bering Straits into Alaska. Only in 1812, by which time they had reached the vicinity of present-day San Francisco, did their eastern march finally come to a halt. With the sale of Alaska to the United States in 1867, the Russians withdrew from North America.

Central to the story of Russia's past is the influence of endemic warfare (which Russia's vast accessible plain, three quarters of it less than 1,800 feet above sea level, has encouraged). War and want and suffering have plagued Russia; they still do.

> Old Russia [Stalin once remarked] . . . was ceaselessly beaten for her backwardness. She was beaten by the Mongol Khans. She was beaten by the Turkish beys. She was beaten by the Swedish feudal lords. She was beaten by the Polish-Lithuanian gentry. She was beaten by Anglo-French capitalists. She was beaten by the Japanese barons.[72]

What Stalin overlooked – with so much Russian blood on his hands he could hardly do otherwise – is that much of Russia's suffering has been its own doing. Listen to the Russian poet, Yevgeny Yevtushenko (1933–):

> She was christened in childhood with a lash,
>   torn to pieces,
>   scorched.
> Her soul was trampled by the feet,
> inflicting blow upon blow,
> of Pechenegs,
>   Varangians,
>   Tatars,
> and our own people –
>   much more terrible than the Tatars.

From these roots stem Russia's melancholia, paranoia, passivity, xenophobia, and national self-pity.

For 250 years, from the thirteenth to the fifteenth century, the Russians made war against the Mongols (and their more numerous Turkic allies, the Tatars). Several times Moscow was overrun and destroyed. The Mongol yoke was a catastrophe of such proportions that Russians have never forgotten it. Dmitri's victory over a Mongol-Tatar army at Kulikovo on the Don in 1380 – the first time that the Russians had beaten a Mongol-Tatar horde – is a hallowed day in Russian history.[73]

The Russians not only had to fight the Mongols; from the thirteenth to the eighteenth century they also had to meet the threats posed by invading Swedes, Germans, Poles, and Lithuanians. At the beginning of the seventeenth century Moscow and Muscovy were constantly under threat from bands of Poles (who wanted to establish the pope's claim to rule the eastern as well as the western branches of Christianity) and Swedes.

The most formidable challenges to Russia's independence, during the next two centuries, came from the French and the Germans. In 1812 the French seized Moscow, but the Russians refused to surrender. Napoleon's effort to conquer Russia failed. Of the approximately three-quarters of a million men who invaded Russia, fewer than 100,000 returned. Wounds, sickness, and the Russian winter accounted for most of the rest. The remnants of Napoleon's army were defeated by a united European army at Leipzig in 1813. At the subsequent peace meetings in Paris in 1814–1815, Russia spoke as the leading power on the continent, Britain as the greatest world power of the time. If Britain made unusual concessions to the French in 1815 (despite its defeat, France was the third greatest power of the time), it was not because they liked the French, but because they feared the Russians. To weaken France was to strengthen Russia. The British had no desire to replace Napoleon with the Czar.

By the mid-nineteenth century growing suspicion by Britain and France of Russia had resulted in the outbreak of hostilities between them in the Crimean War of 1853–1856. Earlier, in 1851, exercising its supposed rights as the guardian of the Orthodox Church, Russia had occupied the Turkish-controlled Danubian provinces. France had responded by pressing its claim as guardian of the western Latin rights (including those of Palestine). The British, alarmed by Russia's invasion of European Turkey and of its growing power in the Black Sea, supported France. In October 1853, encouraged by Britain and France, Turkey (after Britain, Russia, and France perhaps the fourth great power) declared war on Russia. A month later Russia sank the Turkish fleet and took control of the Black Sea. To prevent Russia from subduing Turkey and seizing the Dardanelles (Turkish Straits) which gave it access to the Mediterranean, and which had been closed to Russian warships since the international Straits Convention of 1841, British and French warships were sent into the Black Sea. By March 1854, seemingly in a willy-nilly way, Britain and France had committed themselves to battle. Landings were made in the Crimea. Under the added threat of Austrian intervention[74] (the Habsburgs at that time vied with the Turks as the fourth greatest power), Russia, having lost almost half a million men, was eventually forced to evacuate European Turkey and in 1856 to agree to the neutralization of the Black Sea. The ailing Ottoman Empire was reinstated as a buffer against Russian expansion. Russia's humiliating defeat helped to discredit the Czarist regime.

Before 1914 Britain and Japan had also been concerned with halting the extension of Russian power in the Far East. Russian encroachment into Turkistan in the mid-nineteenth century had already alarmed the British in India. Despite their warnings (Britain had commercial interests in the Yangtze Valley, Japan had similar interests in Manchuria and Korea), Russia insisted on penetrating Manchuria as well as China and Korea. The Trans-Siberian Railway to Vladivostok on the Pacific was begun in 1891 and completed in 1903. In 1898 Russia leased the Chinese port of Port Arthur (Lü-shun) on the southern half of the Liaotung Peninsula. Five days after Russia occupied Port

Arthur, the British occupied the neighboring port of Wei-haiwei. In 1902, with insufficient strength to contain both German advances in the West and Russian advances in the Orient, the British signed an alliance with Japan. Japan was emboldened to request Russia to evacuate Manchuria – a request that was treated with contempt. In 1904–1905 Russia was defeated by the Japanese on land and sea.

Defeated in the East, Russia continued to press its claims in central Asia. For a long time Russia had had its eyes on the warm waters of the Persian Gulf. In 1907, prompted by the revolution in Persia and the growing German threat in south-west Asia, the Russians and the British had reached a compromise and had secretly divided Persia between them. Without consulting the Persians, the British agreed to exercise tutelage over the south-east, which was chiefly desert, the Russians settled for the entire northern half of the country containing three-quarters of Persia's population. The south-western part remained neutral. Britain, the leading sea power of the time, retained control of the all-important Gulf. Ignoring Persian protests, the Russian-British secret agreement on Persia was implemented when war came in 1914. Meanwhile, Russia, Britain, and France had continued to arm against the growing German threat. According to Lenin, it was Russia's massive rearmament from the 1890s onward that caused Germany to strike first.

A year after the Russian-British agreement over Persia, in October 1908, Russia came close to war with Austria concerning the Serbian-claimed territory of Bosnia and Herzegovina, which Austria (thinking it had Russia's informal agreement) had annexed.[75] In support of Serbia, and as mother of the Slavs, Russia called upon Austria to withdraw. Austria refused. Instead it appealed to its ally, Germany. France, with whom Russia had closed ranks against the Germans since the 1890s, showed little interest in becoming involved. Britain watched the growing crisis with studied unconcern. Under threat of war from Germany, Russia capitulated. But the problem remained. The assassination of the Austrian Archduke Francis Ferdinand at Sarajevo, by a Serb on 28 June 1914, brought matters to a head again. This time Russia did not capitulate. And so, after almost a century free of widespread conflict, Europe mobilized and went to war (see Chapter 7). The Serbs were bled white; the Russians lost almost two million men; the Russian, German, Austrian, and Ottoman empires were destroyed; the world was never the same again.

Despite all its trials and tribulations, Russia has endured for a thousand years. During that time Russia's despotic traditions, as well as its penchant for dogma and authority, have been preserved. While Russia is not unique in its disregard for human life – history reeks with human slaughter[76] – it has experienced more than its share of tyranny and brutality. Ivan IV, the Terrible (who from 1547 was Czar of all the Russias), put to death individuals (including his eldest son whom he struck and killed in a fit of rage) and whole communities even remotely suspected of opposing him. Peter the Great, who had his own son tortured to death, once had hundreds of Russians roasted alive. Even Catherine the Great was not immune from the tyranny surrounding the Russian throne. Her own German husband, Czar Peter III, died in mysterious circumstances. Elizabeth Tudor could be as calculating and cruel as the rest, but (in the tradition of *Magna Carta*) she took good care to remain inside the law. Think of the legal devices that her father, Henry VIII, employed to rid himself of his wives. In Russia such action would have been unthinkable. In the three years – 1918–1921 – Lenin's secret police, the Cheka, are charged with having killed seven times as many people as the Czars had executed over the previous hundred years.[77] Stalin is said to have killed more of his own countrymen in the Ukraine, the Volga Basin, the Caucasus, and the area of the Don than had been lost by all the European powers in the First World War.[78] If Russia's traditions appear less humane than those of other parts of Europe, it is not least because, for a thousand years, Russia has been constantly fighting for the right to exist.

The Marxist-Leninist state became a secular version of Russia's earlier omnipotent Eastern Orthodox Church and landed aristocracy. The absolute autocracy of Stalin was a latter-day version of the absolute autocracy of the Czars. For most of the West, the state is the means, the welfare of the individual is the end. In Western society it is not the state's job to prevent the citizen from falling into error, but the citizen's job to prevent the state from falling into error. Even allowing for Gorbachev's perestroika (restructuring) and glasnost (openness), such an outlook is alien to the Russian mind. Security and order, stemming from highly centralized control, have always been paramount. They are what freedom and individualism have meant to the West. Russian history has no Age of Chivalry, no Renaissance, no Reformation, no Counter-Reformation, and no eighteenth-century Enlightenment. Nor did Russia experience the challenge to authority which the French Revolution presented to other parts of Europe. Peter the Great introduced some Western ideas; the German-born Czarina, Catherine the Great flirted with Western liberalization, but the oriental traits in the Russian soul – despite the European inheritance of the Russian Orthodox Church – have remained. In Stalin the oriental traits predominated. Even though educated in a seminary,[79] Stalin stressed not the Sermon on the Mount but the traditional Russian dictum that "It is the pike's job to keep the carp awake."

Stalin's paranoid attitude to foreigners was also the product of Russia's age-old isolation. While, from the fifteenth to the nineteenth century, millions of western Europeans were free to emigrate to America, most Russians remained isolated, bound and hobbled by a rigid serfdom. The Russian serf knew freedom from his master only for two weeks each year. From 1593 onward even this right was revoked. After 1648 a runaway serf had no rights whatsoever. All that was expected of a Russian serf[80] was that he should work and obey; servility and conformity were enforced. Those who did not conform were regarded as a threat to society. Dissidence was feared. The freedom that mattered in Russia – and still does – is the freedom from anarchy, from famine, and from war.

5

The Scientific and Industrial Revolutions

Few events have transformed the modern world as much as Europe's Scientific[81] and Industrial Revolutions.

The origin of Europe's Scientific Revolution can be traced to the shift in emphasis during the Renaissance from authoritative truth – the truth God had already revealed in holy scripture concerning mankind's origin and destiny – to factual, objective truth regarding the processes and laws governing the natural world. Interest shifted progressively from the next world to this; from concern with something affecting our redemption or eternal damnation, to the actual manner of causation in the objective world.

Of incalculable importance in the progress of the Scientific Revolution was the introduction of printing[82] which from the fifteenth century onward made available a vast store of new and accumulated knowledge drawn from an ever-widening area. Written knowledge became more important than the collective memory of a community. The purpose of scientists such as Copernicus, Tycho Brahe (1546–1601), Galileo and Johannes Kepler (1571–1630), with whose writings the Scientific Revolution is most identified, was not to undermine scripture, but to confirm it by revealing God's divine will and purpose in nature as well. Increasingly, what had been the shadow (nature) became the reality. What had been the reality (the soul) became the shadow.

Although the birth of modern science is thought to have begun with the work of Nicolaus Copernicus (who published *De revolutionibus orbium coelestium* [*On the Revolutions of the Celestial Spheres*] in 1543) and Galileo Galilei (whose *Dialogo dei Massimi Sistemi* [*Dialogue on the Great World*

55

Systems] was published in 1632), their writings were themselves dependent upon earlier contributions.[83] Vital to the progress of scientific work in Europe was the translation and literary transmission of ancient Greek and Arabic scientific texts from Arab Spain – including the works of Euclid, Archimedes, Hippocrates, and Galen. Although western Europe had had access to Greek and Arab science and logic from the twelfth century (the reconquest of Toledo in 1085 had yielded an astonishing number of such literary treasures), it was not until the middle of the sixteenth century that the rediscovery of ancient science by the Europeans via Spain reached its climax.

The new spirit of rational inquiry in sixteenth century Europe had much in common with the earlier pathbreaking work of the Arab mathematician Alhazen (AD 965–1038) in optics, and the Florentine architect Filippo Brunelleschi (1377?–1446) in perspective geometry. With the aid of the new perspective drawing, one could not only depict the precise image of the human body; much more important for sixteenth century Europe, one could begin to depict and eventually measure the entire globe.[84] In providing, visually and philosophically, a new view of the world, Alhazen and Brunelleschi caused the arts and the sciences to be pursued much more realistically than heretofore. Man and science became the measure of things, not God.

The significance of the work of Copernicus (a contemporary of Martin Luther and Michelangelo) and Galileo, is that it shattered the geocentric view of the universe. It also shattered the until then respectable science of astrology. Copernicus[85] stated that the earth moved, and was one of the planets revolving around the sun. Fifty years later Galileo labored – almost to the point of losing his freedom and his life – to convince his fellow astronomers and physicists, by accurate observations with his telescope, that Copernicus was right. With the Dane Tycho Brahe he demonstrated beyond any doubt the truth of Copernicus' theory.

The totally different view of the universe held by Copernicus and Galileo helped to overthrow the intellectual traditions not only of the Middle Ages but also of the ancient world. More important for that day and age, their writings challenged church doctrine concerning the nature of the universe and man's place in it. In ignoring authority and tradition, they took the moral component out of science. The church could no longer hide behind theological truths. Moreover, if the church's view of the universe, which was based on Aristotle and Ptolemy, was wrong, what was right?

While it is easy to ask such a question now, it was not widely asked then. The revolutionary nature of Copernican thought was appreciated by neither the church fathers nor Copernicus' scientific contemporaries; great conceptual leaps in scientific thought rarely are. It was not until 1616 (more than half a century after the publication of Copernicus' work) that the Catholic Church placed his book on the *Index of Prohibited Books*.

Despite persecution and censorship, the writings of Copernicus and Galileo gradually released a force of critical inquiry based on scientific observation and mathematical calculation (decimals were introduced in 1585, logarithms in 1614, the slide rule in 1622, and the first adding machine in 1645), which would eventually remodel the whole of Western scientific thought. In time, the gradual rejection of traditional thinking caused a new stress to be placed upon the spirit of inquiry. Empirical observation and experiment – backed by mathematical analysis – became the systematic and logical way of seeking truth. The German mathematician, Johannes Kepler, Tycho Brahe's assistant, eventually reduced the Copernican system to mathematical exactitude.

The Frenchman René Descartes (1596–1650), whose *Discourse on Method*, published in 1637 helped to lay the foundations of modern scientific thought, argued that nothing should be believed, all should be doubted. Only thought, he maintained ("*Cogito ergo sum*" – "I think, therefore I am") was real. Everything should be subject to quantitative analysis and proof. Tangible proof, not medieval faith was what mattered. Everything should be broken down to its constituent parts. The progress of mankind was itself dependent upon taking careful measurements. With the use of mathematics and human reason, order would be imposed on the seeming chaos of the universe. The essence of Descartes' contribution is that he recast the real world into a world of geometrical symbols. His world was bound together by mathematics; for him counting became causation.

Western thinkers like Descartes, Francis Bacon (1561–1626), Baruch Spinoza (1632–1677), and Gottfried Wilhelm von Leibnitz (1646–1716) have had a greater influence upon Western thought and action in the world than most of us realize. Descartes' analytical geometry, his logical progressions, and his overwhelming reliance upon reason have provided Western man with a uniquely different attitude toward life and work. It is this different outlook which has separated Western man from other branches of the human race. Perhaps it is this which in an increasingly scientific, technical, and mechanistic society gave Western man his peculiar powers. The narrow, geometrizing Cartesian attitude toward life, however, has never been triumphant outside the West – holism (the idea that all knowledge is integrated and interdependent), mystery, fate, passion and emotion have had far greater effect. Today the Cartesian attitude is breaking down even among those with whom it originated.

Not so in Descartes' day. Descartes and his seventeenth-century scientific companions were convinced that universal, rational, invariant scientific laws (that, for some, would confirm God's divine purpose every bit as much as scripture had) could be formulated. All phenomena would obey such universally applicable laws. Reality was not beyond the grasp of logical analysis. In his *Mathematical Principles of Natural Philosophy* published in 1687, the Englishman, Sir Isaac Newton (1642–1727), who "was more gifted with the power of scientific demonstration than any man", and who, as a devout Christian, also believed in faith and revelation, provided such a universal, mechanistic, mathematically predictable scientific law governing the majestic clockwork of the heavens. Once having been set in motion, the universal clock did not need the unseen hand of God to keep it going. The Almighty was no longer Almighty. Great as the contributions of Copernicus, Brahe, Kepler, and Galileo had been, it was Newton who first presented "the universe as one great unity operating according to rational, calculable, unalterable principles". He was the originator of value-free system-building in the sciences. To his scientific contemporaries Newton left little to be said that needed saying.

The seventeenth century proved to be a high water mark in Western scientific inquiry. In 1662 the Royal Society of London was founded to advance scientific knowledge. Four years later, in 1666, the Académie des Sciences was established in Paris. In 1675 the Royal Greenwich Observatory was founded primarily to resolve the problem of longitude and thus improve navigation – an appropriate goal in an age of growing world trade and European expansion. This new, detached, mechanistic way of looking at the natural world also influenced the work of the alchemists who began to explain chemical reactions not on a mystical, but on a purely scientific basis. Their work would eventually lead to the founding of chemistry as a separate science in the late eighteenth century. Robert Boyle (1627–1691) led the way in 1661 when he dispensed with Aristotle's theories about substances. Antoine Lavoisier (1743–1794) followed. With Lavoisier, chemical reactions came to be measured more accurately than before.

The publication by Karl von Linné (known as Linnaeus [1707–1778]) of *Philosophia Botanica*, in 1752, which classified plants by genus and species, did something to restore the Almighty to His rightful place as the grand and perfect designer of nature. A century later, following upon the work of Hans Christian Oersted (1777–1851), André Marie Ampère (1775–1836), Georg Simon Ohm (1787–1854), and others, the scientific discoveries of Michael Faraday (1791–1867) provided a tremendous stimulus to the use of electrical energy. Meanwhile, the experiments conducted by the Austrian monk Gregor Johann Mendel (1822–1884), during the 1850s and 1860s, led to the discoveries of the basic principles of heredity and subsequently to the science of genetics.

Until the end of the nineteenth century, Western scientific thinking continued to be developed in the mechanical, atomistic framework outlined by Descartes and Newton. Yet by then Newton's fixed and immutable world had already been challenged by his fellow Englishman, Charles Darwin (1809–1882), with his theory of evolution. To Darwin, natural laws were as valid in the natural sciences as the laws of planetary motion and the law of gravity were in the physical world.[86] Albert Einstein (1879–1955), with his theory of relativity (1905), based on perception and value judgements, as well as his new concepts of time, space, mass, motion, and gravitation, was to shake the Newtonian world to its foundations. The universe, he maintained, might have begun as a great thought; it certainly was not a great machine. Scientists could no longer be considered as custodians of absolute truth which could be found by atomizing knowledge in a mechanistic way. Truth did not reside in the realm of concepts linked with each other. It was much more relative and interdependent than either the Cartesian or the Newtonian approach had made it out to be. There was no final, absolute truth. There was only flux. Truth in science (though not in religion[87]) depended on time, place, and circumstance. Scientific truth was the relation between subject and object. Werner Heisenberg (1901–1976) in his "uncertainty principle" argued that "the observer alters the observed by the act of observing." For the first time since Copernicus, the fundamental faith of Western man in science and the scientific method, and especially scientific truth – the belief that the universe is not chaos but possesses an underlying order, a linear kind of certainty – was questioned.

Differences about scientific truth encouraged rather than halted the course of scientific discovery. So much so that, with the work on atomic particles and nuclear fission by the Englishmen J.J. Thomson (1856–1940) and Ernest Rutherford (1871–1937), and the Dane Niels Bohr (1885–1962), the whole world suddenly found itself in deadly peril. Einstein, by treating matter and energy as exchangeable, had also helped to lay the basis for splitting the atom. Having taken the moral element out of science in the sixteenth century (when the purpose was to perfect man, not matter), man in the twentieth century (whose purpose is to perfect matter not man) found himself facing a moral dilemma. Where we think of man at all, we think of him as another material element whose actions can be predicted and controlled. Only in the West was man first elevated to a dominating position in nature and then equated with matter.

Europe's search for scientific truth since the seventeenth century was assisted not only by the advances in mathematics, and the new stress placed upon logic and reason, it was also furthered by the introduction and improvement of scientific instruments which dramatically extended the range of observation. A close link was forged between scientists and instrument makers. At the beginning of the seventeenth century the telescope and the microscope appeared in Holland. Thermometers were devised. The pendulum clock brought accuracy to the measurement of time. The invention of the micrometer, the barometer, and the air and vacuum pump (also in the seventeenth century), were followed by the eighteenth-century invention of navigational aids such as the chronometer and the sextant. By the end of the eighteenth and the beginning of the nineteenth century, changes in technology[88] were taking place on such a wide front and were becoming so common that later writers would use the term the Industrial Revolution to describe them.

Although the Industrial Revolution was long in forming, it is generally thought to describe the changes taking place in England between the years 1760–1830.[89] From England the revolution later spread to western Europe and to many other parts of the world. The nub of the revolution, through a whole series of improvements in technology, was an enormous increase in Western man's productive power. The outcome was the rapid substitution of mechanized industry for agriculture and the traditional crafts, iron and coal for wood, steam for water and wind, the factory for the cottage, and the urban for the rural scene. The revolution in industry also meant a vast increase in

wage labor, new forms of economic and social organization, the growing power of the market, and the seemingly limitless use of inanimate energy (steam, electricity,
water, petroleum and diesel oil). In all previous history,
human and animal muscle had been the chief source of
energy (on a world scale, they probably still are). The sum
of these changes – though one can argue that none of
them were essentially new – produced a civilization different in kind from that which had preceded it. Unquestionably, they enhanced the military and economic power of
the West.

Prompted by these developments (which were certainly
not as orderly as they appear), western Europe's relative
retardation in the industrial arts underwent marked
change from the eighteenth century onward. In particular,
Britons became inventors and innovators on a scale previously unequalled. Britain's supply of rich deposits of
coal and iron, its improved transport system, its growing
supplies of credit and money, its protection of property by
law, its political stability, its class structure, its expanding
labor and capital, its increasingly ambitious and talented
middle class, its stable government, its Protestant ethic, its
active dissenting religious minorities, its unrivaled navy,
and its ever-growing profitable domestic and foreign
trade, all fostered its lead as the workshop of the world.
Only by inventing labor-saving devices could the British
hope to compete with the great reservoirs of cheap labor
that existed in Asia. Britain also was the state where Adam
Smith's (1723–1790) philosophy of the free market in land,
labor, and capital (expressed in his *Wealth of Nations*) had
taken root. In emphasizing the impersonal role of the
market, he followed Newton's example of value-free
system-building in the sciences. In emphasizing the
wealth of nations rather than that of empires or city-states,
he expressed a new way of looking at economic life. Other
contributing factors were the abundant harvests England
enjoyed between 1720 and 1750, the introduction of new
crops and agricultural practices, and the more profitable
use of land (the enclosure movement). Whatever the
causes of Britain's advance, the technical changes in the

hundred years after 1770 were marked as much by their variety as by their fundamental nature. In that century the ancient skills of the craftsman gradually gave way to first a British and then a European and world technology dependent on metal, machines, fuels, and trained engineers.

The curious thing is that while some scientists were stimulated by the growing problems surrounding the rapid development of Western forms of production, the majority of those who made Britain's Industrial Revolution were practical men, largely unaware of what was going on in the scientific world. Such is true of John Kay, a Lancashire textile machinist who, in 1733, patented the first of the great textile inventions, the flying shuttle. James Hargreaves, who invented the spinning jenny in 1764, was a weaver. Richard Arkwright, who patented the water frame in 1769 was the son of a barber and wigmaker. Samuel Crompton, who in 1779 devised what is essentially the spinning machine in use today, was a spinner. Edmund Cartwright, who in the 1780s mechanized the weaving process, was a country vicar.

This reliance upon practical rather than scientific men did not apply to textiles alone. Neither Thomas Newcomen (1663–1729), a mechanic, nor James Watt (1736–1819),[90] a builder of instruments at Glasgow University, whose names are linked with the development of steam, were scientists as such. Richard Trevithick (1771–1833), another important figure in the development of steam, was a blacksmith and a wrestler. Similarly unschooled were Abraham Darby (c.1678–1717), who improved the smelting and refining of iron ore, John Wilkinson (1728–1808), one of the great iron masters, and Henry Maudslay, who in 1794 invented one of the first lathes for cutting metal. Thomas Telford (1757–1834), who spanned the English landscape with iron bridges was born a shepherd. James Brindley (1716–1772), who laid out a network of hundreds of miles of canals all over England, had no scientific background.

It was these largely self-educated men who set in motion a movement that was to change the world. The outcome of their efforts – especially when steam shipping and steam railways linked the continents – was to create an integrated economic unit of the major countries of the world. Under Western command, the supply and demand of commodities was regulated to serve Western interests. "Free Trade" simply meant freedom for the most powerful to inflict their rule on the rest. It still does. Another consequence of these developments in industry and trade[91] – especially with the rise of Germany and America – was to change the balance of power not only between Asia and Europe, but among the Western powers themselves. The outcome of the subsequent struggle for world power was the First Great War of 1914–1918.

The essential distinction between Western technology of today and that of the eighteenth and nineteenth centuries is the extent to which progress in technology has come to depend on progress in the sciences. They have become integrated to an extent unknown in earlier times. From the second half of the nineteenth century onward, empiricism has given way to exact science. Scientific developments have created many modern industries. In chemicals and electricity (as a source of energy to supplement steam), in the development of the internal combustion and the diesel engines, Germany (united in 1871) led the way. Major British contributions were synthetic dyes, the Bessemer steel converter, the Gilchrist-Thomas basic steel process, and the Parsons' steam turbine. Among many other inventions, the United States contributed the ring-spinning frame, the typewriter, and the telephone.

Science and technology have become the social forces of our time. In the thirteenth century it seemed that all things were possible to faith. Today all things are thought to be possible to science. Especially in this age of space travel, television, and computers, we take it for granted that science can solve all problems, provide all answers. Children of science, we prefer to disregard its transient nature. All that is needed for us to achieve an earthly paradise is to train more scientists.

When men of science find out something more,

We shall all be happier than before,

said the English writer Hilaire Belloc, tongue in cheek. In contrast, the words of Alfred Lord Tennyson:

This truth within thy mind rehearse,
That in a boundless universe
Is boundless better, boundless worse

echo both the cheer and the chill of the scientific age.

Belloc's scientists march toward the Promised Land where man and matter will be perfected. Tennyson is fearful that the Promised Land may turn out to be what T.S. Eliot later called "The Wasteland", the end of which came not with a bang but with a whimper. Fifty per cent of scientific research money spent in the United States in 1986 came from the government. Eighty per cent of it was spent on defense or war preparation. Our much vaunted "scientific progress" has brought us to the point where we may be in danger of destroying planet Earth.

Superficially at least, the Western impact in the world has been practical and material, rather than spiritual. What the West has excelled in has been scientific knowledge and economically productive technology. We have excelled in these things because primarily they came to be the things we honored. Whether these changes in world history were themselves dependent upon novel elements (not least the discovery of the New World), or upon universally applicable elements that other civilizations can follow, is unclear. If the Western scientific and industrial revolutions were prompted by Western expansion and colonization – that is, not by ordinary and continuous events, but by an extraordinary sporadic phase of history – then it behooves us not to use nineteenth-century Western economic growth and development as an example which twentieth century Africa, Asia, and Latin America can follow. Much of the high tide of human progress in the West over the past two centuries – much of what has been achieved in science and technology, which some believe to be the true source of our improved material lot and of our power in the world – cannot be disassociated from the discovery of the New World, from the bringing into cultivation of vast, new, fertile regions of the earth, from the tapping of enormous new mineral deposits, and from the introduction of new forms of transport, communications, and power. These things did not come about because of Western racial superiority or greater Western intelligence, but because the West developed different values and passed through a different historical experience than the people of other continents; an experience that gave full rein to curiosity, inventiveness, and acquisitiveness.

No one can say with complete assurance that the circumstances which saw the rise of the West have not passed, and that the old slower cycle of change might not reassert itself. Surely, we know enough to realize that our confidence in science is rooted in our belief in progress, which is of relatively recent origin. The question remains: whether that "Great Discontinuity of History" – the Industrial Revolution – will prove to be one of the great mutations in history, an ongoing, universal process, or a "Great Abnormality", a historical moment dependent on special circumstances; a phenomenon difficult, if not impossible, to repeat. Only those who follow in the human concourse will know.

6

The Expansion
of the American Empires

Columbus' discovery of America in 1492 opened a dramatic chapter in the history of the human race. The discovery of the New World was fortuitous. In 1506 Columbus went to his grave convinced that what he had found were islands off the landmass of Asia. Not until 1513 when Vasco Núñez de Balboa (1475–1517) set eyes on the Pacific (the whole of which he claimed for the king of Spain) did the Europeans realize their error. By then, the southern half of the continent had been named not after Columbus, but after another Italian, Amerigo Vespucci (1451–1512), who had sailed as far as present-day Argentina. A hundred years later the focus of European attention was still in Asia. It took a long time before Europe conceded the existence of a continent that would radically change its history.

In 1493, one year after Columbus' landfall, Pope Alexander VI divided the world between Spain and Portugal. The Spaniards not only laid claim to most of the southern half of the American continent (Portugal, afraid of being forestalled by the French, secured Brazil by the 1550s), they also made strong claims to the northern half as well. Spain claimed sovereignty over land north from Mexico to Oregon and east to the Carolinas. England and the Netherlands challenged Spanish power by raiding its American possessions, and by harrying it at sea; France disputed the military primacy of Spain in Europe. None of them succeeded in breaking Spain's grip on the New World. In the fifteen and sixteen hundreds Spain continued to rule a great empire with outstanding administrative skill. As late as the eighteenth century, Spain was still expanding into Texas (1718–1720), and California (1770s). The future seaports of San Diego (1769), Monterey (1770), San Francisco (1776), and Los Angeles (1781) were founded by Spain after 1763.

England, the Netherlands, and France failed to bring down Spain in the New World because their minds were not on the task. It was not the conquest of Spanish America that excited Europe's imagination in the sixteenth century. More important were the Turkish threat, the profits to be gained by Asian commerce, and piracy in the Caribbean. European-seized Caribbean islands would eventually yield high profits from sugar and tobacco cultivation. The British, the French, and the Dutch were more concerned with getting around the Americas than with possessing them. Not until the Peace of the Pyrenees in 1659 signalled the shift of world power from Spain to France did the other European powers feel that it was safe to press their claims to parts of the New World.

By 1659 the pattern of European expansion in the Americas had already been formed. Beginning with the settlement of Hispaniola in 1493, the Spaniards went on to establish a base at Panama in 1519. From Panama they sought the route to Cathay (which they thought was nearby). In the same year (1519), Cortez, with 600 men and seventeen horses, arrived in Aztec Mexico. The end of the Aztec empire came three years later. In 1531 Francisco Pizarro (1470–1541), with 180 men and twenty-seven horses, reached Inca Peru (which included modern Peru, Ecuador, northern Chile, western Bolivia, and northern Argentina). Four years later the once great Inca empire was overthrown. Because Mexico and Peru were the chief centers of Indian populations,[92] and also because they were the areas in which immensely productive silver mines were discovered, they became the focus of Spanish conquest. While the conquest of the Mayan Yucatan Peninsula dragged on through the sixteenth and seventeenth centuries, the fate of Guatemala was settled between 1523 and 1542. New Granada[93] (1536–1539) and central Chile (1540–1558) also fell to Spanish arms. By 1659 the Spaniards had taken possession of an area reaching

roughly from northern Mexico to south of the Rio de la
Plata in Argentina.

The pre-Columbian civilizations (see Map I) had a rich
cultural tradition which in many respects was superior to
that of their conquerors. Although the Mayas had long
since passed their peak when in the 1520s Pedro de Alvar-
ado (1485?–1541) reached Guatemala, and Francisco de
Montejo (1473–1553) reached Yucatán, they are credited
with having developed the most advanced pre-Columbian
society of all. The Maya calculation of the solar year
developed before AD 1000 is said to have been more
accurate than the much more recent corrected western
Gregorian calendar. In mathematics, they had developed
the idea of place value and the concept of zero. Their
hieroglyphic system of writing was the most complex in
the New World; their art styles were brilliant; their architecture unparalleled. While they did not possess precious
metals on the scale of Mexico or Peru, their agricultural
resources were adequate to guarantee their independence.
Relying as they did on the whim of the gods, religion
pervaded the whole of their culture. In a state of continuous warfare, their rulers possessed near-absolute powers
in government, religion, war, and commerce.

In contrast to the Mayas, the Aztecs were probably at
their peak in 1519 when Cortez arrived in Mexico. Their
capital Tenochtitlán (Mexico City) with a population in
excess of any European capital, was the wonder of the
Spaniards. While iron and steel, the plough, draft animals, the rotary quern and the wheel were unknown to
them, they had all that was necessary to live well and
extend their conquests. Religion was the dominant factor
in their lives. It was to obtain victims to sacrifice to their
principal god of the sun that caused them to wage war
constantly. As war was the guarantor of the survival of the
universe, a long peace to the Aztecs was a disaster.

The richest, most integrated and dynamic pre-Columbian state of all in the 1500s was that of the Incas. Some
regard it as the most successful totalitarian state the world
has known. When Pizarro appeared in 1531, the Inca
military organization, systems of transport (though they

did not make use of the wheel) and communication, engineering, stone and metal-working skills, architecture, medicine and surgery, textiles and ceramics were all highly developed. Nor did their lack of a system of writing prevent them from developing an efficient imperial administration. In the *quipu* (long ropes made of knotted cords) they possessed an effective system of calculation. In relation to existing scientific knowledge and techniques, no other pre-Columbian civilization used its resources more productively, and with such concern for the general welfare. Governing through an absolute theocracy, the Incas imposed their rule upon all they conquered. Their sense of empire was more comprehensive and coherent than that of either the Mayas or the Aztecs. From their capital Cuzco in Peru they united the different peoples of their far-flung realm by the use of a common tongue. Their aim was one language, one nobility, one emperor.

The overwhelming defeat of the pre-Columbian empires by the Europeans must be ascribed to the superior weapons of the invaders and to the audacity and fanaticism of the Spaniards. Propelled by their individual missionary role for Christianity, by their desire to serve their king, by their unmatchable warlike pride, by their lust for plunder, and their own desperate situation, the Spaniards fought ferociously. Aiding them were dissident tribes, the low morale of the native warriors, and the utter dependence of their opponents on leaders such as Moctezuma and Atahualpa. These men were the pillars upon which rested the Aztec and Inca states. When they fell, the states fell. The Spaniards also took advantage of the natives' ritualistic and ceremonial way of fighting. Further weaknesses of the native societies were class hatreds, tribalism, and political and religious schism. Diseases[94] and prophesy also played a part. All these societies – Mayan, Aztec, and Inca – had a legend of a returning white god. In the last resort, shock (gunpowder and horses terrified the Indians) coupled with treachery, ensured Spanish victory.

The policy followed by Portugal in the colonization of Brazil (which they had secured by the 1550s, and which a hundred years later they were to defend successfully from Dutch intrusion) differed from that of its Spanish neighbor. There were no Portuguese conquistadores. Portuguese colonization which was closely directed by the Crown was concerned with plantation agriculture (it was the world's first great plantation economy). No country received more slaves from Africa than Brazil. Showing more interest than the Spaniards in developing the country rather than searching for gold and silver, though gold and diamonds were discovered in the eighteenth century, the Portuguese were able to extend the frontiers of Brazil beyond the line established at Tordesillas in 1494.

From a world point of view, the conquest by western Europeans of the pre-Columbian cultures of central and south America is a story of gain and loss. The loss was the destruction of indigenous cultures and the extension of war, sickness, and slavery. Thus were laid the foundations of the tumultuous, unstable world that would follow. The gain was the widening of the world economy and the stimulus given to the North Atlantic region through increased trade and monetary resources (precious metals) at a critical moment in Europe's economic development. The Iberians also imposed on the region a common religion, and in certain areas a common language.

At the end of the seventeenth century Latin America was divided into the empires of Spain and Portugal. At the end of the eighteenth century there were four major divisions in Spanish America: the vice royalties of New Spain (founded in 1535), Peru (1542), New Granada (1717), and Rio de la Plata (1776), located respectively at Mexico City, Lima, Bogotá, and Buenos Aires. Brazil remained a Portuguese colony.

In the early nineteenth century, encouraged by the example set by the American and French revolutions, as well as by new opportunities rising from the preoccupation of the Spanish and Portuguese crowns with European wars, the Iberian colonists of the New World won their independence. In 1822 Brazil became an independent empire. The Spanish empire broke up into fifteen new states. After 1850, with the exception of an independent

Cuba and Panama (both created by the United States) the map of Latin America remained virtually unchanged.

Having obtained their independence from European imperial rule, the countries of Latin America displayed a fierce determination to retain it. Efforts made at economic or political union always came to naught. Disunity and dispute in internal and external relations, and dictatorial rule, have marked the course of Latin American history into the twentieth century.

The initial aim of the English, the French, and the Dutch (who explored and settled the northern half of the American continent), was also to find a route to Cathay. With such a purpose, in 1524, the British sent Giovanni da Verrazzano (1485?–1528?) up the east coast of North America. In 1535 the French navigator Jacques Cartier (1491–1557) followed the St Lawrence thinking it would lead him to the Pacific and China. Arriving in New France in 1603, Samuel de Champlain (1567?–1635) drove the French spearhead further west. With the accession of Louis XIV (1643–1715) the search for a new passage to the Golden East was abandoned; the development and settlement of New France was earnestly begun. Before the seventeenth century had ended, New France, though always with a much smaller population than the English colonies, stretched crescent-like from the mouth of the St Lawrence to the mouth of the Mississippi.

While the first successful English colony was planted at Jamestown in Virginia in 1607, England's search for a northwest passage to the East was not relinquished until the 1630s. With the arrival of the Puritans at Cape Cod in 1620, an English colony also took root in New England. By 1642, 20,000 Puritans – a description covering many kinds of religious dissent – had settled on the New England coast. Maryland became a refuge for English Catholics; the Carolinas a refuge for French Protestants, as well as for English, German, and Swiss settlers. In addition, New Jersey (1664), Pennsylvania (1681), and Delaware (1704) were founded. Georgia (1733) was meant to be a buffer state between the southern colonies and Spanish Florida.

Instead of being faced with an immediate life and death struggle with large and powerful native civilizations[95] (such as Spain had met with in the southern half of the continent), the English were able to encroach piecemeal on scattered native Indian domains. Unable to halt the incursions of the Europeans, the Indians found temporary relief by escaping to the Plains.

Like the French and the British, Dutch interests in North America began in 1609 with Henry Hudson's search for a northwest passage. It ended in the mid-seventeenth century with the founding of trading colonies on Manhattan Island, in Connecticut, New Jersey, Delaware, and Pennsylvania.

Of the European contestants for power in North America, the two strongest soon became Britain and France (see Map VI). Compared with France (who possessed a valuable gateway to the interior in the St Lawrence), or the Dutch (who possessed an equally valuable gateway in the Hudson), the claims of the small, isolated pockets of Englishmen on the Atlantic seaboard to inherit the continent appeared improbable; especially after the English had been cut off from the interior by a line of French forts which stretched from the St Lawrence via the Mississippi to New Orleans. But Britain's triumph over the French on the heights of Abraham outside Quebec in 1759 changed all that. After the Treaty of Paris (1763), which ended the near-global Seven Years War between the two leading powers, and under which all Canada and the land east of the Mississippi were ceded to Britain, the French flag disappeared off the political map of North America altogether. Britain, at one time the least likely contender for supremacy in North America, had outrivaled the rest.

While the colonization of the Americas by the white man has its credit as well as its debit entries, the price of European expansion into the Americas was an enormous toll in human lives and suffering. In the fight to possess and exploit the New World, unknown millions died.[96] Countless numbers of Indians in North and South America died in battle, others from the epidemic diseases

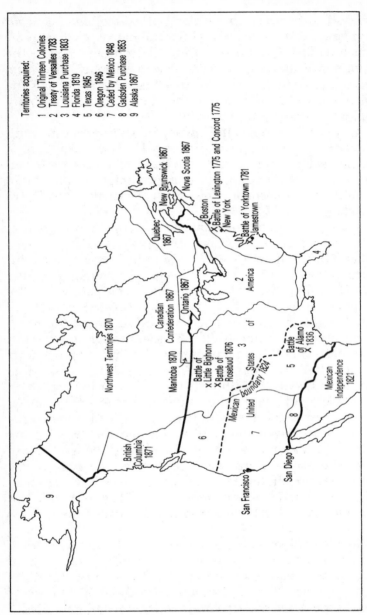

NORTH AMERICAN EXPANSION
Map VI

brought by Europeans (such as smallpox, measles, chicken pox, whooping cough, influenza, tuberculosis, and diphtheria) and Africans (such as yellow fever and malaria). Against these diseases – which killed off native populations faster than European arms or liquor – the much older and far more distinguished Amerindian civilizations of the Mayas, the Incas, and the Aztecs had no immunity. It has been estimated that within 130 years, eighty-five per cent of the native population of Central Mexico had died out.[97] We are not sure whether syphilis was inflicted upon the aboriginal Americans by the Europeans or vice versa. We do know that syphilis spread across Europe like a scourge shortly after the discovery of America.

The discovery and exploitation of the New World also altered Europe's relations with Asia. The enormous quantity of precious metals[98] – constituting one of the greatest windfalls in history – which reached Europe from Peru and Mexico could now be exchanged for the luxuries of the East. As a result, the first true world economy was established. In addition, the arrival of so much gold and silver in Europe caused great inflation – prices in Spain increased fourfold in less than a century – and a business boom which influenced the course of European economic development for some time to come. In 1795 the German publicist and statesman Friedrich von Gentz wrote: "The discovery of America and a new route to the East Indies opened the greatest market, the greatest inducement to human industry, that had ever existed since the human race emerged from barbarism."[99]

The British victory at Quebec in 1759, which ended the struggle between the British and the French in North America, proved to be short-lived. The destruction of French power in New France was, in fact, instrumental in the destruction of British power over the thirteen American colonies. Being no longer vital to the defense of the colonists, British power could now be discarded. The enforcing of half-forgotten mercantile regulations that threatened the profits of American commerce, as well as the introduction of new measures (including restrictions on western settlement, interference with the profitable American West Indian trade, and the obnoxious Stamp Act of 1765), only served to make the need for a break with the mother country all the more urgent.

Hostilities between the colonists and British troops began at the battles of Lexington and Concord, Massachusetts on 19 April 1775. On 15 June 1775 George Washington (1732–1799) was appointed commander of the Continental Forces. On 4 July 1776 the colonists declared their independence. Thenceforth, with the indispensable help of the French (whose fleet played a crucial role in the defeat of the British), the Spaniards, and the Dutch, the struggle was continued until on 19 October 1781 the British surrendered at Yorktown. The only major war Britain had fought without an ally, it had lost.

For the French, the Dutch, the Spaniards, and even the Russians on the Baltic, the outcome at Yorktown meant the settling of long-standing grievances against the British. More particularly, for the French, who had invested vast sums in the struggle, it meant the re-establishing of French power in North America in the Louisiana Territory. Had the War of Independence not been part of a much wider European power struggle, in which each country fought for what it considered to be its own interests, the American colonists might have had to wait longer to achieve their independence. As it was, their success in overthrowing an imperial power inspired revolutions in France and elsewhere.[100]

The American Revolution neither displayed the same savage brutality, nor broke with the past as did the French Revolution of 1789. The American Revolution was based on the English Enlightenment which sought to enlarge individual freedom and parliamentary government, whereas the French Revolution was based on the continental Age of Enlightenment which tended to subordinate the individual to absolute monarchy. Whatever their differences, both events brought *the people* to the forefront of world political history.

Under the subsequent peace settlement of 1783 between

the United States and her allies and Great Britain, all the land between Canada and Florida east of the Mississippi was assigned to the Americans. Florida was ceded to Spain. American territory doubled overnight from 400,000 to 880,811 square miles. At that time only about 25,000 white settlers were strung out in the new area from the Appalachians to the Mississippi.

The next great acquisition of territory by the Americans was the Louisiana Purchase of 1803. For $11.3 million (raised chiefly in London) Jefferson obtained from the French (who had previously obtained it from the Spaniards) the whole of the Louisiana Territory – a tract comprising 828,000 square miles stretching from the Mississippi to the Rocky Mountains. The price paid by the Americans was under three cents per acre. Any rights which native Indians – the occupants of the land – had, were ignored. Again overnight, and without bloodshed, the United States had doubled its territory. In 1804 President Thomas Jefferson (1743–1826) dispatched the explorers Meriwether Lewis (1774–1809) and William Clark (1770–1838) to find out what he had bought. They were also charged with the search for a water route from the Missouri to the Pacific coast.

Soon, called by the promise of free land, by trade, by a sense of adventure, by the expanding mining, farming, cattle, and (later) railway frontiers, the white Americans began their westward march. Unlike the Spaniards, who had had little interest in founding a new homeland in South America, the North American colonists were intent on creating a "New Jerusalem" for themselves and those who followed them. Theirs was a manifest destiny assigned by God. Nothing should be allowed to impede its unfolding. When friction between the growing number of American settlers and Mexican authorities came to a head in Texas in 1845, Congress responded by annexing 390,000 square miles of Mexican territory (the size of France and Germany combined). At little cost to itself, the United States had added to its territory the equivalent of the original thirteen colonies.

A year later, in 1846, on the pretext of a Mexican invasion, the United States declared war on Mexico. Understandably, the much weaker Mexico was defeated. By the Treaty of Guadalupe Hidalgo, of 2 February 1848, on payment by the United States of $15 million, Mexico relinquished all claims to Texas above the Rio Grande and ceded New Mexico and California to the United States. A further 1,193,061 square miles had been added to the United States' national domain, which now stretched from the Atlantic to the Pacific.

The other groups to be dispossessed as a result of American westward expansion were the aboriginal Indians of North America, who had fought a continuing battle to retain control of their communal lands since shortly after the white man had arrived. Sometimes the Indians won temporary relief, as Crazy Horse did for the Sioux and the Cheyenne at the Battle of the Rosebud in 1876, or when Sitting Bull annihilated Colonel George Custer and his troops at the Battle of the Little Bighorn; but eventually the white tide returned to engulf them. Propelled by overwhelming numbers, by a most extraordinary aggressiveness, by superior arms, by a righteous belief in their race, their cause, and their destiny, nothing could hold the white man back. In contrast to the profound respect that the Indian had for nature, the white man was determined to subdue it and anyone who stood in his way.[101] For the red man there was no escape, no compromise he could make, no terms he could accept other than death or exile. By the 1890s, most Indian chiefs were dead, the people decimated, torn apart, scattered to the winds. Indian resistance had ended. "Hear me, my chiefs," said Chief Joseph, a great Indian warrior and statesman in 1877, "I am tired . . . my heart is sick and sad. From where the sun now stands, I will fight no more forever." Judged by deeds and not by words, the ultimate arbiter in the disposition of North America was naked force.

Meanwhile, America's territory had been rounded out by a compromise with the British in 1846 over the Oregon territory, which added a further 285,580 square miles to the United States. In 1853, under the Gadsden Purchase, the United States bought what is now southern Arizona and New Mexico (a mere 29,670 square miles) from a bankrupt Mexican government at a cost of $10 million. In 1867 it also purchased Alaska's 586,400 square miles from Russia for the sum of $7,200,000 (about two cents an acre). Never was so much territory obtained so quickly and at so low a price.

By 1868, eighty-five years after the peace treaty with Britain and the other powers in 1783, United States territory had grown from 393,152 square miles to 3,608,787 square miles; a more than ninefold increase. By the 1890s the continental expansion of the United States was complete. The United States now occupied an area equivalent to the whole of Europe (including European Russia). States such as Texas and California were larger than the largest European countries. Increasingly, Americans felt that their manifest destiny called them not only across the continent but across the seas.

The more one ponders the expansion of the white man's empire across North America, the more one is struck by how relatively easy it was – especially when compared with Russian expansion across Asia. Except for the colonization of Australia, there is no other example in world history of any group coming into possession of such a vast, rich area so swiftly and at so little human cost. While each death represents a tragedy which cannot be expressed with statistical detachment, American casualties in the period of its most rapid expansion were minimal. At Yorktown the Continental Army and its French allies lost 262 men. The War of 1812 with Canada, the Mexican War of the 1840s, and the Spanish American War of the 1890s were all minor clashes as far as American losses were concerned. The Battle of the Alamo (187 dead), and the battle of the Little Bighorn[102] (246 dead), are chiefly of symbolic importance.

Not only were America's wars low on casualties, they also conferred considerable benefits on the United States. The war of 1776–1783 had brought independence; the War of 1812 had extended that independence to the high seas as well as to the Mississippi Valley; the wars against

Mexico [103] in the 1840s had brought great territorial gains; the Civil War of the 1860s, scourge as it was, had safeguarded the unity of the nation, abolished slavery, and stimulated development; the Spanish American War of the 1890s had made the USA a world power.

The relative ease with which the white American obtained what he considered to be his true inheritance has left its mark. While environment is only one of the factors explaining a people's outlook, the ease with which the territory of the United States was obtained must surely help to explain the American's sense of confidence and optimism (the belief in a happy ending). Moreover, America had only two neighbors, Canada (unified in 1867) and Mexico, both of whom were weak and (if left alone) peaceful.

In contrast to the settling of Russia (or of Europe generally), which is a story of fortified villages and towns, the settling of America in the nineteenth century entailed the clearing of the forests and the dividing of the plains. The ease and speed with which territory was won has no better example than in the whirlwind occupation of Oklahoma in 1889:

> At the sound of a gun . . . a flood of 50,000 white settlers poured like an avalanche into the last great Indian reservation. By nightfall, under conditions of utter pandemonium, almost 2,000,000 acres of land had been claimed, most of it to be sold again. Within half a day, Guthrie and Oklahoma City, each with an instant population of 10,000, had come into being.[104]

Nowhere else in the world has this ever happened.

The conquest of North America had repercussions across the entire world. Politically, it resulted in the appearance of a new great, industrialized power. Having in the 1860s fought the first modern war, the Americans, according to the London *Spectator* on 17 February 1866, had become "a power of the first class, a nation which is very dangerous to offend, and almost impossible to attack". Henceforth,

America's viewpoint was taken seriously in the world. It says a great deal for the growth in the actual and the potential power of the United States that the Americans were able to bundle Napoleon III's imperialistic-minded French troops out of Mexico once the Civil War was over.

The United States not only became a great political and industrial power; through the crucible of its Civil War (1861–1865), which more than any other historical event defined the American character, it became a unified power. Had President Abraham Lincoln (1809–1865) not insisted on unity – had the principle of unity been lost – the history of the western world would have been very different. A dis-United States could never have intervened as decisively as it did in the two world wars.

The economic consequences stemming from the colonization of the North American continent were as significant as the political. Not least, it released a torrent of cheap food and supplies upon the world. By the late 1860s the United States was producing a bushel of wheat for about half the cost of a European bushel. From 1852 to roughly the end of the century, the average American exports of wheat and wheat flour grew from nineteen to 197 million bushels; in the same fifty years exports of corn and corn meal rose from seven to over 200 million bushels. The export of chilled and refrigerated meat of all kinds to Europe became a veritable flood. By 1900 American farm produce made up three quarters of the country's total exports. By 1914 the United States (although – because of its foreign debt – still a net debtor nation) had vast trade surpluses with Europe. All of which – coupled with the increasing immunity to epidemic diseases in Europe after 1750 – helps to explain the impoverishing and subsequent restructuring of western European agriculture[105], as well as the falling death rates, and the unusually rapid growth of the European population. Thanks to America's riches, famine in the Western world became a thing of the past.

Accompanying the avalanche of food to Europe were immense quantities of minerals, metals, and raw materials which provided a powerful stimulus to the growth of Western industrialism. The United States production of crude petroleum rose from three million barrels in 1865 to more than fifty-five million in 1898. The availability of large quantities of Californian gold enabled the Western world to abandon a bi-metallic standard of silver and gold in favor of a common gold standard,[106] which further facilitated the economic integration of the Old World and the New.

Whether we are considering the unprecedented migration of Europeans and enslaved Africans to the New World, or the transfer of capital and skills from the Old World to the New, or the tremendous improvements in land and sea transport and communications, or the resulting cornucopia – the outcome was a reallocation of the world's resources and white hegemony around the globe. Little wonder if the white people of the world came to think of themselves as superior.

Blessed by its resources, by its abundant supplies of capital and labor, by its political stability, by its work ethic, and its aggressive entrepreneurial spirit, by 1914, almost comet-like, the United States had become the agrarian, industrial, and financial colossus of the world.[107] Its *per capita* income of $377 in 1914 soared above all the rest.[108] Never has any country become so rich so quickly, or so easily, as the United States did in the half-century before 1914. No other country has set aside the basic law of political economy – the law of diminishing returns – as America did. No other country had such economic potential. By moving labor and capital from Europe (where they were relatively plentiful) to the United States (where they were relatively scarce) the world – especially the white world – was economically better off.

Long before 1914, America's manifest destiny had carried it far beyond its shores. In 1867 it annexed Midway Island; in 1878 it established a semi-protectorate over Tutuila in Samoa. In the 1890s it annexed Hawaii (which foreshadowed its clash with Japan at Pearl Harbor in 1941), Wake Island and Guam, and, led by President William McKinley (1843–1901), conquered Spanish Cuba, Puerto Rico, and the Philippines. At the turn of the century, unsuccessful efforts were made to lease Samsah Bay, opposite Formosa, from China. United States Secretary of State John Hay proclaimed his Open Door Policy whereby economic opportunities in China should be available to the Americans on equal terms with Britain, Germany, and Russia. Americans began to talk about Manchuria becoming America's "new West" (which is partly why, in 1907 and 1910, Russia and Japan divided it between them). In 1902 Cuba became a protectorate. There followed in 1903 the seizing of Colombian territory by American-backed Panamanians and the eventual construction of the Panama Canal which was completed in 1914. As a "corollary" to the Monroe Doctrine, President Theodore Roosevelt (1858–1919) announced the right of the United States to intervene in Latin America to prevent "chronic wrongdoing", and European interference. Thus the door was opened to the subsequent military intervention of the United States in Nicaragua, Cuba, the Dominican Republic, Haiti, Panama, Mexico, and Grenada. In 1907, to demonstrate how powerful the United States had become, Roosevelt sent his "Great White Fleet" (the world's third most powerful) around the world. In 1911 United States Senator Taft and several congressmen caused a storm in Canada with their talk of annexation.

Encouraging the Americans' expansive urge was the belief in their role as God's chosen people – that they had a mission not only to the American continent but to the world. Most Americans took it for granted that it was all part of God's plan. That is why America was called "God's country". "God," said Senator Beveridge ". . . has made us the master organizers of the world to establish system where chaos reigns." (Much later President Harry Truman (1884–1972) would repeat Beveridge's theme: "We're going to run the world the way the world ought to be run.") In his book *Our Country* (1885), Josiah Strong wrote:

This race . . . having developed peculiarly aggressive traits calculated to impress its institutions upon mankind, will spread itself over the earth . . . this powerful race will move down upon Mexico, down upon Central and South America, out upon the islands of the sea, over upon Africa and beyond.

Strong thought the expansion of Americans and American commercial and financial interests would usher in a golden age of justice, democracy, and economic well-being. The idea of a manifest destiny to the world was not peculiarly American. Most nineteenth century Europeans felt the same. Throughout history, the most powerful country of the time has always felt it had a duty to save the rest. The British spoke of a "white man's burden", to raise up the rest of the world; the French stressed their "mission civilisatrice"; the Germans and the Belgians also thought that they possessed a superior civilization and that they had a right and a duty to tell the world what to do. To save the world was the God-given right of all the Western nations.

On the eve of war, in 1914, most Americans would have agreed with the sentiments expressed by Senator Beveridge. No mention was made, at the time, that America's gains had been won at a high cost to the Mexicans, the American Indians, and the African blacks. That would, of course, have smacked of imperialism – which was not what American history was about. The truth is that while Americans have been more idealistic and moralistic in their outlook on the world, they have essentially been involved with the struggle for power that has affected all other expansionist nations. If imperialism means taking other people's land by force, if it means imposing one's will on others, if it means considering oneself superior, then Americans – the moralistic rhetoric of Presidents Theodore Roosevelt, William Howard Taft (1857–1930), and Woodrow Wilson (1856–1924) aside – were imperialistic. Where they differed from the so-called imperialist nations of Europe is that they ascribed to themselves a purity of motive that no expansionist nation can possess.

7

The Great War: 1914–1918

On 28 June 1914 a nineteen-year-old Serbian terrorist, Gavrilo Princip, assassinated the Archduke Ferdinand of Austria at Sarajevo, the capital of Bosnia, then under Austro-Hungarian rule. Convinced that Princip had the secret backing of the neighboring kingdom of Serbia, a month later, on 28 July, regardless of Serbia's willingness to make concessions, Austria declared war. Sarajevo had provided Austria with the excuse it sought to crush Serbia once and for all. The next day Russia mobilized in support of the Serbs. As mother of the Slavs, she had no choice; especially as she had given in to the Austrians over an earlier Balkan crisis in 1908-1909.[109] On 1 August Germany declared war on Russia. Faced by war on two fronts, Germany dared not delay. On 3 August Germany declared war on France. On 4 August Britain declared war on Germany; its dominions were quick to rally to its support. In a highly industrialized, mechanized Europe, the whole time sequence of war had changed. Before 1870 the methods of projecting armies into battle were secondary; after 1870 they became primary. Mobilization depended on intricate movements of troops by rail which could not be stopped and started at will – at least not if one hoped to win the war.[110] "The lamps are going out all over Europe," said Sir Edward Grey, British Foreign Secretary, "we shall not see them lit again in our lifetime."

Overnight, the military alliances earlier agreed upon between the powers came into effect. (See Map VII) Britain, France, and Germany were not directly involved in the Greater Serbia question – the basis of Austro-Russian antagonism in the Balkans – but their allies were. Germany was committed to supporting Austria and Italy (1882). France was committed to supporting Russia (1894). Britain was committed to France in 1904 and to Russia in 1907. The

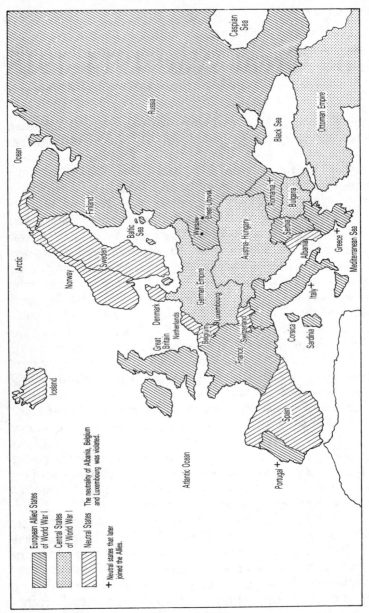

EUROPE IN 1914
Map VII

Ottoman Turks and the Bulgarians eventually came in on the side of Germany because the Turks were the traditional enemies of the Russians, and the Bulgarians held grievances against the Serbs. The Japanese followed Britain's example in declaring war on Germany because they were committed to do so under the Anglo-Japanese treaties of 1902 and 1905. Japan's primary concern was to seize the German-held Shantung province of China and German islands in the Pacific. Although Italy (unified between 1859 and 1870) was committed, under the Triple Alliance of 1882, to go to the aid of Germany and Austria, it held back. Not until 23 May 1915 – after the Allies had made all kinds of secret promises – did Italy switch sides (as it would do in the Second World War) and throw in its lot with the British, the French, and the Russians. By then the fire lit by Gavrilo Princip at Sarajevo in the fateful summer of 1914 had engulfed the Western world. In Europe only Norway, Sweden, Denmark, the Netherlands, Switzerland, and Spain remained neutral.

Although the war seemed to burst upon Europe out of a clear summer's sky, it had, in fact, been long in forming. It was the culmination of all that was dangerous in Europe's excessive nationalism. Two nationalist wars, the Balkan wars of 1912 and 1913, involving Serbia, Greece (which gained its independence from the Turks in 1831) Bulgaria, Romania, and Turkey had preceded it. Although the war of 1912 had largely expelled the Ottoman Turks from Europe, neither war had provided a permanent solution to the Balkan problem. On the contrary, egged on by Russia, Serbia, whose national territory had doubled as a result of the recent wars, had begun to exert even greater pressure on an already weakened Austro-Hungarian Empire. It was Serbian national aspirations that made "the Eastern Question" insoluble except by war. It only required the fateful spark of the Archduke's assassination to kindle the flame of war again. Monumental stupidity, cowardice, existing alliances, miscalculations, impulsiveness, mobilizations, and ultimatums did the rest.

While the Archduke's death was the spark that lit the

flame, the situation in the Balkans was not the sole cause of war. Tensions between the great powers had been growing since the turn of the century. Nothing irked the British in the twenty years before 1914 as much as Germany's naval challenge. "Germany's future," Kaiser Wilhelm II (1888–1918) had declared, "lies on the water." The German fleet had moved from sixth to second place – immediately behind the British Royal Navy. The fundamental concept of British foreign policy had always been control of the seas around its shores. This control was now threatened. In challenging British mastery on the seas and oceans of the world, Germany was trying to change something which the British thought had been settled in 1805 at Trafalgar. The Germans were also outstripping the British in the size of their merchant marine, in ship-building,[111] in the production of textiles, chemicals, coal, iron, and steel, and in the volume of world trade.

What really upset the British was that the Germans were challenging what the British regarded as their God-given right to rule. Winston Churchill expressed it best in 1914 when he said:

We have got all we want in territory, and our claim to be left in unmolested enjoyment of vast and splendid possessions, mainly acquired by violence, largely maintained by force, often seems less reasonable to others than to us.[112]

But Germany saw no reason why the world's destiny should be determined by Britain alone. Despite the fact that for most of the nineteenth century Germany was a group of petty states, which under Bismarck's leadership, first as Minister President of Prussia (1862) and then as German Chancellor (1871–1890), had united to become a great power, Germany was not a "Johnny-come-lately".[113] The Germans, having overwhelmed Denmark (1864), Austria (1866) and France (1870), formed their Second Empire in 1871. (The First Empire – the Holy Roman Empire of the German Nation – had been founded a thousand years earlier). In building a large fleet to defend its seaways and its shores, in exercising military and industrial power, in claiming an ever-growing share of world trade, in demanding its place in the sun, Germany was only doing what Britain had done. But what was right for Britain was wrong for Germany.

The trouble with Britain was that it bore its responsibilities as the world's superpower too lightly. To be able "to float downstream, occasionally putting out a diplomatic boat hook to avoid collisions", which is how Lord Salisbury described British foreign policy, may be an enviable way of conducting foreign affairs, but it does not say much for Britain's sense of responsibility as the world's leading power. When the crisis came in June 1914, Britain acted as a bystander rather than a leader of world affairs. By the time Sir Edward Grey, Britain's Foreign Secretary, proposed a conference, Austria could not turn back without humiliation. Britain entered the fray because she feared that Germany would overwhelm France and Belgium and reach the Channel. Only Germany could unseat Britain as a leading power in Europe. Germany's alliance with Turkey also threatened one of Britain's chief arteries to the East.

In Germany's violation of Belgian territory, Britain found the necessary pretext to make war. The basic problem between Britain and Germany, however, was not the violation of Belgian territory, but a much more all-encompassing struggle for world power. For Germany to obtain more power meant that Britain would have less, and on that point Britain would not compromise. A country like Britain, which was already losing ground in production and trade,[114] had little to gain by reducing its power still more. In any event, a change in the *status quo* has always been resisted by the leading power of the day.

France (whose economic and military power in 1914 was far inferior to that of either Britain or Germany) had even more reason than Britain to fear Germany. France had never accepted Prussia's overwhelming victory of 1870, which involved the loss of its territories of Alsace-Lorraine. Nor was France willing to surrender its primary role in Europe. Although Germany's military and industrial power exceeded that of France,[115] another struggle with the Germans was considered inevitable. In preparation for such a struggle, in 1894, France compromised its principle of Republicanism by allying itself with Czarist Russia. To foster better relations with the British, it accepted British power in Egypt (1904) and, unlike Germany, deliberately remained neutral (in word and deed) while Britain fought the South African War (1899–1902). If Britain could be committed to France and Russia (as it was in the Triple Entente of 1907) Germany must become the common enemy. For France to survive, Britain had to be committed. On that all else depended. At the outbreak of war, France had no choice but to follow where its Russian partner led. France, not Serbia was at stake. It was now or never; either the Triple Entente (Britain, France, and Russia) intervened, or Germany would dominate the continent and perhaps the world.

Some writers, such as the non-Marxist J.A. Hobson (whose book *Imperialism: A Study*, appeared in 1902) and the Marxist Vladimir Lenin (whose book *Imperialism, the Highest Stages of Capitalism* was published in 1917), saw the march to war before 1914 as springing more from economic than political roots. They thought that the search for privileged spheres of foreign trade and investment in the decades preceding the First Great War – the economic jostling and undercutting going on between the powers in Europe and the world – stemmed more from the changes taking place in the structure of the Western industrial economies than from politics. The "scramble" for parts of Africa and Asia by the European powers was the logical and inevitable outcome in the development of Western capitalism trying to escape from its own inner dilemma. The armaments race that preceded the war was simply a profitable substitute for more peaceful forms of manufacturing, such as railroads, the demand for which had declined.

While the economic explanations of Hobson and Lenin have much to recommend them, it is difficult to separate the economic from the political factors at work. If we must deal with the economic factor apart from the political, then it is evident that the great powers had more to lose than gain by going to war. In 1913, next to India, Germany was Britain's best customer. Britain also bought more from Germany than from any other country except the United States. Austria-Hungary's best markets were in the British Isles. As for the growing friction among the powers in Africa and Asia, European colonial trade and investments (while they might have been a matter of life and death to the colony itself) played only a minor role in world commerce and international investment. Trade and investment have not necessarily followed the flag. In any event, the strong commercial links that existed prior to 1914 did nothing to prevent war or alter the alignment of the belligerents.

The truth is that Europe's leaders seemed bent on war in the early years of the twentieth century with or without the aid of political and economic factors. Governments outdid each other in their preparations for war. The people who would eventually be sacrificed were not consulted. Incredible as it may seem, since 1870 European civilization had come to be measured not by art, learning, or religion, but by a country's ability to win a war.[116] Most of Europe's scientific and industrial talent was increasingly absorbed in the war industries. In the decades prior to 1914, every aspect of sea and land warfare was revolutionized. The best battleships existing in the 1880s would have been a match for the entire British fleet existing in the 1870s. The use of steam and oil had raised the speed of 6 knots in the 1870s to 36 knots in the 1880s. Armor-plating, first introduced in the 1850s, had by 1905 reached a thickness of 24 inches. The "Dreadnought", which Britain first launched in 1907, with its 18,000 tons of steel, its twenty-one knots, and its ten twelve-inch guns, had mesmerized the world. World power in 1914 rested as never before or since on the capabilities of a nation's battle fleet.[117] Paradoxically, the vessel that came closest to cutting Britain's lifeline with the world – the submarine – was the most neglected of all when the war began.

As for land warfare, by 1914 the Western powers had devised mechanized slaughter.[118] The intensity, range, and accuracy of side arms, shoulder arms, and artillery had all undergone sweeping change. In the war against Austria in 1866, Prussia had used a breech-loading gun, in contrast to Austria's muzzle-loading gun, with deadly effect.

Few doubted that the war, like most wars after 1865, would be swift and sure. Despite the fact that both civil and military indices of power pointed to French weaknesses, the French plan called for an attack on the entire front with unprecedented speed. The danger of a German attack on the exposed French left flank, which eventually took place, was wished away. With a complete disregard for the evidence before them, the German General Staff intended to end the conflict in three weeks. Morale and dash would settle matters. By 1913, with war clouds gathering, the Europeans had begun to assemble great armies for the coming fight.[119] If the worst came to the worst, war was still an acceptable way of settling a dispute. It was taken for granted that, as in all the other wars of the nineteenth century, there would be no shortage of people willing to fight. Increasingly, the question asked in the chancelleries of Europe was not "Will there be war?" but "When will there be war?"

The preparations for war in Europe in the twenty years before 1914 did not go unchallenged. In 1910 the English writer Norman Angell published his influential book *The Great Illusion*. The economic and financial complexity of the modern world, he argued, made a major war between the powers obsolete. It was a message that growing numbers of Europeans found consoling. The Socialist International[120] (which by 1912 had nine million members) swore it would oppose a capitalist war with every means at its disposal. In an attempt to stem the mill-stream race to war, the Hague Peace Conferences of 1899 and 1907 were organized; the Olympic Games were resumed; Esperanto was introduced; students were exchanged; commerce and travel were encouraged. None of these efforts succeeded; the war clouds grew. Oddest of all, when war came it was not treated as the scourge it proved to be, but as the hope of European civilization. At the outset idealism was paramount. Through sacrifice, the world would be saved. The only fear most European males felt in 1914 is that they might reach the front after the war had ended.

Alas, the war did not end in three weeks, or three months, or three years. This time there was to be no repetition of the swift, decisive, military victories obtained by Germany against Austria in 1866, and against France in 1870. Instead, there ensued a seemingly endless, exhausting, dogged struggle similar to some of the drawn-out wars of the eighteenth, and the American Civil War of the nineteenth century, in which the power of the purse became all-important.[121] The men did not come home for Christmas. Millions of them never saw their homes again. For four terrible years the war continued to consume the best that Europe had to offer. In 1916, for a few square miles of shell-torn ground on the Somme, hundreds of thousands of lives were sacrificed. Ten months of struggle at Verdun, also in 1916, cost almost a million casualties. The "red sweet wine of [Europe's] youth"[122] drenched the earth. Old men's errors were redeemed with young men's blood.

The nine to ten million who died at the front far surpassed the total of those lost in all European wars since the outbreak of the French Revolution. Of the 65 million mobilized the greatest losses were sustained by Germany (1,808,000 dead), Russia (1,700,000), France (1,385,000), Austria-Hungary (1,200,000), Britain (947,000), Italy (460,000), Romania (335,706), Ottoman Empire (325,000), Serbia (45,000), Bulgaria (87,500), and Greece (5,000). Many more millions were disabled, seriously wounded, taken prisoner, or died from sickness and privation. The United States, which had entered the war in April 1917, lost 112,432 – a remarkably small percentage of the 1.2 million doughboys who reached France.

The war took the monstrous toll it did because industrial Europe[123] practiced mechanized butchery. On 1 July 1916, at the Battle of the Somme, the attacking British lost 60,000 before noon on the first day – sixty per cent of the officers, forty per cent of the men. The machine-gun, capable of firing six hundred bullets a minute, had by now made defense systems almost impregnable. Moreover, as those giving the orders were too far away to witness or be affected by the carnage, the killing was repeated the next day, and the next, and the next, for month after ghastly bloody month. Alas for those involved, the Great War was the first major conflict in history to be directed by remote control. Battle commanders such as Marlborough, Washington, Napoleon, and Wellington, who shared the perils of battle with their troops, would never have permitted such endless, pointless killing. Only when mutiny threatened did the politicians order the staff to halt the slaughter. But the killing was soon renewed, with no visible effect on the war. For three years on the western front the line of battle hardly moved. Whereas all the European wars since 1815 had been short and decisive, this war dragged on.

In an effort to break the stalemate, everything was tried. In 1915 the Germans used poison gas; they also bombed from the air. The first German Zeppelin raids on London in 1915 were condemned as barbarian.[124] The British soon stifled their sense of outrage and bombed back again. At Gallipoli, in 1915, British, Australian, and New Zealand troops made a desperate but disastrous attempt to force the Dardanelles and seize Constantinople, capital of Turkey. In 1916 the British Navy fought an inconclusive battle with the German Kriegsmarine off Jutland. On land, equally inconclusively, the British tried tanks. Lured by promises of territorial aggrandizement, Bulgaria and Turkey joined the Central Powers; Italy, Romania, and Greece joined the Allies. Under the Sykes-Picot Agreement of 1916, Italy was promised the Turkish Dodecanese Islands, as well as the south-eastern and western coasts of Turkish Asia Minor; Russia would be given Constantinople and parts of north-east Asia Minor. This secret agreement (divulged by the Bolsheviks in 1918) also showed that while the Allies were promising the Arabs independence after the war, their true intentions were to enrich themselves at Arab expense. Arab hopes that their revolt against the Turks would culminate in a united Arab kingdom with the Sharif of Mecca at its head were sacrificed to Western interests. The Arab world was subsequently divided on terms that suited the Western powers.

Although it carried with it the risk of bringing America into the war, in February 1917 the Germans again resorted to unrestricted submarine warfare,[125] which had been abandoned after the sinking of the Lusitania[126] in May 1915. By May 1917 the German U-boats were sinking British ships faster than they could be replaced. In the first three months of that year more than four hundred British vessels were sunk, leaving the United Kingdom with six weeks of food and supplies.

Fortunately for Britain, help was on the way. A month earlier (April 1917), following the German announcement of unrestricted submarine warfare, the United States had decided to enter the war on the side of the Allies. The pro-Allied sentiment pervading Wilson's Administration had at last openly declared itself. The world's third greatest navy had entered the fray; a vast new army had become available. Yet the mobilization and training of the United States army was so painfully slow that a year later, in March 1918 (Germany having forced a treaty upon Russia at the Polish frontier town of Brest-Litovsk, under which Russia surrendered the Baltic provinces, Poland, Ukraine, Finland, and parts of Transcaucasia), the German General Staff felt it could afford to stake everything on a spring offensive in the West. While American troops rushed across the Atlantic, German troops raced westward from the eastern front.

Despite heroic efforts, the German spring offensive failed. Germany was forced to sue for terms. But instead of the "just peace" that President Wilson had promised, Germany suffered total humiliation at the Peace Conference at Versailles in 1919. Chicanery and hatred triumphed over Wilson's vision of a world governed by the rule of law. The stage was set for the rise of German national socialism and Adolf Hitler.

It is now more than seventy years since the First Great War ended. Yet it continues to dominate European thinking – sometimes even more than the Second World War. It does so because the years 1914–1918 have come to be recognized as one of the great watersheds in world history. The bullet which killed the Archduke Ferdinand of Austria also helped to kill Western supremacy in the world. The Europeans could not expect to recruit Africans and Asians to kill Europeans without lowering their own prestige in non-European eyes. Nothing equals the First Great War in prompting Asians and Africans to rid themselves of European rule.

Not least, the war remains alive in the memory of the West because of its terrible irony. It began with unbounded idealism; it ended with cynicism and disgust. At the outset, the English poet Rupert Brooke thanked God for having

> . . . matched us with His hour,
> And caught our youth, and wakened us from
>   sleeping, . . .
> To turn, as swimmers into cleanness leaping,
> Glad from a world grown old and cold and
>   weary . . .[127]

Thomas Mann, spokesman of German humanism, looked upon the war as "a purification, a liberation, an enormous hope . . ." Older, wiser men, who knew these hopes were false, lacked the imagination to warn those who were to be sacrificed; the young lacked the imagination to believe.

And so hope died and disillusion and disgust took its place. Poets like Wilfred Owen (who himself died in the inferno), wrote not of heroic war but of death:

> If you could hear, at every jolt, the blood
> Come gargling from the froth-corrupted lungs . . .[128]

"It must be all lies," wrote Erich Maria Remarque (in his novel *All Quiet on the Western Front*), "and of no account when the culture of a thousand years could not prevent this river of blood being poured out."

More than anything else, it was this "river of blood"

which helped to drown Europe's nineteenth-century faith
in the future. The providential nature of progress, which
had dominated nineteenth-century Europe, gradually
gave way to the feeling of doom later expressed by Os-
wald Spengler in his *Decline of the West*.[129] Even Spengler's
critics had to agree that much of what the Renaissance and
the Age of Enlightenment had bequeathed to Europe had
been lost for good in the mud of the western front. Europe's belief in reason and the Christian belief in the
reverence for life were never to be the same.

Not only did the Great War prove – in starting out with
idealism and ending with disgust – to be ironic; for many
Europeans it came to be identified with hypocrisy. The
glowing promises made by the leaders of both sides were
(in Remarque's words) "downright lies". Despite the sac-
rifices, and all the fine words, the First World War did not
prove to be "the war to end all wars". While Wilson
retreated to an increasingly isolated America (an isolation
that carried with it tremendous implications for the future
of world affairs), wars went on; an even greater catastrophe befell the world twenty years later. By then, however, the Western world had become callous, not idealistic
as it had been in 1914. Nor did the war "make the world
safe for democracy". Instead, it fostered the rise of revolutionary communism in Russia, fascism in Italy, and
national socialism in Germany. And while the Treaty of
Versailles, and the treaties that followed, promised (and in
some instances gave) "self-determination" to Czechs,
Poles,[130] Serbs, Croats, Slovenes,[131] Catalonians, Basques,
Finns, Latvians, Lithuanians, and Estonians, it denied it to
Asians and Africans. Indians who had been fit enough to
fight for Britain, were not thought fit enough to govern
themselves. Appeals for self-determination by Germans
absorbed by Italy and Czechoslovakia, or by the Irish[132]
who had fought a running battle with the British for
centuries, were given equally short shrift.

In particular, the earlier promises of independence
made by Britain to the Arabs (the Hussein-McMahon
correspondence of 1915)[133] together with the joint British-
French declaration of 1918 to the people of Syria and

Mesopotamia, "promising national governments drawing their authority from the initiative and free choice of the native populations", were disregarded by the Allies once the war was over. Britain held on to Iraq, Trans-Jordan and Palestine (euphemistically called mandated territories); France took Syria which included Lebanon. The mandate for Palestine approved by the League of Nations in 1922, incorporated the Balfour Declaration,[134] which was Britain's wartime promise to the Zionists to support the creation of a national home for the Jews in Palestine. For many Arabs of the Fertile Crescent there followed a struggle against Britain and France (and now against the United States) which has gone on from 1920 until the present day.

The economic promises of Europe's leaders proved to be just as hollow as the political. Far from providing "homes for heroes", most European countries emerged from the war too impoverished to provide food. Hundreds of billions of dollars had been spent on the war, and most European treasuries were empty. Britain and France never regained their pre-eminent position in the world. Both nations experienced a relative erosion of their economic strength. The international system of trade and investment upon which pre-war European economic greatness had been based was impaired. (Between 1928 and 1935 the value of European trade was more than halved from $58 to $20.8 billion). Britain experienced dramatic declines in the production of textiles, iron and steel, coal, and shipbuilding. In contrast, the war gave a tremendous stimulus to the industrialization of India, China, and Japan. Not least important for the outcome of the future struggle for world power, by transferring control of the German colonies – the Mariana, Caroline, and Marshall Islands – to Japan, it enlarged the Japanese presence in the Pacific; an outcome which some Australian leaders looked upon with more alarm than their British or American counterparts.

American attempts to replace Britain's economic leadership in the world proved to be ill-starred. No sooner had the United States provided a measure of economic stability in Europe, through its Dawes and Young Plans[135] of the 1920s, than a speculative frenzy in the United States in

1929 brought an economic slump to the whole of the Western world. President Roosevelt's refusal to agree to the stabilization of currencies at the World Economic Conference in London in 1933 resulted in the further disintegration of the world economy. Without the economic chaos of the postwar years, the Italian fascists and the German national socialists might never have triumphed at the polls.

The end of the First Great War left Europe physically, emotionally, intellectually, and morally exhausted. National fears, national pride, and national honor had led to international disaster. In place of the earlier romanticism and innocence, a vast fatigue dominated Europe. The war did, in fact, divide two periods of Western history – one of optimism, the other of disillusionment. While it took the devastating economic depression of the 1930s to bring the lesson home, politically and economically, Europe's period of overwhelming ascendency was over. Temporarily at least, economic and political might had passed to the United States. The war not only pushed America to the front of the world stage; it also made Russia a leading power – one whose example would inspire revolution everywhere. In addition, it stimulated the resurgence of Asia. The five great powers at Versailles in 1919 were Britain, France, Italy, the United States and (for the first time an Asian power) Japan. The war had provided Japan with an excellent opportunity to develop its industries (especially textiles) and supplant European traders in the East. For those with eyes to see, the shape of world politics, self-evident at the close of the Second World War, was already visible in 1918.

In 1918, at the eleventh hour of the eleventh day of the eleventh month, while Europe waited in hushed silence, the Armistice was signed. The most monstrous war was ended. Men being what they are, and history being tangential, Serbia and Belgium had long since been forgotten. The dynastic and imperial domination of the Romanovs, the Hohenzollerns, the Austro-Hungarians, and the Ottomans, had all been swept away. At the instigation of the

Allies, the Ottoman Empire was dismembered in 1920 by the Treaty of Sèvres. (Its dismemberment had been secretly agreed upon by Britain, France, and Russia in May 1916.) The Treaty of Sèvres, rejected by Turkish nationalists led by Mustapha Kemal Atatürk (1881–1938), was replaced in 1923 – after a successful fight by Turkey against the Allies – by the Treaty of Lausanne which recognized the territory and independence of the new Turkish Republic. More important, while Britain and France seemed to have emerged from the war with a semblance of political power, the initiative in world politics had passed to the capitalist United States and to revolutionary Russia. The Bolshevik Revolution of 1917 – which created the world's first revolutionary, socialist government – marked a new era in the world power struggle. From the start, it promised revolutionary support to colonial peoples everywhere.

8

1917: Communism – A New World Religion

The Russian Revolution of 1917 changed the political outlook of much of the human race. The uprising began on 8 March 1917, when a handful of hungry housewives rioted in the streets of Petrograd (St Petersburg), capital of Czarist Russia. The economic hardships and the stupendous losses suffered by the Russians at the beginning of the First Great War had already aroused widespread dissent among all classes and it was not long before the bread riots became anti-government demonstrations. On 11 March soldiers of the Petrograd garrison mutinied. On 12 March, in a vast, unexpected explosion of feeling, the people of Petrograd took to the streets. Unplanned, unforeseen, and uncoordinated, the revolution was underway. This time, unlike the earlier uprising of 1905, which had followed Russia's defeat by Japan, nothing could stem it. Troops were called out to put down the revolt, but they mutinied and joined the people. Panic seized the city. In an attempt to restore order, the Duma[136] formed a Provisional Government. On 15 March Czar Nicholas, who was hurrying back to the capital from the front, was forced to abdicate.

A month later, in April 1917, the Russian communist and revolutionary, Vladimir Ilyich Ulyanov, alias Lenin (1870–1924), who for most of the past seventeen years had lived in exile, reached Petrograd from Switzerland. The German High Command, hoping that Lenin would undermine whatever strength the Russian Provisional Government had left, and thus take Russia out of the war, did everything (including providing a sealed train) to get Lenin back to Petrograd. It is thought that secret German funds were made available to the Bolsheviks. Hastening to

101

join Lenin were two other Bolsheviks,[137] Lev Davidovich Bronstein, alias Trotsky (1879–1940)[138], from New York, and Iosif Vissarionovich Dzhugashvili, alias Stalin (1879–1953), from Siberia. Although only Stalin was of working-class origin, the Bolsheviks intended to establish a dictatorship of the proletariat along Marxist lines. Contrary to the Provisional Government's aim to continue the war against the Germans, the Bolsheviks called for peace, land, and bread. Appeals to nationalism were conspicuously absent. In spite of their appeals, the Bolsheviks did not succeed in unseating the Provisional Government. By July, Lenin had been driven into exile again; Trotsky was jailed on charges of treason; Stalin and other leading Bolsheviks had gone to earth.

For a moment it looked as if the head of the Provisional Government, Alexander Kerensky (a socialist), had succeeded in closing the floodgates of revolution. But then came the abortive attempt by the ex-Commander-in-Chief of the Russian Army, General Kornilov, to overthrow the Provisional Government from the right. To help fight Kornilov, Kerensky turned to the Bolsheviks for help. Lenin was allowed to return. Trotsky was released from jail. In recruiting the Bolsheviks, Kerensky had replaced Kornilov's challenge from the right with a much more dangerous threat from the left. By September the Bolsheviks had won control of the Moscow and Petrograd Soviets (the councils of delegates from the factories and barracks). In October Lenin decided that the time was ripe to overthrow the Provisional Government, which would, he hoped, ignite a revolution throughout Europe. According to Marxist doctrine, unless the revolution was taken up elsewhere, the Bolsheviks themselves would fail. On the night of 23–24 October at a meeting of the Central Committee of the Bolshevik Party attended by Lenin, Trotsky, Stalin, and nine others, the decision to seize power was made.

On the eve of 7 November 1917,[139] almost without bloodshed, the Bolsheviks seized the centers of transport and communications, energy and government in Petrograd. The Provisional Government, having neither the

strength nor the will to defend itself, was forcibly dis-
banded; the Winter Palace, its last stronghold, was overrun. The Duma died. Overnight, the Soviet of the People's
Commissars, with Lenin as Chairman, Trotsky as Foreign
Minister, and Stalin as Commissar for National Minorities,
became Russia's only legitimate central government. All
others, including the freely elected Constituent Assembly[140] which met on 18 January 1918, and which was
forcibly dispersed by Lenin's militia in the early hours of
19 January (never to reconvene), were treated as counter-
revolutionary. Marxism was declared the official doctrine
of the state. Under Lenin terror was substituted for popular support. Russia's first real experiment with democracy
had been destroyed by Lenin at its birth. Without the
interim experience of bourgeois democracy, Russia had
passed from feudalism to socialism. Russia's foreign
debts, amounting to between $3–$4 billion, were repudiated. In place of orthodox Christianity, atheistic communism was declared Russia's new secular religion.

Earlier, on 15 December 1917, Russia had been forced to
sign a humiliating armistice with Germany at Brest-
Litovsk.[141] The choice for Lenin was either humiliation or
the failure of the revolution. Unlike Trotsky, he insisted
on peace at all costs. But there was to be no peace for
Russia. No sooner had hostilities against the Germans
ceased, than the Russians fell upon each other. Beginning
in May 1918, in what came to be known as the Great Civil
War, Russia proceeded to tear itself to pieces. Untold
numbers (from thirteen to twenty million) perished. The
idea that Lenin was unaware of slaughter on this scale is a
Soviet myth. Where the elimination of opponents was
concerned, Vladimir Lenin[142] could be as ruthless as his
successor Joseph Stalin. There is no radical discontinuity
between them. In the summer of 1918, while counter-
revolutionary armies controlled most of the country from
the Volga River to the Pacific Ocean, the Romanov imperial family was assassinated. In 1917 and 1918 an Allied
force, led by Britain, and including French, American and
Japanese contingents, invaded Russia[143] in an attempt to
strangle the revolution at its birth. Lenin and the Bolshevik

leaders fled inland from Petrograd to Moscow. It was there, in 1919, that the Third Socialist International was formed with its aim of world revolution. Moscow had become the center for all socialist and anti-imperialist forces.

Because the anti-communist forces in Russia could never unite, and Allied support was half-hearted, by 1919 communism had triumphed: a new experiment in living had begun. Supporting the experiment was the Marxist doctrine which had first appeared in the *Communist Manifesto*, written by two German emigres in England, Karl Marx (1818–1883) and Friedrich Engels (1820–1895), and published in German in 1848. (The English translation did not appear until 1888). Marx, the son of Jewish middle-class parents who had converted to Christianity, was a freelance writer, a born agitator, and a political revolutionary. Banished from Germany because of his political activities, driven from France, often beset by poverty, he eventually found asylum in London. Engels was the son of a well-to-do Manchester textile manufacturer who later provided Marx with an annual allowance. It was in London that Marx wrote his most important work *Das Kapital*, first published in German in 1867. The book was translated into Russian in 1872. The Russian censor felt the work was so dull that he allowed it to appear. It was published in English in 1886. Neither the *Communist Manifesto* nor *Das Kapital* attracted much attention. *Das Kapital* remained almost unknown to the European labor movement until Marx's writings became the holy writ of the Russian Revolution.

Adopted by Lenin as the new Russian ideology, the *Communist Manifesto* and *Das Kapital* became two of the most influential pieces of writing in world history. They not only recounted history; they made history. Their central message is clear: the whole of history (since the dissolution of primitive tribal societies) has been a history of class struggle, a contest between exploiters and exploited, between oppressor and oppressed. To that extent, economic injustice is the sole cause of human conflict. To Marx, drawing upon the German philosopher Georg W.F. Hegel

(1770–1831), the process of history is fundamentally a dialectic (a conflict of opposites producing progress). Marx argued that history is the history of the economic process; all is derived from the material conditions of life. From the conflict between the feudal lord and serf, to the conflict between capital and labor, the eternal antagonism between classes develops its changing forms. Its last and most virulent form is precipitated by the capitalistically inspired European Industrial Revolution of the nineteenth century. Because the capitalist system polarizes the enmity between capital and labor, as no other conflict has ever done, revolution – a violent climax – is inevitable.

Marx provided a most convoluted explanation why this must be so. In a capitalist system, he held, the laborer must sell his labor in such a way that the difference between the value which the laborer creates and the bare cost of his own subsistence inevitably accrues to the capitalist in the form of surplus value. It is a process in which, inexorably, the rich must get richer and the poor poorer. Despite the productive power of the bourgeoisie,[144] for which Marx had only praise, the condition of the poor must worsen until they are forced to revolt. With the revolt, the injustices which had caused the conflict, would be abolished. "Workers of the world," Marx cried, "you have nothing to lose but your chains." The right to rebel, nay, the necessity to rebel, was established.

Marx thought that with the decisive dictatorship of the proletariat, private property and the resultant class conflict would end. The dialectic process – the conflict of opposites – would be no more. The state (hitherto the political implement of the bourgeoisie) would wither away. As Darwin had discovered a law of the evolution of organic matter, so Marx thought he had discovered an economic law of motion which would carry the oppressed of the world to a new communal Utopia.

Where Marx differed from earlier communalists or communists, such as Plato, St Luke, St Thomas More, and countless Benedictine monks, is that he sought a solution through violence. He also differed from them in his belief that the ultimate reality is economic – that God was dead.

At least it is to his credit that he was concerned with the whole of mankind rather than a particular nation. In an age of growing nationalism, he was one of the first to appreciate that the spread of European capitalism and European systems of production were creating problems of a world-wide nature. "Capitalism," he concluded, "knows no flag." One cannot help feeling that Marx would have been fascinated with the manner in which foreign capitalists are today buying up United States industry and real estate.[145] According to Marx, the social problems of nineteenth-century Europe would eventually spread to the world; under capitalism, social injustice would not lessen but grow.

Marx was not alone in protesting the social conditions of the time. Many others, including the German Catholic social pioneer Bishop Wilhelm von Ketteler (1811–1877) and the French sociologist Gustave le Bon (1841–1931), were also concerned with the growing social evils accompanying societies in transition from a rural to an industrial way of life. They too were appalled at the terrible working and living conditions that the Industrial Revolution had created in England, France, and Germany. Like Marx, they deplored the degrading working conditions, the regimentation of workers, the growing industrial unrest, and the alarming injustice and instability associated with a capitalist economy. It did not require Marxist analysis for them to be able to recognize capitalist exploitation. While upholding the right to private property, they opposed capitalist wage slavery as much as they had opposed African slavery. The two great papal encyclicals on social conditions, Rerum Novarum (1891) and Quadragesimo Anno (1931) show that the Vatican was aware of the momentous consequences of the economic and social changes taking place. Where the Christian message differed from Marx was in its attempt to reduce class conflict through charity and understanding, rather than enlarge it through violence. The church rejected Marxist atheism outright. It rejected the Marxist tragic view of life which must end in blood and fury. The hope of the world lay not in class hatred – in godless malice – but in Christian love.

While the study of Soviet communism must begin with Marx, the conclusions reached will depend as much on one's faith (or lack of it) in the Marxist system as on one's intellect. The true Marxist does not recognize bourgeois objectivity. He will defend the Marxist economic law of motion, which to him is gospel truth, with the same faith and fervor as that shown by a religious fundamentalist waging war for the literal interpretation of the Bible. The inevitability of Marx's perfect society must be believed, it cannot be proved.

Indeed, there is about Marxism the same dogmatic orthodoxy, the same apocalyptic vision, found in the Old Testament. One cannot help being struck by the fact that, for Marx, the eventual and inevitable destruction of the bourgeoisie by the proletariat was simply another way of restoring the chosen people (in this case the proletariat) in an earthly rather than a heavenly messianic kingdom.[146] A myth, of course, but no less powerful for that. In his dogmatism, in his condemnation of evil (capitalism) in his belief that right will prevail, in his grandeur of conception, in his vision and his messianism, in the blazing passages which from time to time light up his often turgid prose, in the white-heat of his moral judgements – in all these things Marx is like an old Testament prophet whose voice thunders across the world.[147] He realized, as the early Christians did before him, that we must not only have something to live for, but something to die for as well. He was a prophet among prophets, yet unlike Jesus or Mohammed he was a prophet without a god.

Marxism is ethical judgement rather than economic history. *"Das Kapital,"* said the famous economic historian Lord Keynes, "is an obsolete economics textbook which I know to be not only erroneous, but without interest or application for the modern world." Economics alone – as Marx would have it – are not the cause of human conflict; human beings are. The conflict between economic classes is not the only conflict. Ethnic, religious, linguistic, and national differences are also the source of discord. Indeed, Max Weber[148] maintained that an economy is derived from a society's underlying ideology and ethics, and not the

other way round. Even if Marxism had been deduced from
history, which it was not, by the nature of things, it could
not provide the positive prescription (the ability to be
clever for the next time) which Marx expected of it. Irrational, emotional nationalism has often been a far more
powerful force in history than rationalistic, scientific
socialism.

Moreover, as with all visionaries, some of the things
Marx predicted never materialized. His prediction that the
revolution would not come in Russia, but in the advanced
countries in the West (particularly Germany and Britain
which had undergone the Industrial Revolution) proved
false. But then, he had a low opinion of the Russians: "I do
not trust any Russian," he wrote to Engels. "As soon as a
Russian worms his way in, all hell breaks loose." He was
equally wrong in believing that the state would "wither
away" as an instrument of oppression; the Soviet state, in
fact, became more powerful than ever – even more powerful than that of the Czars. He erred in stressing the
primacy of economics at all times, in all situations. History
is not merely the story of class conflict as he believed it to
be (if it is, he certainly does not prove it). The First Great
War, 1914–1918, the greatest slaughter in history until
then, did not arise because of poor and rich nations, or for
that matter because of poor and rich classes. It was false
for him to assume that change would come about because
of class conflict. Change is always the work of a small
resolute minority – regardless of class. Finally, he was
wrong in ascribing selfishness and greed to the middle-
class (the bourgeoisie) rather than to incalculable human
nature, as he was in placing so much stress upon the
power of the intellect and so little upon the power of
passion and feeling. Marx not only misread history, he
misread human nature as well. Private property, profit,
and individualism are not particularly bourgeois qualities,
but the outcome – in many parts of the world – of human
instincts.

Regardless of whether one is a supporter or a critic of
Marxist doctrine, our world would have been a very different place had Marx never lived. Without him there would
still have been a labor movement in Europe – perhaps a

revolution in Russia – but it would have been a different labor movement, and a different revolution. Had Lenin never heard of Marx he would have lived and worked and perhaps made history, but it would not have been the history it came to be under the influence of Marxist doctrine. Indeed, it is as difficult to think of Lenin without the doctrinal background of Marxian orthodoxy as it is to imagine Paul of Tarsus without the doctrinal background of Jesus of Nazareth. Lenin did for Marx what Paul did for Christ. Without Lenin and the Russian revolution, Marx might have remained unknown.

However heretical it may be to say so, the Great Socialist Revolution of 1917, far from being the outcome of Marxist doctrine of historical and social determinism, was, in fact, one of the greatest accidents of history. At best it was the result of a straightforward coup. It depended more on a disastrous war, the desperation of the common people, mutiny at the front, the excesses of capitalism, the social and political decay of the Romanov dynasty, an enfeebled aristocracy, self-seeking politicians, and a corrupt officialdom, than on doctrinal exactitude. The strength of Marxism (and the communism to which it gave birth), does not rest on doctrinal exactitude. Marx's influence in the world does not depend on his theory being proved true or false. Communism grew because Marx provided a weapon (in the *Communist Manifesto*) with which the poor of the world (particularly the poor of the non-Western world) could fight the rich – a psychological weapon which no other political system had devised. For the underdeveloped, agrarian countries of the world, such as China, Marxism was a revolutionary call to arms – a philosophy of action designed to change the world, not to interpret it.

In the 1980s one and a half billion people lived under communist rule. They represented more than a third of the world's population, occupying more than a quarter of the earth's land surface. Until the explosion of sentiment in eastern Europe in 1989 (when Hungary and Czechoslovakia actually abandoned communist doctrine), communism, with atheism as its official belief (a belief abandoned on 1 October 1990 when the Supreme Soviet approved the freedom of religion by a vote of 341 to 2), had been one of the world's most rapidly growing faiths.[149] Between the 1940s and the 1980s, Marxist-Leninist communism had become the official doctrine of fifteen countries. Marx's scientific and historical accuracy is open to question; his impact on the world is not. Facts can be disputed; the influence of Marx and Lenin is before our eyes. No fact can overthrow a legend or upset a faith. The present setbacks in the communist world, dramatic as they are, do not necessarily mean the end of Marxist-Leninism. It remains to be seen whether the abandonment of communism in eastern Europe in 1990 will become world-wide. Nor does the failure of communism automatically ensure the success of democracy and the free market.

Since 1917 Marxism has given way to Leninism, Leninism to Stalinism, Stalinism to the policies of his successors. Doctrinally, the changes have been slight. True, Lenin converted Marx's doctrine of dialectical, historical materialism into a practical instrument of revolution. In order to seize power it was permissible to transcend the economic situation – to leap across the historical stage. "A Marxist," Lenin said, "must take account of real life . . . and not hang on to the tails of the theories of yesterday." It was the Party's job to lead the proletariat in the revolutionary struggle. Lenin also developed the theory that Western imperialism would prove to be the final stage of capitalism. After Lenin's death in 1924 Stalin made changes in communist doctrine whereby socialism could be built in one state without – as Marx had assumed at the outset – its being sustained by world revolution. It was one thing to sing the "Internationale"; it was another thing to implement it. It was this change in doctrine which caused the clash between Stalin and Trotsky (who, like Marx and Lenin, supported the idea of ecumenical, worldwide communism). The argument was concluded in 1940 with Trotsky's assassination in Mexico City. The Third Socialist International founded in 1919 was formally abolished by Stalin in 1943.

Meanwhile, the so-called inevitable Marxist historical process remains a vision. Until the assumption of power by that extraordinary individual Mikhail Gorbachev, there had been no real will in the Soviet Union to move beyond elaborately centralized socialism (prescribed by Marx as the precursor to the true communist era). Five years ago when Gorbachev came to power, (like Martin Luther and the Christian church) his object was to reform communism, not to destroy it. His book *Perestroika*[150] published in 1987, while critical of the economic stagnation in Soviet society, which he hoped to change in the direction of a market economy, did not altogether abandon the communist approach to geo-politics. Like Luther, he ended up destroying the institution he set out to reform. His acceptance of the profit motive, free enterprise, and a market economy (both domestic and global), as well as private property and the freedom of religion, flies in the face of Bolshevik and Stalinist history. Like Luther, he was overtaken by a whirlwind which he was powerless to control. He resigned his position on 25 December 1991.

Far from Russian communism fulfilling Marxist predictions, far from it creating a new civilization, since the death of Lenin, it has reverted to Russia's earlier status: that of a great autocratic power choosing its allies and its enemies not on grounds of ideology, but to suit its national interests. In this, Gorbachev is akin to Nikita Khrushchev (1894–1971) and Leonid Brezhnev (1906–1982) who in 1964 succeeded Khrushchev as First Secretary of the Communist Party. What is at stake in the Soviet Union's relations with the rest of the world is not Marxism – not ideology – but power politics and expediency. Marxist ideology became the camouflage for purely national aims, national prestige, national aspirations, and above all national security. Little wonder if the communists of Spain and Italy criticized the Soviets for ideological back-sliding; or that the Chinese communists repeated Trotsky's slur against Stalin: that in putting national interests before the interests of world communism he had "betrayed the revolution". Perhaps in its increasing Westernization, which gained new life under Gorbachev, Russia is succumbing not to the Marxist dialectic, but – as Peter the Great did – to Western culture.

9

"White Peril" in the East: The Response of China and Japan

In 1515 a group of Portuguese traders and buccaneers – Arab, Persian, and Indian sea-traders had long preceded them – appeared off the southern Chinese coast. In 1543 a group of Portuguese merchants, bound from Indonesia to China, were blown off course and shipwrecked at Tanegashima, an island off Kyushu, the southern island of Japan. By the mid-sixteenth century, the Chinese government having forbidden its subjects to trade directly with Japan, the Portuguese at Macao on the Chinese coast controlled the carrying trade between China and Japan. By then, the western invasion of eastern Asia by sea was underway.

At first the Chinese, conscious of their age-old, superior civilization, did their best to keep the foreign barbarians at bay. Except for gold and silver specie, and entertaining items such as mechanical clocks, the West had nothing that the Chinese wanted. Besides, the merchant class in China had always been considered socially inferior. It was not until 1601 that several Jesuit priests,[151] led by Matteo Ricci (1552–1610), who had spent seven years proselytizing on the coast, decided to penetrate the imperial bureaucracy in Peking. Prompting the Chinese decision to allow the Jesuits to stay in Peking was the scientific knowledge which they had brought with them. In due course, Ricci and his companions translated several important Western scientific works into Chinese. In helping to reform the Chinese dynastic calendar, which was crucial in regulating every aspect of the emperor's life, they altered the whole outlook of Chinese astronomy.

113

So impressed were the Jesuits by the civilized conduct and bearing of the ruling Mandarin class, that they extolled the Chinese as superior among orientals. In particular they noted the contrast between China's tolerance toward other beliefs and seventeenth-century European religious strife. The reigning religion in China in 1500 – Confucianism – was not so much a religion as a system of order. The Confucian social code was as rational and reasonable as the Christian code was dogmatic. The different world outlooks of East and West were noted by Ricci in his diary:

> To begin with, it seems to be quite remarkable . . . that in a kingdom of almost limitless expanse and innumerable population, and abounding in copious supplies of every description, though they have a well-equipped army and navy that could easily conquer the neighboring nations, neither the King nor his people ever think of waging a war of aggression. They are quite content with what they have and are not ambitious of conquest. In this respect they are much different from the people of Europe, who are frequently discontent with their own governments and covetous of what others enjoy . . .
>
> Another remarkable difference . . . is that the entire kingdom is administered by the Order of the Learned, commonly known as the Philosophers . . . The army, both officers and soldiers, hold them in high respect . . . Policies of war are formulated and military questions are decided by the Philosophers only . . . From the beginning and foundation of this empire the study of letters was always more acceptable to the people than the profession of arms, as being more suitable to a people who had little or no interests in the extension of the empire.[152]

In Ricci's view the Chinese were justified in calling their country the "Middle Kingdom" – the center of the earth. European leaders of the Enlightenment, such as Voltaire, Quesnay, and Leibnitz, looked upon China as a model that Europe should imitate. The fact that the Confucian social code stressed conformity, and hence was less stimulating to the development of scientific thought, was glossed over. A passion for things Chinese swept through eighteenth-century Europe. With the help of the Jesuits, the Chinese examination system was adopted first by France and then by the other European powers.

It took time before the Jesuits began to notice aspects of Chinese life – such as ancestor worship – which they were less willing to praise. Some Jesuits thought ancestor worship idolatrous. They also wondered aloud about the emperor's spiritual authority in relation to that of the pope. Priests in the emperor's employment faced the problem of serving two masters. In 1715 the pope appeared to insult the emperor by telling him how the word "God" should be translated into Chinese. Worse, the rival Christian orders began to squabble among themselves about the compromises being made by the Jesuits to Confucianism. By 1722, by which time the emperor K'ang Hsi (1662–1722) had wearied of the Western presence, the propagation of Christianity in China by the Jesuits had been dealt a severe blow. The quarrel over rites – a theological dispute among the Christians rather than a political threat to the Chinese throne – eventually put an end to more than a hundred years of almost unbroken Jesuit presence at the Chinese court.[153]

Thenceforth, for more than a century, China remained largely closed to Western influence. The Chinese themselves were forbidden to go abroad. Foreign trade was proscribed or severely restricted. Chinese shipping was confined to coastal waters. When in 1793 George III of England sent Lord Macartney, his Ambassador Extra-ordinary, to negotiate improved foreign trading conditions in China, the emperor, seeing no reason why Britain or any other European nation should be granted rights other than those of a tributary state, politely turned him away. Another British mission sent in 1816 suffered the same fate. There was simply nothing that China needed of the West. Instead of fostering its links with the West, China directed its energies to extending and maintaining

its relations with surrounding areas, including the Amur
Valley, Mongolia, Nepal, Tibet, Siam, Burma, and Vietnam.
The only link with the West – and that a tenuous one –
was that maintained by a handful of European traders at
Canton. Here ever-growing quantities of tea, silk, fine
cottons, highly valued porcelain and lacquerware were
traded for Western goods and specie. Foreign imports
were looked upon by the Chinese governing class as
tribute. Only neighboring Russia succeeded in maintaining the right to trade regularly with China (Treaty of
Kiakhta, 1727), and this only annually and overland. Not
until the British forced open the Chinese door to Western
commerce in the Opium War (1839–1842) was China's
policy of isolation abandoned.

Until the mid-nineteenth century, Japan's response to
Western intrusion stands in marked contrast to that of
China. The Japanese made no pretensions of cultural
superiority toward the West. On the contrary, they greeted
the foreigners with wonder and awe. The Japanese were
eager to learn from them, especially about weaponry. In
the sixteenth century they quickly adopted and put the
Portuguese musket to use. The port of Nagasaki, opened
to Western commerce in 1570, became the meeting-place
of an ever-growing throng of Portuguese, Spanish, Dutch,
and British merchants. Chinese gold and silk, luxuries
from India and Persia, and firearms from Europe were
brought to Japan in exchange for Japanese silver and
copper. It looked as if the traditional geographic isolation
of Japan might end.

The Japanese displayed the same interest in Western
religion as in Western commerce. Christianity (first introduced into Japan by the Jesuit missionary St Francis Xavier
in 1549), received the protection and the seeming encour-
agement of two of Japan's military leaders: Oda Nobunaga
(1534–1582) and Toyotomi Hideyoshi (1537–1597). The role
of both these men in deciding Japan's relations with the
West was paramount. With their tolerance, and sometimes their help, in less than fifty years, the Christian

missionaries had made an astonishing 300,000 conversions. With a population of about twenty-five million at the beginning of the seventeenth century (as against approximately sixteen million for France, seven million for Spain, and four and a half million for England) Japan[154] came to be regarded as the most promising field of Christian evangelism.

Yet the very success of the Europeans in Japan proved to be their undoing. The growing Christian presence began to alarm the Japanese leaders (especially Toyotomi Hideyoshi) who came to suspect the church as an agent of Western imperialism. The Jesuits in Japan came to be looked upon as the secret agents of Spain. Loyalty and authority were at stake. Increasingly fearful that the Europeans might try to seize power in Japan, as they had done in the Philippines (1565–1571) and Formosa (1624), the Japanese proceeded to reverse their attitude toward Western commerce and Christianity. By the mid-seventeenth century European merchants had been banished from the mainland. Christianity was denounced as a threat to the state in 1587. In 1614 the Tokugawas decreed that all missionaries must leave; their converts were ordered to renounce their faith. In 1636 a seclusion Edict was proclaimed.[155] In 1637 the Japanese stamped out a Christian insurrection at Shimabara (close to Nagasaki) in which 37,000 Christians died. Everything was done to exterminate Christians and Christianity. At issue was the extent to which the growing Western presence had become a threat to the state.

Henceforth, the only Europeans allowed to stay in Japan were a few Protestant Dutch traders in virtual imprisonment on the islet of Deshima in Nagasaki harbor. To prove that they were not true Christians, and therefore not agents of Western expansion, this small group was required annually to trample on the Christian cross or an image of Christ. With a few Chinese, and two supply vessels a year from Holland, they remained Japan's only link with the outside world. The Japanese themselves were forbidden to travel abroad. Any Japanese returning from abroad was put to death. For two centuries (relatively peaceful centuries for Japan) Japan was isolated from most of the world.

All of this was consistent with the defensive nationalism which Japan has practiced since the earliest times. Through a policy of exclusion Japan had sought earlier to escape from the pressures of the Chinese Empire; now it sought to escape from the pressures of the West.

The Japanese, and later the Chinese, deceived themselves in believing that Western expansion in the Orient could be so easily halted. Britain was determined to obtain commercial access to the "Middle Kingdom" and end China's isolation. Western traders demanded the right to trade where they wished. The traditional Chinese view that China was superior to the other nations of the world could no longer be tolerated. In British eyes, China should not be allowed to refuse the civilizing medium of Western trade, Western diplomacy, and Western religion. Certainly, it should not be allowed to exclude either Britain's manufactures or opium from British India. It was purposeless for the Chinese to protest that they wanted none of these things; that their traditional, agricultural way of life gave them all they desired; that Britain's talk of freedom of trade made no sense to them; that all they wanted was to be left alone. But how could they when so many Westerners coveted their wealth, or were consumed with the idea of dominating China? In the Opium War of 1839–1842 the British used cannon and gun powder (Chinese inventions) to force open the Chinese door.

What staggers the imagination about the British invasion of China is how a country of approximately twenty million people could impose its will upon a far older country of enormous size and numbers. In 1840 China's population was about 430 million – far more than the whole of Europe, including Russia. The answer is that whereas Britain was technically superior, unified, well-armed, and overwhelmingly aggressive, China, was technologically backward, tradition bound, disunited, ill-led, and ill-armed. What Britain lacked in numbers they made up for with superior weapons. Cannons made of bronze and bamboo were no match to British gunboats. The chaos resulting from severe population pressure, endless rebellions, corruption, inefficiency, and growing poverty also made China too weak to resist.[156]

If Britain chose to use opium as a pretext for invasion, it was because opium (regardless of its pernicious effect upon the populace, and the fact that it had been outlawed by the Chinese government) was the only commodity the West had to obtain a favorable balance of trade with a largely self-sufficient China. Subsequent events, coupled with overwhelming military and naval victories, were to prove the British right. As ever-increasing opium imports exceeded China's exports of tea and silk, a net inflow of silver was converted into a net outflow.[157] No sooner had the British gained commercial and legal concessions in China under the humiliating Nanking Treaty of 1842[158] than the other Westerners, including Russians and Americans, hastened to obtain similar privileges. The Americans were quick to exploit the opium trade, bringing supplies from Turkey and the Levant.

Russia's expansion in China differed from that of the other Western powers not in methods but in aim. Profits did not interest them as much as territory. Taking advantage of growing Chinese disorder, in 1858, under the Treaty of Aigun, Russia laid claim to all the territory north of the Amur. The following year, in 1859, it seized the province of Manchuria. In 1860 Vladivostok, an earlier dream of Peter the Great, was founded. Also in 1860 the Maritime Provinces north of Korea were annexed (territory which Russia still holds and China is determined to recover). In contrast, the first treaty between the United States and China in 1844 aimed not at expanding the American frontier overseas but at enlarging American commerce.

From 1842 onward intermittent hostilities between China and Britain and France continued. Under the Treaties of Tientsin, 1858, between China and Britain, France, the United States, and Russia (which included China's Treaty of Aigun with Russia) China was forced to open still more ports to Western traders. Also forced upon China was the establishment of foreign legations at Peking, and the unhindered activity of foreign trade (including the now legalized and immensely profitable opium trade). The unhindered activity of Christian evangelists in China was also conceded. To ensure that the large indemnities demanded by the British would be paid, the English took control of all customs duties levied on foreign goods. In 1860 British and French troops occupied Peking and burnt the Summer Palace. The outcome was still further concessions on the part of China.

An added indignity for China was the recruiting of coolie laborers to work in European colonial territories. By the 1860s, 100,000 Chinese had been shipped to Peru in conditions not far removed from slavery. Another 150,000 had gone to Cuba. Although some efforts were made from the 1870s (by sending students abroad and by establishing overseas diplomatic missions) to learn something about the basis of Western supremacy, the Manchu elite never took such efforts seriously. Most of them scorned Western science and technology. Failing to understand the Western challenge, they saw no reason to abandon their traditional ways.

And so, against a background of war (in 1884–1885 France fought China over Indo-China), famine[159] and internal rebellions – the worst of which was the Taiping Rebellion (1851–1864), which aimed to free native Chinese from the predations of both the Manchus and the intruding Europeans, and in which twenty million Chinese lost their lives – the despoiling of China by the West continued. Because of Western intrusion, civil war, and famine, population in China at the end of the century was little more than it had been in the 1830s.

The final humiliation for China in the nineteenth century came not from the West but from the East. In 1894 a war broke out between the Chinese and the Japanese over Korea in which the Western-style Japanese army disastrously routed the Chinese. As a result, Japanese influence became paramount in Korea; Chinese Formosa was annexed. Beset and exploited by East and West, with all reforms blocked by the conservative Manchus who had ruled the country since 1644, with corruption at every level of its government, the Chinese state could do nothing else but collapse.

By the end of the nineteenth century, Western exploitation of China was rampant. By then, the Western nations had established claims in thirteen of China's eighteen provinces. When the Chinese rebelled against Western exploitation in the Boxer Rebellion of 1900, the foreign powers, including Britain, France, Germany, the United States, Japan, and Russia (which seized the opportunity to occupy most of Manchuria) quickly put it down. Still more concessions and a huge indemnity followed. Having failed to master Western technology, China was forced to succumb to it. Until the First Great War drew the West's attention elsewhere, despite the reform movement which received a setback with the overthrow of the emperor in September 1898, a disunited China remained the prey of all. In October 1911 a revolution broke out under the leadership of Sun Yat-sen (1866–1925). In 1912 the Manchu Dynasty was overthrown. The Republic which followed soon foundered. Power was once more assumed by the provincial warlords.

Japanese reaction to the renewed nineteenth-century Western challenge (the American expedition, commanded by Matthew C. Perry, arrived in 1853), differed markedly from that of the Chinese. Japan's martial Samurai traditions, its intense nationalism, its strong sense of self-identity, its deeply ingrained "work ethic", its remarkable homogeneity, its morale and its discipline, its good government, its insularity, and its prosperous conditions, made it difficult to coerce. Of the greatest importance was the Tokugawa Shogunate's (1603–1868) ruthless exclusion of Western influence, which spared Japan the fate suffered by the Philippines, India, China, and Formosa. Japan met the signing of the shameful "Unequal Treaties" forced upon it by the Europeans and the Americans in 1858, with a strategy of procrastination. Being the only nation on record to have given up using the gun,[160] it could hardly do otherwise. Baffled by the Japanese genius for fore-stalling, in the 1860s an angered West (including the United States) responded by bombarding the Japanese coast. The bombardments, however, only served to undermine the Tokugawa regime (1603–1868) which, like the Manchus, had failed to meet the challenge of Western technology.

With the overthrow of the Tokugawas in 1868 and the recovery of imperial power by Emperor Meiji, Japan abandoned its policy of exclusion and began a process of Westernization. Instead of shunning Western ways, as the Manchus had done, the Japanese eagerly studied Western systems of government, Western systems of industry (which had produced such material wealth), and Western military and naval technology, the backbone of Western power. The army was modelled on the French and later the Prussian military; the navy was built on British lines. In 1871 feudalism was abolished. In 1872 a national education system was introduced. In 1873 the Samurai, the hereditary warrior class, were replaced by a regular Western-type conscript army. With the aid of this conscript army, in 1877, the new government was able to quash the last of the Samurai uprisings. Between the 1870s and the 1890s a modern court and legal system, based first on French and then on German models, was established. Western dress, first adopted by the military, spread to other parts of Japanese society. The beard, military uniform, and medals worn by the Meiji emperor were innovations all borrowed from Western royalty. Japanese scholars and travelers were sent to the West in search of knowledge. At great expense to the state, foreign technicians and experts were brought to Japan. Countless Western books were imported and translated. Far from spurning the West, without abandoning its own traditions and virtues, Japan consciously, zealously, and pragmatically sought to adopt Western ways. In 1889 Japan provided itself with a new constitution based upon the German Imperial Constitution of 1871. In 1897 Japan tied its currency to the European-devised gold standard. Increasingly, the cry became: "Japanese spirit, Western talents".

The Japanese were encouraged in all these efforts by their victory over China in 1895, and by the Anglo-Japanese Alliance of 1902.

Emerging from 250 years of isolation, Japan's task of catching up with the West was immense. Whereas Europe's Industrial Revolution had been a step-by-step organic process, growing naturally out of traditional crafts and the Scientific Revolution of the seventeenth century, Japan's ability to meet the West on its own terms depended on its taking giant strides. Possessing the necessary human qualities, as well as the required pre-industrial skills and technology, the challenge was met. By the First Great War Japan had become one of the world's great powers. Its status as such was confirmed by the role it was accorded by the Western powers at Versailles in 1919. Japan and the United States were the true victors of the First Great War.

Meanwhile, Japan had launched itself upon a course of territorial expansion. In the 1870s it attacked Formosa, annexed the Ryukyu Islands (including Okinawa), exchanged part of Sakhalin with Russia for the Kuriles, and with subtle support from the British who feared Russian more than Chinese expansion, began to contest China's interests in Korea. In 1894 it invaded Korea and overwhelmed a much larger Chinese army and navy. Under the Treaty of Shimonoseki, 1895, China was compelled to open four more ports to international trade and pay an indemnity of $20 million (obtained from the British at 5 per cent). Japanese rule was extended over Korea, Formosa, the Pescadores Islands, the Liaotung Peninsula (which the now apprehensive European powers later persuaded it to give up) and Southern Manchuria. Impressed by the Japanese performance, in 1899 the Western powers ceded their extraterritorial rights in Japan. In the Anglo-Japanese Alliance of 1902 Japan became an ally of the most powerful nation of all: Britain. To meet growing Russian power in the Far East, Britain had increased Japan's power. The move, insofar as it enabled Britain to bring home most of its eastern fleet to guard its own shores, also strengthened Britain's hand against Germany.

In 1904 Japan decided to end the growing impasse

between itself and Russia over Korea and Manchuria by force. Backed by Britain, it struck suddenly at the Russian fleet stationed in the ports of Chemulpo (Inchon) in Korea and Port Arthur (Lü-shun) on the Liaotung Peninsula. Landings were made; the Russian army was pursued and eventually overwhelmed at Mukden in February 1905. The annihilation of Russia's northern battle fleet at the Tsushima Straits off Japan in May 1905 completed the Russian disaster. The destruction of Russia's sea power in the East made it feasible for Britain to subsequently transfer some of its eastern fleet to stations in the North Sea.

For the first time in modern history an Asian people had defeated a European power both on land and sea. The myth of Western omnipotence had been exploded. Asian nationalism in India, Persia, and Turkey was given a tremendous stimulus. The Russian revolution of 1905 provided added impetus to the movement, especially in India. With Japan's victory over Russia, the balance of power on the Asian landmass, as well as in the Pacific, was dramatically altered. Under terms of the Treaty of Peace of 1905 Russia acknowledged Japan's paramount interest in Korea. It also restored Japan's lease of the Liaotung Peninsula (including Port Arthur and the existing mining and railway privileges there), and ceded the southern half of Sakhalin. Manchuria was divided into spheres of Russian and Japanese influence. The return of Asia to the forefront of world history had begun. Not surprisingly, in 1905 Britain expressed its willingness to renew the Anglo-Japanese Alliance for another ten years. In August 1910 Japan formally annexed Korea.

The First Great War added further wealth and glory. Quite apart from providing Japan with new trade opportunities, the war resulted in Japan's occupation of the Shantung Province of China and of Germany's colonies in the Pacific. While few Americans realized it, a new and deadly threat to the United States had appeared.

Japan's experience during the crucial 1860s demonstrates the complex set of circumstances which determine a nation's destiny. If Japan had not put its own house in order with the political reformation of 1868, if the spread of clan warfare had robbed the nation of all leadership in national affairs, if any further serious provocation of the Western powers had been made after the allied naval demonstration at Osaka in November 1865, if Japan had been unable to alter its social structure – if any of these things had happened (and the 1860s were critical years when anything might have happened), Japan could have suffered the same fate as the rest of Asia (see Map IV). Japan also had extraordinary luck in being able to meet the Western threat when it did. Mutiny against the British in India in the 1850s, civil war in the United States in the 1860s, and the struggle between France and Prussia in the 1870s, all helped to deflect the attention of the West from Japan and preserve Japanese independence.

Whereas Japan profited from the First Great War – it emerged as a major power with a permanent seat on the Council of the League of Nations – the conflict left China in greater chaos than ever. In 1919, at Versailles, China lost its Shantung Province to Japan. In retaliation, the Chinese ordered their delegates home, boycotted Western products, and discarded Western democratic ideas. The grossly unfair terms of the Peace Conference provoked a massive upsurge of nationalist feeling expressed in the 4 May Movement. So divided had China become (not least as a result of Western and Eastern oppression[161]), so weak did it remain, that by 1923 (eleven years after the Republic had been established) whatever unity it possessed had been shattered by the competing claims of warlords, nationalists and communists. In the resulting confusion, the Chinese provinces of Tibet and Outer Mongolia broke away.[162]

The collapse of order in China in the inter-war years, coupled with the harsh terms meted out to China at Versailles in 1919, caused the one-time, liberal-minded leader, Sun Yat-sen,[163] to advocate the adoption of the Russian Communist Party system. He conceded that the liberal and democratic ideals espoused in the revolution of 1911 had proved impracticable. Out of necessity, he argued, China would have to return to its traditional way of life based on the collective rather than the individual; the controlled rather than the free; the hierarchic principle rather than the egalitarian. The authoritarian ideology of the state, implied in Confucian doctrine, must be exchanged for the parallel authoritarian ideology summed up in communism. In contrast, the Western historical pluralism upon which the West's liberal democracy depended, and upon which the Chinese experiment in Western republicanism had been based, was largely alien to Chinese thought. Western republicanism had nothing in common with Chinese traditions, hence its failure. In 1923 Sun Yat-sen and other one-time advocates of Western republicanism allied themselves with the infant Chinese Communist Party founded three years earlier. In 1924, coincident with the calls for industrialization being made in Turkey, Persia, and India, Sun Yat-sen advocated the industrialization of his country. Thanks partly to the impulse provided by the Russian Revolution of 1905, industrialization was about to become the alchemy of the modern age.

In 1925 Sun Yat-sen died. Replacing him as head of the national government was his deputy, Moscow-trained Chiang Kai-shek (1887–1975).[164] The struggle for power in China now lay between the warlords, the Russian-led communists, and the nationalists (which included the remnants of Sun Yat-sen's republican movement) led by Chiang. Having formed an alliance with the communists, Chiang carried out a successful expedition against the northern warlords. In 1927 he turned around and proceeded to slaughter his allies. Three hundred communist leaders died in Shanghai alone. Having put his enemies to flight, and having captured Peking, between 1928 and 1937 Chiang extended his rule to the whole of China. His abolishing of the hated extra-territorial rights of Westerners gained him support in his drive to create an independent, unified, progressive China. Foiling his efforts was widespread corruption,[165] and Russian and Japanese intervention. The Russians invaded Manchuria in 1924, and directed communist insurrection within China itself. In an effort to prevent China becoming united under

Chiang, the Japanese army annexed Manchuria in 1931. The puppet state of Manchukuo was subsequently established.

Henceforth, China was divided between the nationalists led by Chiang (based on Nanking), the communists led by Mao Zedong, operating as guerrilla bands in the southern provinces, and the Japanese. In 1937 Japan dropped all pretense and began a general war against China. By 1938 its troops occupied north and central China.

As the Second World War approached in the West, Russia's influence in the struggle for power in China declined. With the outbreak of war between the Western allies and Japan in December 1941, the Chinese nationalists and the communists (who after their earlier 6,000 mile "Long March" in 1934 had reached Yenan in the far north-west) made what proved to be largely unsuccessful efforts to form a common front to fight the Japanese invader. There matters rested until 1945 when – the Americans having forced the Japanese to surrender – the nationalists and communists began a fight to the death for supremacy.

Between 1918 and 1941 Japan's conduct toward the rest of the world oscillated between peaceful and warlike intentions. For most of the 1920s it gave the other powers little to grumble about. In 1921 it amicably accepted Britain's decision to terminate the Alliance of 1902 – an alliance never accepted by the United States or Australia. Until it left the League of Nations in 1933, it was a loyal and active member. It became conciliatory toward China, even handing back the Shantung Province (which it seized again in 1928). It co-operated with the United States and Britain in the Washington Naval Disarmament Conferences of the early 1920s by scaling down its naval armaments and by accepting a ratio of major warships favorable to the Western powers; a decision that resulted in anti-American and anti-British feeling in Japan. A spate of assassinations of Japanese political and industrial leaders took place. With the London Naval Treaty of 1930, Japan extended to its heavy cruisers the three to five ratio it had accepted with the United States and Great Britain at the earlier conferences. With Britain and the United States, it pledged itself to maintain the *status quo* in the Pacific. The Americans and the British reciprocated by agreeing not to increase their bases at Pearl Harbor and Singapore – a decision they, and Australia and New Zealand, would later regret.

Forces were at work, however, that would eventually undermine whatever goodwill was established between Japan and the Western powers. Following the policies already introduced in the British Dominions, the United States Immigration Quota Acts of 1921–1924 deliberately penalized Asians such as the Japanese.[166] The introduction of the measures was greeted in Japan as a "Day of Shame". Serious misunderstandings and differences arose about naval disarmament. Growing world autarchy resulted in the exclusion of Japanese products from American and other Western markets. The commercial and financial crash in the United States in 1929 led to the Smoot-Hawley Tariff Act of 1931, which caused the further decline of international trade upon which Japan greatly depended. Protective measures taken by the Dutch in 1932 and by the British in 1933 further restricted the sale of Japanese goods. With vastly increased numbers (between 1873 and 1918 Japanese population rose from thirty-five to sixty-five million), and with its population growing by a million a year, Japan had to find – either through the expansion of world commerce, or by territorial aggrandizement in Manchuria – a solution to its demographic and economic problems.

To the detriment of future world relations, the economic problems besetting Japan strengthened the hands of the militarists and ultra-nationalists. Condemned by the League of Nations for its occupation of Manchuria in 1931, and the establishment of the puppet state of Manchukuo in 1933, Japan abandoned the League in the same year. The flouting of the League Covenant by Japan undermined the League's authority. In 1936 Japan withdrew from the London Naval Treaty. In the same year it signed the

Anti-Comintern Pact with Germany; Italy joined the following year. In 1937, taking advantage of the fact that Europe was preoccupied with the Spanish Civil War, it began its long-prepared invasion of central and southern China. In 1938 the League of Nations, prompted by the Americans, declared Japan an aggressor. In 1939 the United States rescinded its Treaty of Commerce and Navigation with Japan. The American Pacific Fleet was moved from its base in San Diego to Pearl Harbor. The Americans had by now the world's greatest fleet. In 1940 Japan signed a tri-partite Pact of Mutual Assistance with Rome and Berlin. President Franklin Delano Roosevelt (1882–1945) responded with economic sanctions, including the cutting off of scrap iron and steel supplies. In September 1940 Japan began its expansion in the Pacific by occupying northern French Indochina. Roosevelt's response was to ban vital oil shipments. Denied oil supplies by America, Britain, and the Netherlands, Japan faced a stark choice. It either had to abandon its stake in China (which the Americans demanded), or seize the oil of Indonesia, then called the Dutch East Indies. In 1941, though nominally still at peace with Japan, the United States banned virtually all normal trade and froze all Japanese assets in the United States. For Japan the die was cast.

By then the United States had come to be regarded by many Japanese as their country's chief enemy. The only crime Japan was committing in expanding onto the land mass of Asia was to upset the division of world territory already settled in the West's favor. It was doing nothing the West had not already done. Only the United States – satiated with territory – prevented Japan from fulfilling its destiny as the leader of East Asia. In November 1941 Japan made the fateful decision to attack all the major Western powers in the Pacific. According to the Japanese General Staff, the war would have to be won in four months. The longer the war, the less likely it was that Japan would win it. As in its earlier contests with the Chinese (1894) and the Russians (1904–1905), war against the Americans had to be won quickly or not at all. Time was the crucial element.

The Japanese military had no illusions about America's

far greater productive capacity. In the 1920s, before the effects of the Great Depression had been felt, America's output had exceeded the combined output of several of the European powers as well as that of Japan. Although severely under-utilized in the 1930s, America's productive capacity was still in a class by itself.

On 7 December 1941 the Japanese made their successful surprise attack against the United States' fleet at Pearl Harbor and United States' installations in the Philippines. In doing so they entered the final stage of the great venture in aggression they had begun in Manchuria in 1931 – a venture which proved beyond their strength and in which more than two million Japanese perished. It ended with the atomic bombardments of Hiroshima and Nagasaki in August 1945. With the use of nuclear weapons, a new era in warfare had begun. The horrendous destruction of Hiroshima and Nagasaki recall the words of Hindu scripture: "I am become death, the destroyer of worlds."

10
The Second World War: 1939–1945

In the early hours of 1 September 1939 Germany attacked Poland on land and from the air. Two days later, on 3 September, Britain and France declared war on Germany. The Second Great War of the twentieth century – the greatest single slaughter in history – had begun.

The Second World War must be seen as a continuation of the First. It was the direct outcome of the spiritual malaise, the economic chaos, and the political barbarism engendered by the First. The resulting catastrophe – and the false peace that followed the Treaty of Versailles in 1919, in which Germany suffered ignominy and humiliation – made a further clash between the nations of the West almost inevitable.[167] If there is one reason more than any other why the Germans supported the radical agitator Adolf Hitler (1889–1945),[168] it was because he expressed better than anybody else the real or imagined grievances of the Germans under the Versailles Treaty.

Even without Versailles, the worsening of conditions in postwar Europe made a confrontation between the liberal Western democracies and the totalitarian states unavoidable. Lenin, Stalin, Mussolini, and Hitler triumphed as they did because the First Great War led to economic collapse[169] and the almost total destruction of the middle class in Russia, and its partial destruction in Germany and Italy. Out of the unparalleled conditions prevailing in Russia emerged Lenin and the dictatorship of the proletariat. The Bolshevik Revolution, like the French Revolution before it, and the Chinese Revolution after it, saw the triumph of the merciless revolutionary masses. For those it crushed it offered neither hope nor consolation.

While communism was entrenching itself in Russia, a

rival ideology of fascism was emerging in Italy. In 1922 a former school teacher from a remote Italian village, Benito Mussolini (1883–1945),[170] made his farcical but effective "March on Rome". In the election of 1924, as conditions deteriorated, the fascists obtained two-thirds of the total poll. Fascism became the official ideology of Italy. The outcome was the establishment of an authoritarian, all-powerful state.

Germany, like Russia and Italy in the postwar period, was ripe for revolution. The country was in turmoil; armed insurrection and political slayings were common. By the end of 1923 – when some prices were a billion times their pre-war figure – in December 1923 it cost between eight and nine hundred million marks to buy a three pound loaf of bread – financial collapse was widespread. In 1923 – as leader of the National Socialist German Workers Party – Hitler tried to seize power and, having failed, went to jail. His subsequent rise might have been avoided if the Genoa Conference of 1922, at which more than thirty nations were represented (and during which Germany and the USSR made their own separate treaty at Rapallo) had not foundered. Nor was the postwar German government, the Weimar Republic, able to hold the balance. Like Kerensky's Provisional Government in Russia, it proved to be too weak to survive.

On 6 June 1920, the parties most identified with the republic – the Social Democrats and the Roman Catholic parties – received a severe set-back at the polls. The nationalists and the People's Party on the right, and the Independent Socialists on the left, achieved considerable gains. Henceforth, the demands for the overthrow of the republic and its leaders became unrestrained. In coalition after coalition, the Weimar Republic fought to stay alive. The Western democracies – far from going to its help – hastened its fall. The French and Belgian occupation of the Ruhr in 1923, coupled with the Allies' demands for reparations (made all the more urgent by America's demands upon the Allies), precipitated its collapse. The volatility of United States financial leadership at this time made matters worse. In the election of 1930, as the nation became desperate, and the vast army of unemployed grew, the national socialists (Nazis) increased their seats in the Reichstag from twelve to 107.[171] Forced to choose between what many of them saw as freedom and chaos on the one hand, and the Nazis on the other, the Germans supported Hitler. Not even the demagogue Hitler, it was thought, could make matters worse than they were.[172] Anarchy – as always – had opened the door to despotism.[173]

In 1932, with the deepening of the world depression,[174] the Nazis became the largest party with 230 seats. On 30 January 1933 Adolf Hitler was appointed Chancellor of Germany. A system of government by terror and duress, especially against the Jews and the communists, followed. In March, using the Reichstag fire of 27 February as evidence of a communist plot to overthrow the state, the Reichstag was eliminated as a political force. Hitler became an absolute dictator.

Like all the other dictators, Hitler did not create the chaotic conditions or the enthusiasm which brought him to power. He was endowed with power because he offered a solution to the unbelievably desperate conditions of the times; he never ceased emphasizing Germany's postwar humiliation. Having lost faith in a democratic solution, the electorate bestowed upon Hitler a blind faith.[175] They thought that the crises which had shaken German society since 1918 would now end. Through Hitler national and social redemption would be achieved. All of which proved to be a disastrous illusion.

Once in power, Hitler substituted propaganda and terror for public support. The National Socialist German Workers Party (Nazi Party) was declared the only political party. The judicial and administrative systems of the country were concentrated in Nazi hands. The power of organized labor was likewise broken. Political, racial, and religious persecution became the order of the day. Everything was sacrificed to the welfare of the party and the security of the state. Racist laws[176] were introduced excluding Jews from government, the professions, and many walks of cultural life. In the great purge of 30 June 1934 Hitler in one fell swoop assassinated about 180 political opponents. In July Austria's Chancellor Engelbert Doll-fuss was murdered by Austrian Nazis. In 1935 Hitler denounced the Versailles Treaty (Germany had left the League of Nations in October 1933) and began rearming the German people. The League's attempt to bring about general disarmament, which had begun in 1928, was abandoned in 1932. The Saar territory was recovered by plebiscite, the remilitarization of the Rhine begun. Coupled with Italy's invasion of Abyssinia (Ethiopia)[177] in the same year, Hitler's repudiation of the Versailles Treaty in 1935 probably marked the point beyond which war could not be avoided. In 1936 Hitler repudiated the Lo-carno Agreements (concluded in 1925 between Britain, France, Germany, Italy, and Belgium) which had guaran-teed the frontiers of Germany with Belgium and France, and reoccupied the Rhineland. The Rome–Berlin Axis was formed. The year 1936 also witnessed the outbreak of the Spanish Civil War which ended in 1939 with the victory of the insurgents under General Francisco Franco (1892–1975). The war provided Germany and Italy with a dress rehearsal for the world conflict that was to follow.

In 1938, with no one prepared to use force against him (and with the Romanov and Austro-Hungarian empires no longer in existence to restrain him), Hitler seized both Austria and the German-speaking areas of Czechoslova-kia.[178] The surrender of parts of Czechoslovakia to Ger-mans, Poles, and Hungarians which followed the Munich meetings in 1938 was described by the English Prime Minister Neville Chamberlain as "peace with honor". It was, of course, appeasement.[179] As a result, Germany, without a major war, had become the strongest power on the continent of Europe.

In 1939 Hitler proceeded to annex the whole of Czecho-slovakia and the port of Memel on the Baltic. Intent now on conquering Poland, he made the "Pact of Steel" with Italy in May 1939. Although in 1934 Germany had signed a non-aggression pact with Poland, in August 1939 Hitler agreed with Stalin (who desperately needed time to pre-pare for the feared German onslaught, and who despaired of Britain's lukewarm overtures) to divide Poland. Stalin even pledged material support to the Germans. Russia's share of the spoils was to be eastern Poland, Bessarabia, the northern Baltic states and parts of Finland.[180] (See Map VIII) On 1 September, having been warned that an invasion of Poland would bring Britain and France into war against him, Hitler attacked Poland. Two days later, on 3 September 1939, conscious now that they were in deadly peril, Britain (joined at once by its Dominions) and France declared war against the German Reich.[181] On the same day, Roosevelt, although anti-isolationist, declared that the American people would stay neutral.[182] On the contrary, Roosevelt's actions in supplying Britain with war materials and warships were anything but neutral. On 8 December 1941, the day after Japan's attack on the United States fleet at Pearl Harbor, America declared war on Japan. Hitler declared war on the United States on 10 December.[183]

While Hitler bears major responsibility for the Second World War, he could never have done what he did had he not been faced by weak, divided French and British leaders.[184] Not even a fanatic such as Hitler could have gained total power if the Western leaders had stood fast. Hitler knew they would yield under threat, and he exploited their moral weakness. Not one of them stood up to him. Few, like Winston Spencer Churchill (1874–1965), were even prepared to think the worst of him. Only when it was too late did they see through his guise of talking peace while preparing for war.[185] While Hitler and Mussolini sought victory at any price, the democracies sought compromise. The decent, middle-class shopkeeper mentality, epitomized by Chamberlain, who was already overwhelmed by the seemingly intractable political and economic problems facing his country, was pitted against the bullying, militaristic mentality of the dictators. Whereas Chamberlain and the rest wanted to reconcile conflicting interests as one would do in business, the dictators wanted, by one ruse or another, to triumph over their rivals. Knowing only national law and national interests, talk of the supremacy of international law was an anathema to them. Outside of war, the democracies could not hope to win. The best thing that can be said for the British and French leaders is that having experienced the horrors of the First Great War they could not believe that anyone would plunge the world into war again. The next best thing that can be said is that they bought for Britain the vital time needed for rearmament (especially in the air) and the development of what became indispensable to Britain's defenses: radar. In March 1938 the British Joint Chiefs of Staff urged Prime Minister Chamberlain ". . . no matter what the cost, war must be averted until the rearmament program began to bear substantial fruit".[186]

The democracies' belief that no one could be evil enough to begin a second world war proved false. War followed on a scale such as the world had never seen before. In a month (September 1939) Poland was conquered. With Poland occupied by Germany and Russia (the Soviets had invaded eastern Poland on 17 September 1939), Hitler turned west. Ignoring the Copenhagen Declaration of Neutrality of July 1938, by means of which the smaller European states[187] had hoped to stay out of the upcoming war, in April 1940 he struck at Denmark and Norway. In May he overran Belgium, the Netherlands, and France. In a "lightning war" (Blitzkrieg) all these countries fell one after the other. In ten days the Germans were at Calais and Boulogne. On 15 May, Churchill, who had replaced Chamberlain five days earlier, wrote to Roosevelt: ". . . the weight may be more than we can bear". Saved by a miracle, the British army held out on the sands of Dunkerque for another ten days.[188]

In five weeks Germany had overrun western Europe; Paris had fallen; Britain had been called upon by Hitler to surrender. On 10 June 1940 Italy, turning a deaf ear to the appeals of President Roosevelt,[189] also attacked France. For Britain, France was the greatest loss.[190] It brought the possibility of a German victory much closer. On 15 July Hitler offered peace terms to Britain which were rejected,[191] not least because they consisted of vague generalities. Also in July, the United States abandoned neutrality by providing the British with fifty destroyers. Meanwhile,

French resistance continued under General Charles de Gaulle (1890–1970) from London and Algiers.

Determined to knock Britain out of the war, Hitler gave orders for its invasion in the summer of 1940. The battle for Britain began in the air. The German bombing of London and other parts of Britain lasted eight months and accounted for about 30,000 dead.[192] (Later Hamburg and Dresden would lose more than that number in single air raids).

Defeated by the British air force ("Never in the field of human conflict was so much owed by so many to so few", said Winston Churchill on 20 August 1940), and unable to penetrate Britain's naval defenses, Hitler (like Napoleon in 1805) turned around and attacked the Soviet Union. The hoped-for colonization by Germans of Slav lands, about which Hitler had written in *Mein Kampf*, had begun. Hitler's action - however stupid it might appear now - was prompted by the fact that Germany had defeated Russia in the First World War. Despite its much larger numbers (roughly 181 million against Germany's 69 million), Russia was expected to fall as France and Poland had done. "Kick in the door and the house will collapse", Hitler kept saying. Germany's military might, its productive capacity, and its general strategy were all superior to that of the Soviet Union. As Hitler saw it, with Russia out of the war, and the oilfields of the Caucasus in German hands, Britain's fate would be sealed; final victory for the Germans in the West would be assured. America would be forced to come to terms. Furthermore, Russia's failure to conquer Finland in 1940 had demonstrated that the time was ripe.

Germany's invasion of Russia in June 1941 - code name "Barbarossa" - had been planned since December 1940. Hitler had been talking about it since July of that year. But the original plan had called for an invasion in May, not June. It was delayed a crucial six weeks partly because Hitler, in response to an anti-Axis coup in Belgrade in March 1941, had invaded Yugoslavia. He had also decided (against the advice of his generals) to go to the aid of Mussolini who had become embroiled, and who now faced almost certain defeat in Greece and North Africa. Such

diversions of men and materials had been specifically pre-
cluded by those who had planned "Barbarossa". Another
factor causing postponement was climate. In the spring of
1940 unusually heavy floods hindered movement across the
Polish-Russian river areas.[193]

The decision to go to Mussolini's aid opened a chapter
of disasters which played no small part in Germany's
ultimate defeat in 1945. Mussolini may have boasted
"eight million bayonets", but, over the long haul, his
country proved to be an economic and military liability to
Germany. In an effort to reinforce the imperiled Italian
army in Albania and Greece,[194] the Germans were compelled to fight a prolonged and difficult campaign in
Yugoslavia.[195] Having rescued the Italians in Greece, the
Germans then fought the British in Crete (where the
backbone of the German airborne troop command was
permanently broken). From Crete the Germans went to
the aid of the Italians who by now were being driven by
the British, Australians, and New Zealanders from Libya.
Under General Erwin Rommel, the German Africa Corps
was formed. Step by step, largely on Italy's account,
Germany found itself committed to war in the Mediterranean and the Middle East. Seemingly disregarding any
overall, long-term strategy, the Germans fought in every
campaign they could find. When, at last, the main German Army was unleashed against Russia in June 1941, it
was already too late. Moscow was still in Russian hands
when winter set in. Taking the view that it was better to
have Russian control of part of Europe (the Soviets had
invaded Poland whose independence Britain and France
had guaranteed) than the whole of it under German control, the British joined ranks with the Soviet Union. Disaster was afoot for Germany.

With Germany's invasion of Russia in June 1941 and
Japan's attack on Pearl Harbor[196] on 7 December of that year
(about which the Germans were not consulted), the
war became global. These two actions sealed the fate of
the Axis powers. The Japanese attack ensured that the
Americans would enter the war. The German attack on
Russia commited Germany to a prolonged, limitless war

which, with all its other military adventures, it could hardly hope to win. It was the eastern front that accounted for most of Germany's military casualties.[197] Without the eastern front, it is doubtful that there would have been a D-Day on the western front in 1944. The failure to seize a quick victory on the eastern front, followed by overwhelming defeat, weakened German morale everywhere. Yet, not even after the United States had entered the war were the Axis powers halted. In 1942 Germany's armies still stood outside Moscow in Russia and Alexandria in Egypt. Only at the end of 1942 and the beginning of 1943, with the Allied victories at Stalingrad (now Volgograd), El Alamein,[198] and in the Pacific against Japan (especially at Guadalcanal in August 1942) was the Axis tide turned. In 1943, with far superior forces at their disposal, the Allies defeated the German army in Africa and invaded Italy. In July 1943 Mussolini fell from power. In November, Churchill, Roosevelt, and Stalin met at Teheran to coordinate strategy. By June the following year (1944) Rome had been taken and Italy had switched sides (as it had done in the First Great War) and declared war on its ally, Germany.[199] With the failure of the German offensive at Kursk-Orel in July 1944, initiative on the eastern front was taken out of German hands.[200] By then the Allies were using long-range aircraft (equipped with radar) to help win the battle against German U-boats in the Atlantic.

In the summer of 1944, once more with far superior forces at their disposal,[201] Allied armies landed in Europe. The French contingent was led by General de Gaulle. The long-awaited D-Day had arrived. Overnight, the resistance movements of German-occupied Europe came out into the open. (Unlike in 1918, there could be no question of Germany being able to switch its eastern army to the western front). Germany was now besieged from the east – where more than anywhere else the outcome of the war was decided – the west and the south. By now, in manpower, in productivity, in armaments, and without effective allies, Germany was hopelessly outclassed. Nor was Germany able to stem the invasion by the use of its newly-developed guided missiles. Instead, the horror of war began to spread across the German Reich. Hundreds of thousands died from Allied air bombardment.

The German attempt to recover the initiative in the west – by striking through the Ardennes in the fall of 1944 (the Battle of the Bulge) failed as the spring offensive had failed in 1918. On 25 April 1945, the Allied and Russian forces met on the Elbe. On 30 April, in a bunker in Berlin, Hitler committed suicide. On 7 May the Germans surrendered unconditionally. Mussolini had already been shot by Italian partisans. With his mistress he was hung by the heels by an excited, bloodthirsty mob in Milan. The war in Europe was over.

It remained to defeat the Japanese who, in a series of brilliant campaigns[202] had overrun Southeast Asia and had reached India, New Guinea, and Guadalcanal. Their first setback on land was in New Guinea (September 1942) where the Australians halted the Japanese drive. Fearing invasion, the Australians appealed to the United States for help. In May 1942 the battle of the Coral Sea, won by the American Navy, saved Australia. The battle of Midway (June 1942) marked the turning point in Japanese fortunes. Until then Japan had never lost an important battle in the Pacific; after that it never won one. By October 1944 the Americans, under the command of General MacArthur, had island-hopped across the Pacific and retaken the Philippines. The accompanying sea battle of Leyte Gulf – the greatest sea battle of its kind – ended the threat of Japanese sea power in the Pacific. The capture of the Marianas, Iwo Jima, and Okinawa provided land bases from which the Americans bombed Japan. From November 1944 till August 1945 the skies above Japan were rarely free of hostile American aircraft. On 16 July the United States detonated its first atomic bomb at Los Alamos in New Mexico. On 6 August an atomic bomb was dropped at Hiroshima, and on 9 August at Nagasaki. In Hiroshima 92,000 died instantly; 130,000 were injured.[203] Perhaps the most powerful consideration in dropping the bomb was to end the war before the Soviets could stake a claim for the joint occupation of Japan (as they had done in Germany).

Simultaneously, on 8 August, the Soviets attacked Japanese positions in Manchuria.[204] Within a week all hostilities between Japan and the Allies had ceased. On 14 August 1945 the Japanese – as the Germans had done in May – surrendered unconditionally. In allowing their ambitions to run wild, they had become committed to undertakings far greater than their strength could support. For the Japanese, the threat of conquest posed by the invading Mongols in the thirteenth century had now come true.

Thus ended a cataclysm without parallel. War related deaths were about fifty-five million, most of them in eastern Europe.[205] Unbelievable mass exterminations had also been practiced against minority groups and political opponents. The number of European Jews, by flight and genocide, had been reduced by two-thirds. The Jews now speak of this as a holocaust – a holocaust demanding a special place in the history of twentieth century barbarism, an event that surpasses understanding.[206] While Nazi zeal to achieve the total extinction of European Jews warrants such a claim, one should guard against making Jewish suffering exclusive, and the holocaust the sole measure of postwar Jewish identity. Certainly, it was an event that would change both Jewish and world history. It undoubtedly led to the establishment of the state of Israel in 1948 and to the present discord between Arab and Jew in the Middle East; which in turn has affected United States relations with the rest of the world. The war uprooted and dispersed millions of other people (including 14 million Germans). The use of saturation bombing which – official rhetoric aside – was meant to terrorize the civilian population, greatly increased the number of casualties. World War II is the first war in history where the civilian losses outnumbered those of the military. It is one of the great turning points in the history of warfare.

Germany and Japan emerged from the war at the mercy of the Allies. Japan was stripped of all the Pacific islands acquired before 1941, and of all possessions seized since 1941. The Soviet Union annexed the Kurile Islands north of Hokkaido, the United States took Okinawa (the Ryukyu Islands). Had not President Truman (1884–1972) and

General MacArthur (1880–1964) resisted Soviet proposals, Japan, like Germany, would have become a divided state. The trial of Japanese and German war criminals followed. The Axis powers had been fully warned by Churchill and Roosevelt that they would be held responsible; and they were.[207] In bringing the Axis leaders to justice, the trials assembled the damning evidence of a uniquely barbaric age. Other than shooting people out of hand, which was the traditional way of meting out punishment to the vanquished, it is difficult to see what else could have been done. Yet it was a victor's justice – with no guarantee that the victors were necessarily the most just. Without neutral judges, it assumed that truth and justice were on the victor's side. United States chief justice Stone called the Nuremberg trials "Jackson's lynching expedition" (Jackson was United States associate justice of the Supreme Court[208]). The defendants (22 at Nuremberg, 28 in Tokyo; of whom twelve were sentenced to death by hanging in Europe, seven in Japan) were not allowed to cite Allied crimes as justification for their own acts. The Soviets' Katyn Forest massacre in Poland in 1939, Britain's war in Norway in 1940, and the terror bombing by the Allies of Germany and Japan all went uncited. As the Japanese were tried with a complete disregard for Japanese values and traditions, in particular with a disregard for Bushido or the Samurai code, the Tokyo trial has come to be regarded by some writers as little more than a farce.[209]

The chief legal criticism levelled at the trials, particularly where judgement was rendered for crimes against humanity, was that the laws applied were created retroactively. The General Treaty for the Renunciation of War (the Kellog-Briand Pact of 1928, of which Germany and Japan were signatories) had not made war, as such, illegal. What it had censured was aggressive war, and that was a matter of interpretation. Men were sentenced for deeds which were not crimes when the acts were committed.

Ironically, the trials may have enlarged rather than limited war. Having established that guilt in war will be personal and that military necessity or the receipt of orders from a superior[210] will not be admitted in defense, it means that those who are engaged in war will either emerge victorious (whatever the cost), or they will run the risk of being hanged.

Unfortunately for human kind, the evidence since 1945 (despite the United Nations General Assembly's approval of the Convention of the Prevention and Punishment of the crime of Genocide in 1948, and the Geneva Conventions in 1949, which grew out of the Nuremberg trials, and which tried to obtain more humane treatment of war prisoners and civilians in time of war) suggests that the Nuremberg and Tokyo trials have had limited effect. Crimes against humanity have gone on; even genocide persists.[211] As long as there is no international tribunal empowered to uphold international law, for covenants without swords are useless, as long as we are unable to reconcile universal laws with the wishes of national sovereignty, crimes against humanity will continue.

Power abhorring a vacuum, in 1945 the United States and the USSR emerged as the two greatest world powers. Although the five great powers of the time – the United States, the USSR, Britain, France, and China[212] included western European powers, the Eurocentric world system, which had prevailed since the sixteenth century, was over. A bi-polar world had replaced the multi-polar world of nineteenth-century geopolitics. The concessions made to Stalin at Teheran (1943), Yalta and Potsdam (1945), which gave Russia parts of Germany and Poland, and gave Poland parts of Germany,[213] and divided Germany itself, had greatly enlarged Russian tutelage in eastern and central Europe.[214] (See Map VIII) Despite what Hitler intended, for the first time in its history, central and eastern Europe were at the mercy of the Russians. By 1948, except for Greece,[215] Turkey, and Yugoslavia, eastern Europe had come under Soviet control. By then communist power had been established in Poland, East Germany, the Baltic states (except Finland), Romania, Yugoslavia, Hungary, Bulgaria, and Albania. Except in Albania, Soviet power was never extended without military pressure from Moscow. Also in 1948, in order to keep

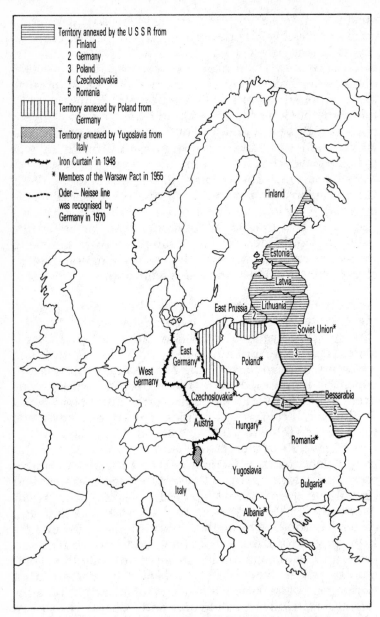

EASTERN EUROPE AFTER THE SECOND WORLD WAR
Map VIII

its outer defenses intact, the Soviets seized power in Czechoslovakia.

One of the astonishing outcomes of the war was the way communist Russia was able to reach out and seize control of so much of Europe. In 1939 Britain and France had gone to war because Hitler had invaded Poland whose independence they had guaranteed. Russia's invasions, which began with the conquest of eastern Poland in 1939 (seventeen days after the German invasion), and ended with the seizing of Czechoslovakia in 1948, raised no such furor in the West. Similarly, the atrocities commited by the Soviets in their rapid expansion in Europe, especially in eastern Poland in 1939, have been glossed over. The West seems to have had a double standard: one by which to judge the diabolical actions of Hitler; the other by which to judge the conduct of "Uncle Joe" (Stalin). Hitler's invasion of Poland meant war; Stalin's invasion of Poland meant that he became an ally of the West. Yet Stalin altered the European map more than Hitler did. All of which seems to confirm the age-old dictum: *"Inter arma silent leges"* – "In times of war the law is silent". Political expediency prevailed.

Western attitudes toward Stalin are partly to be explained by Russia's severe losses – the greatest of all – during the war. They are also to be explained by the attitude of the West toward Hitler. More importantly, from 1939 to 1948, nobody had the will, or the power to halt the Soviet transgressions. Certainly, in the postwar period, there was no desire on the part of the United States to challenge Stalin's policy of imposing the communist system as far as the Red Army could reach. Regardless of America's superlative economic and military power, the vital factors determining the redrawing of the map of Europe after 1945 were communist strategy and Stalin's determination to impose his will. It was out of the question for war-shattered Britain and France to stop Stalin. Britain not only lacked the physical resources to wage another war; after six years of war, it also lacked the fighting spirit it had shown in 1940. Britain and France could no longer be thought of as first-class powers.

Regarding war as episodic, rather than continuous, all that the Americans wanted to do was to end the war and go home. This time there was no great peace conference (such as Versailles) to settle the problems of the postwar world. In 1947 peace treaties were made with Italy, Hungary, Romania, Bulgaria and Finland; in 1951 with Japan; in 1955 with Austria; and in 1990 with Germany. Yet before the unparalleled scramble of American forces to leave Europe, the United States had held the balance of power there. The war had pushed America to new peaks of military, economic, commercial, financial, and technical power. Only the United States had the atomic bomb. Moreover, quite apart from its formidable land, sea, and air forces in Europe, its domestic strength was unimpaired. In contrast to the 31.5 million civilians killed elsewhere, the continental United States lost six individuals from enemy bombing. The United States was the only country to emerge from the war with a higher standard of living that it had had when it began to fight.[216]

In the civil war that broke out in China in 1945, the Americans (and, peculiarly enough, Stalin) went to the aid of anti-communist forces led by Chiang Kai-shek. As it turned out, they backed the loser. With the victory of Mao in 1949 (the first communist revolution among non-white peoples), the American presence in China ended.

The revolution in China in 1949 changed both the political structure and the underlying Chinese way of thinking. Until 1949 Chinese history had always been an ongoing struggle between bureaucrats and peasants. One of the reasons for the Cultural Revolution in the 1960s and 1970s was Mao's fear that the revolution was at stake, that it had fallen into the hands of a bureaucracy which, like all the bureaucracies that preceded it, was becoming stagnant and oppressive. Unlike Lenin's revolution of 1917, which had been a revolution from above, Mao (whose revolution had been from the bottom up) clung to his peasant base. He distrusted elitism and intellectualism.

With Mao's triumph, the People's Republic of China ceased to exist in the official American mind. Chiang Kai-shek's government in Taiwan became the only Chinese government officially recognized in Washington. This absurd situation continued until communist China took its rightful place at the United Nations in October 1971. China and the United States did not re-establish diplomatic relations until January 1979.

In the summer of 1945 the line between the Western democracies and the Soviet Union had still to be drawn. At that time most Western peoples' hopes were pinned on the United Nations Organization which, under American auspices, had just been established to guarantee world peace. Unlike in 1919, the United States now embraced the idea of collective security. President Truman's words: "Oh, what a great day this can be in history", echoed the hopes of mankind. But the dream of world peace soon gave way to the Cold War. "From Stettin on the Baltic," warned Winston Churchill at Fulton, Missouri, on 5 March 1946, "to Trieste in the Adriatic, an Iron Curtain has descended across the continent." (See Map VIII) Henceforth it took a balance of terror to keep a third world war at bay.

11

The Balance of Terror

Ever since The Bomb, "Little Boy", destroyed Hiroshima at 8.16 am on 6 August 1945, we have lived under the threat of apocalypse. Only the balance of terror has saved us from a third world war. We now have enough nuclear weapons to destroy the world's population many times over. In 1987 the United States alone turned out five new nuclear weapons a day. It has produced 11,000 nuclear warheads and bombs since 1981 – some 60,000 since 1945. The nuclear arms industry in the United States in 1987 was a $7.5 billion a year industry employing 90,000 people.[217] For the first time in history we have the means of destroying the entire planet. In 1986, the year declared by the United Nations to be the Year of Peace, the world spent $900 billion on arms, six per cent of the world's gross national product. The United States' share was $268 billion, the Soviet Union's $237 billion. The total in 1989 was in the region of $1,000 billion. Probably the most important capital product of both superpowers was weaponry. Without economic collapse, there is no way that either great power could suddenly stop producing arms on this scale.

The surrender of the Axis powers in 1945 brought the unprecedented conflict of the Second World War to an end. Henceforth the world would no longer rotate around a European sun. For the first time in its history, Europe became a large armed camp divided into spheres of Russian and American influence. It was the Soviet Union's attempt to fill the vacuum caused by the collapse of German power in eastern Europe, and the United States' attempt to fill it in the West, that resulted in the division first of Europe and then of much of the world into communist and non-communist spheres of influence.[218] This confrontation became known as the Cold War.

149

Yet in 1945 the USA and the USSR had emerged from the war as supposedly close allies. Roosevelt was prepared to go to any length to keep the alliance[219] between the United States and the Soviet Union intact. Nothing was allowed to divert him from that end. At Yalta, in February 1945, he willingly agreed to Stalin's proposals for territorial expansion and hegemony in eastern Europe. It is difficult to see how he could have done otherwise outside of war. Ultimately to the shame of those involved, the British and the Americans also agreed to Russian demands to return those Russians who had either fought for Germany, or fled to the West; though it was realized at the time that many of these men would be executed.[220] Roosevelt was much less suspicious of the Soviets than he was of British and French postwar imperial ambitions Churchill, with more historical insight, tried to get the American president to see things differently. He suspected that Stalin was not primarily concerned with world peace but with the postwar security of the Soviet Union. As seen from Moscow in 1945, the capitalist West, with the atomic bomb at its disposal, was a far greater menace to Russian communism than it had been in 1918. Roosevelt died in 1945 believing that he had bequeathed to posterity the means of obtaining lasting world peace.

Churchill's premonition that the realities of power would invalidate Roosevelt's view of Stalin was soon confirmed. By the end of the war, the Soviet Union was already in occupation of the territories needed for its future defense. War to the Russian leaders was a continuum; they wanted to be prepared for every contingency. Their's was a paranoid, suspicious, tragic view of life. Before the United Nations had been able to devise a common and effective strategy, Stalin had consolidated his hold on the whole of eastern Europe. Although, at Yalta, Poland had been promised "free and unfettered elections", a communist regime was soon imposed. The Allies formally protested the Russian occupation of Poland, but took no steps to prevent it. Hitler had been condemmed for invading Poland; Stalin acted with impunity. By 1947 the Soviets dominated Hungary, Poland,

Bulgaria, and Romania. But not Tito's Yugoslavia , which in June 1948 was denounced and expelled from the Moscow-controlled Cominform.[221] In February 1948 they invaded Czechoslovakia. Territory that Hitler had fought for, Stalin took almost without bloodshed. Emboldened by its successes, Moscow further tested the Allies' resolve in Greece (where in 1947 it went to the help of Greek communists in their attempt to overthrow the state), and in 1948 in Berlin. In 1949, having obtained critical data through espionage in the United States, it exploded its first atomic bomb. Having fought the war to get rid of one kind of despotism, the Allies now faced another.

Stalin was able to do what he did because the Allies feared war more than they feared him. Despite Churchill's warning, Roosevelt did not suspect Stalin's true motives, any more than Chamberlain had suspected Hitler's. While Truman – who succeeded Roosevelt on 12 April 1945, and who represented the United States at the inconclusive Potsdam Conference of July-August 1945 – did not share Roosevelt's illusions about Stalin, it would have been political suicide for Truman to have begun a war with Russia. The American people had set out to defeat the Germans, the Italians, and the Japanese, and they had done it.[222] For them the war was over.

The turning point in United States-Soviet relations came in 1947 when the Russians began to assert pressure on Greece and Turkey. Faced by Britain's inability to protect these countries, President Truman announced his policy of containment. A Cold War was declared against world communism. Roosevelt's exaggerated belief in the possibility of lasting United States-Soviet co-operation was exchanged for an even more exaggerated belief in military and economic confrontation. In the late 1940s the danger that parts of western Europe – France and Italy, for example – would become communist was taken very seriously. In the immediate postwar years communists were deliberately excluded from the cabinets of both countries. Fearing total economic collapse, in 1947, under American auspices, a start was made to rebuild Europe's economic strength under the Marshall Plan.[223] The Soviet's response

(1949) was COMECON, an organization which coordinated the economic policies of Soviet bloc countries in eastern Europe as well as Mongolia and Cuba (and since 1978, Vietnam). In 1948 the United States and its allies met the Soviet Union's threat to incorporate Berlin into East Germany with the Berlin Airlift (June 1948 until May 1949).[224] In 1949 Germany was divided between East and West. Also in 1949 the United States was instrumental in establishing the anti-Soviet front known as the North Atlantic Treaty Organization. NATO[225] was not strictly a North Atlantic Alliance (Italy was a member), nor was it in defense of democracy (Portugal's presence made that claim invalid[226]), nor was it a treaty among equals (the United States had no intention of sharing control of its atomic and hydrogen bombs, first exploded in 1945 and 1952 respectively). When, in 1955, West Germany was included in NATO, the Soviets responded with the Warsaw Pact, which henceforth formed the basis for mutual defense co-operation within the Soviet bloc.

By the 1950s the Cold War between the United States and the Soviet Union had become world-wide. The North Korean invasion of South Korea in 1950, following Mao Zedong's[227] victory in China in 1949, and the signing of a thirty-year alliance with the USSR was seen by the Americans as the first move by the Soviet Union and China to extend communist power to the whole of Eastern Asia. There was much talk of the "Domino Theory" and of the new "Red Peril". Thanks to the fact that the Soviet ambassador to the United Nations was in Moscow at the time (and was therefore unable to veto American action), an American-led, United Nations force immediately intervened. After initial North Korean successes, the Americans counterattacked under General Douglas MacArthur and took up positions close to the Chinese frontier on the Yalu. Convinced that the Americans were about to invade China, in October 1950 the Chinese directly intervened in Korea. The Americans could have ended Chinese intervention with the use of the nuclear bomb, but they hesitated to use it. With millions of casualties, the war dragged on with neither side winning a decisive victory.

Meanwhile, the Americans shored up their defenses in the area. In 1951, while the Korean war was still being fought, the United States signed a peace treaty and a mutual security pact with Japan. Between 1945 and 1952 the United States granted $1.7 billion of aid to Japan. (The mutual security pact was renewed in 1960 and 1970). Gradually, Japan and Okinawa became American bastions in the east.

In 1953 the Korean War ended in stalemate. After endless negotiations, the country was partitioned (as it had been originally in 1945) between communist and non-communist forces at the 38th parallel. For the Americans the war had been an object lesson in communist expansion. It stimulated American efforts to complete its encircling alliances and bases around the communist world. In 1953 the United States signed a ten-year military and economic agreement with Spain (led by General Franco) under which America obtained military bases. (The death of Franco in 1975 and the accession of Prince Juan Carlos, grandson of Alfonso XIII, to the Spanish throne has further cemented US-Spanish relations). In 1954, to deter possible future Chinese aggression, the South East Asia Treaty Organization (SEATO[228]) was formed. This was followed in 1959 by the Central Treaty Organization (CENTO[229]) which replaced the Baghdad Pact of 1955. By the 1960s the United States had more than 1000 bases in thirty-one countries. It also had a far larger nuclear stockpile than the USSR, and had supremacy at sea.

On 5 March 1953 Stalin died. So ended twenty-five years of despotic rule of such ruthlessness as to be unusual even in Russian history. In the brutal execution of all who opposed him (especially in the merciless killing of fourteen million of his countrymen[230]), his infamy parallels the horrendous conduct of the Nazis toward the Jews. Yet Stalin left behind him a far more powerful USSR than he had inherited. Glorified as an omnipotent and infallible genius, he was laid to rest alongside Lenin in the Red Square.

In 1956,[231] three years after Stalin's death, Nikita

Khrushchev shocked the communist world by denouncing Stalin's wartime policies. Far from having saved the USSR, he contended that Stalin had brought the country to the brink of defeat. Khrushchev also condemned Stalin's "brutal violence . . . [and his] capricious and despotic character".[232] With Khrushchev's accession to power in 1958, Stalin's body was removed from Lenin's side and buried elsewhere. The following year, in a spirit of competitive coexistence, Khrushchev became the first Soviet ruler to visit the United States. His friendly behaviour on that occasion contrasted sharply with the ruthlessness he had shown in putting down the revolts in East Berlin (1953), Poland (1956), and Hungary (1956). Nor did his proposed coexistence with the West discourage him from strengthening the Warsaw Pact, building the Berlin Wall (1961), or offsetting the United States' aid to Israel by assisting the Arabs.

Khrushchev is especially responsible for changing Soviet relations with eastern Asia. Under his leadership Soviet influence in Korea, India, and Vietnam grew; in China it declined. The tremendous assistance which Russia had given China during the late 1940s and early 1950s was reduced. Irked by personal taunts made against him by the Chinese for his adventurism in placing missiles in Cuba, and for his cowardice in removing them, Khrushchev cut off all aid to China and strengthened Russian defenses along the Chinese border. In 1964, as relations between the Soviet Union and China worsened, he tried to discredit the Chinese before a world conference of communist organizations.

It was during Khrushchev's regime that the USA and the USSR came close to a nuclear confrontation over Cuba. In an attempt to offset America's advantage in intercontinental ballistic missiles, the Soviet Union placed medium-range ballistic missiles in Cuba. Suddenly, in 1961, America found itself exposed to Soviet nuclear weapons. Only by bringing the world to the brink of a nuclear war were the Russians compelled to remove their missiles the following year. The Cuban crisis not only caused the Russians to challenge the Monroe Doctrine, under which the United States had held a protectorate over the western hemisphere for 150 years, it also caused the Soviets to begin a naval building program that by the 1970s had ended American supremacy at sea. For the first time since 1945 the Soviet Union became a superpower not only on land and in the air, but at sea as well. The Cuban missile crisis also caused a shift in emphasis for the Russians from medium range to intercontinental ballistic missiles.

In 1964, partly because of his loss of credibility over Cuba, Khrushchev was forced to relinquish power to the collective leadership of Brezhnev, Kosygin, and Podgorny. No sooner had he been removed from office, than his denunciation of Stalin came under attack. Partially at least, Stalin's image as the savior of the USSR was reinstated. Within two years, Brezhnev had assumed full power in the USSR.

Even more important than Cuba in helping to shape the postwar outlook of the American people toward itself and its adversaries was the war the United States fought and lost in Vietnam. Until Vietnam, all of the United States' wars had been moral, righteous, and victorious. World Wars I and II had stimulated the entire economy. America emerged from both wars with a higher standard of living than it had when it entered. Only the Vietnam War proved to be an unmitigated disaster. It caused the deaths of 57,000 Americans and – while the threat presented by North Vietnam was never direct or vital to American interests – it came close to tearing the fabric of American society apart. The United States' withdrawal from South East Asia in 1975 – precipitated by its defeat in Vietnam in 1973 – ended the Truman Doctrine of containing communism begun twenty-eight years earlier.

Since the Vietnam War, new great centers of powers have appeared in Germany, Japan, communist China and (collectively) in the Third World. The bi-polarism of 1945 has given way to the multi-polarism of the 1970s and 1980s. Not only have new centers of power appeared in the West and the East, the balance of terror, existing since 1945, has been greatly affected by the proliferation of nuclear, chemical, and biological weapons. Following upon American and Russian developments, Britain exploded an atomic bomb in 1952, France in 1960, China in 1964, India in 1974.[233] Only India or Japan can seriously affect the moves of China or the USSR in eastern Asia, and India has the manpower which Japan lacks. India and the Soviet Union have already declared that they will not stand by if Pakistan, the United States' ally, obtains the bomb. Israel is also thought to have nuclear potential which Iraq and Libya seek to offset by mobilizing a chemical arsenal. In October 1989 United States government sources confirmed that South Africa, aided by Israel, had successfully launched a ballistic missile. Other countries have the atomic bomb or, like Iraq, are working to obtain it. The proliferation of ballistic missiles is also affecting every region of the world. Increasingly, the danger of widespread war lies not in a superpower confrontation, but in the actions of minor powers armed with advanced technological weapons. The world is moving into an entirely different and perhaps even more dangerous era of armed conflict in which Cold War thinking will no longer serve.

The post World War II growth of communist power in the world, the resurgence of Asia and Europe, and the proliferation of nuclear weapons have all helped to erode the military supremacy which America held in 1945. In the western hemisphere Canada maintained an independent stance. It declined US nuclear weapons, developed friendly relations with communist Cuba and China, and ignored America's trade boycott of the communist world. In the 1970s it refused to support the United States in the Vietnam War. America's technical supremacy was challenged in 1957 when the Russians launched the first artificial satellite (Sputnik). Since 1962 there has also been a decline of American political and economic influence. The first real sign of western Europe's growing sense of neutrality was Europe's lukewarm support of United States Middle East policy in 1973 at the time of the Arab-Israeli War. The United Nations (once a forum for praising the United States' actions) became a tribunal before which American actions were often criticized or condemned. An exception was the world-wide support given to President Bush's call for sanctions against Iraq following that country's invasion of Kuwait in August 1990.

Economically, partly because the United States and Europe have increased their trade with other parts of the world, trade between Europe and the United States accounted for a relatively smaller share of world trade. Europe was strengthening its economic ties more with the eastern bloc than with the United States. The post-World War II economic hegemony of the United States was conclusively ended by the Arab oil embargo of 1973. For the first time in modern history the initiative in world economic affairs was wrenched out of Western hands. There has also been the extraordinary economic challenge presented to the United States by the resurgence of Germany and Japan. Economically, Germany has become the strongest power in Europe; Japan has become the leading creditor nation of the world. By 1987, primarily because of fiscal profligacy which began with President Johnson's refusal to finance the Vietnam War through additional taxes, the United States had become the world's largest debtor nation. Rarely has the United States' trade, budget, and debt situation[234] been in greater disarray. In the short space of twenty years the United States has passed from the point where it felt it could dominate the world economy to being increasingly concerned about the effect of the world upon itself. America is still the richest country; its absolute level of productivity is still the highest in the world.[235] While America, economically speaking, no longer possesses the overwhelming power that it held from 1945 until 1973, it is the absolute level of productivity, not the comparative, that must ultimately determine America's future standard of living.

The postwar period has also witnessed a relative decline of Soviet power vis-a-vis the rest of the world. The Soviets experienced political setbacks in Egypt, Algeria, Somalia, Guinea, Zaïre, Iraq, Yugoslavia, Romania, and Berlin. By the late 1980s, ethnic minorities in the Baltic states and in central Asia were demanding their independence.

eastern European states have broken away from the Soviet bloc. The old sure balance of Soviet power vis-a-vis the United States has certainly been eroded. Since 1949, China has challenged the USSR militarily and ideologically. Decisions made during the 1980s by the Americans, the British, and the French to sell arms to China, coupled with the visits made by Chinese leaders to Europe and the United States, have added to the Soviet Union's paranoia about its security. However, the massacre of Chinese students by the military in Tiananmen Square, Beijing (Peking) on 4 June 1989 (which like the Cultural Revolution of the 1960s and 1970s demonstrated the Chinese goverment's disregard for the rule of law) caused relations between Washington and Beijing to deteriorate.

Despite its theoretical commitment to the destruction of capitalism, the Soviet Union's first priority after 1945 was to safeguard its own national interests (see Map IX). Except for its invasion of Afghanistan in 1979 – in support of a communist regime – the Soviet Union has undertaken few direct foreign adventures. In Korea, Vietnam, Angola, and the Middle East it has let its communist allies do the fighting. By and large, since 1945 the USSR has steadfastly protected its own national interests in the world power struggle. "Russia," said Winston Churchill in 1939, "is a riddle wrapped in a mystery inside an enigma. But perhaps there is a key. That key is Russian national interest." Nationalism may be eroding, but it is obvious that it is likely to remain the greatest force in world politics for some time.

Between 1949 and 1973 the Cold War fought between the superpowers dominated world history. The conclusion of a Four Power Agreement on Berlin in 1971, coupled with the improved relations between East and West Germany, and the United States withdrawal from Vietnam in 1973, foreshadowed its end. Major landmarks in the ongoing world-wide struggle between the USSR and the USA since 1949 were the Truman Doctrine of Containment, the Marshall Plan, and the Greek, Hungarian, and Czechoslovakian crises. The two superpowers also came close to war in

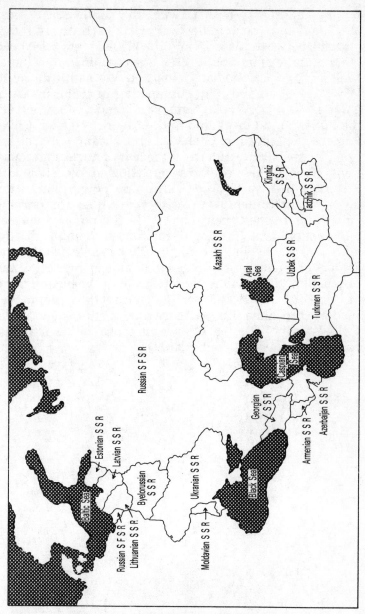

THE SOVIET REPUBLICS AFTER 1945
Map IX

Berlin. Landmarks in Asia were the conflicts in Korea, Vietnam, and the Middle East. Besides the continuing struggle between the USA and the USSR, there have been other conflicts in South East Asia (China and India, Vietnam and Cambodia, China and Vietnam), in South West Asia (Iran and Iraq, culminating in 1988), in Africa (Algeria, Kenya, Angola, Namibia, Uganda, Mozambique, the Sudan, and Libya), and in the Americas (Cuba, Chile, Panama, El Salvador, Grenada, and Nicaragua). Yet because of the balance of terror – the fear of nuclear annihilation – none of these conflicts were allowed to escalate into a third world war. Faced with crude power that is too awesome to contemplate, neither the Russians nor the Americans pushed their interests to the point of nuclear annihilation. One blessing of the nuclear bomb is that he who uses it will almost certainly die by it. As long as the leaders of a nation remain as vulnerable as the rest of the population, there will be no repetition of the blood-letting of 1914–1918 and 1939–1945. The concept of victory in war died at Hiroshima in 1945. Since then, until the end of the Cold War in 1991, the balance of terror rather than the balance of power was our guard.

12

The Resurgence of Asia

The resurgence of Asia dates from Japan's defeat of Russian land and sea forces in the Russo-Japanese War of 1904–1905. The West had been defeated earlier by Mongols and Turks but never simultaneously on land and sea. The Japanese victory over the Russians was a clarion call to the people of Asia – especially to the Turks, the Persians, and the Indians – to rise up and shake off the fetters of European and (in the Philippines and other islands in the Pacific) American imperialism.

In the Second Great War (1939–1945) Japan, once more spearheading Asian hostility, broke the West's grip in the East. In June 1941, taking advantage of Germany's assault on the Soviet Union, Japanese troops overran what was then called French Indochina (Vietnam). In December 1941 they attacked the Americans in Hawaii and in the Philippines, the British in Hong Kong, Malaya, and Burma, the Dutch in Indonesia, and the Australians in New Guinea. In early 1944 Japanese troops stood poised before Imphal on the Burmese-Indian border. This was the furthermost point of Japanese expansion. They were routed there by British and Indian troops in the spring of 1944.

Following Japan's defeat in the Pacific, and its surrender in 1945, the Europeans, unable to realize that the Japanese had destroyed their power in the East for good and that the age of European dominance in the world had ended, hastened to regain their Asian empires. (See Map X).

The first European colonial territory to gain its independence in the postwar period was British India; and this not because of Japanese invasion, but because of the idea of nationalism which the British themselves had introduced to India at an earlier point.[236] When the Japanese began

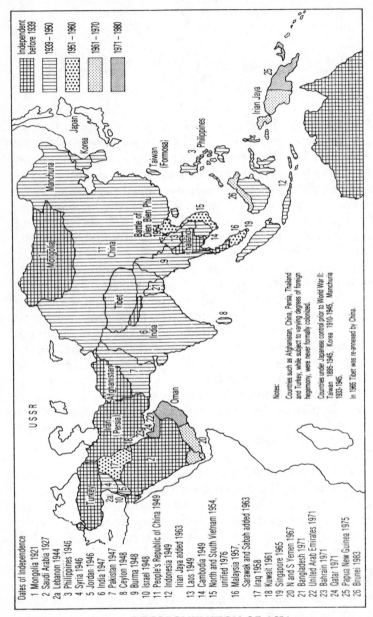

DECOLONIZATION OF ASIA
MAP X

their conquest of south-east Asia in 1941, the century-old struggle for the independence of India was still underway. Although English educated Indian leaders, such as Mohandas Karamchand Gandhi (1869–1948)[237] and Jawaharlal Nehru (1889–1964), shared Britain's apprehensions at the Japanese advance, discord between the nationalist movement and British authority in India could not be stilled. By 1942 the growth of civil disturbance had led to the imprisonment of Gandhi (who had begun his movement of non-violence in 1920), Nehru and other nationalist leaders. Faced by growing insurrection in India (in 1944), the British Labour Party – which had adopted a policy of anti-imperialism – promised independence for India if it gained power. In 1945 the Labour Party (having won the election) kept its promise. In 1947 British power in India was relinquished. (Ceylon obtained its independence the following year.) So ended British imperial rule in India which had taken hundreds of years to build.

Unable to obtain agreement between the Indian National Congress Party, led by Nehru, and the Muslim League, led by Muhammed Ali Jinnah (1876–1948),[238] the Viceroy, Lord Louis Mountbatten (1900–1979), was forced to agree to the tragic division of India between Hindu and Muslim. Against Gandhi's warnings, the Muslim areas of the Punjab in the north-west were joined with the eastern sector of Bengal (now Bangladesh) to form Pakistan. In the subsequent exchange of populations, half a million Hindus, Muslims, and Sikhs lost their lives. The slaughter was not halted even by the shock of Gandhi's assassination on 30 January 1948. Henceforth, until his death in 1964, Nehru[239] was the dominant figure in Indian politics. It was he who first coined the terms "neutralism", "Third World", and "non-aligned countries". He played a leading role in founding the Third World bloc of African and Asian states at Bandung, Indonesia, in 1955. By the 1970s the Third World had become the most politically powerful group at the United Nations. Although Nehru did his best to cultivate cordial relations with communist China, the latter's conquest of Tibet in the 1950s, with its deliberate attempt to destroy traditional Tibetan culture, as well as its invasion of India's northern territory in 1962 (territory which China still holds), undermined his work of peace.

Burma, which had also been under British rule for a century, welcomed the Japanese as liberators rather than as conquerors.[240] They resented the return of the British in 1945. The British, having yielded power in India, could hardly reconquer Burma. Following the anti-imperialist policy they had adopted in India, they yielded to Burmese demands for home-rule just as quickly as they could. The Union of Burma came formally into existence on 4 January 1948. Since then the country has been torn by internal rivalries (from ethnic minorities and from communist opposition). Although it broke Chinese (and Indian) control of the economy, Burma was the first country to acknowledge Mao's victory in 1949. In 1960 the Burmese signed a treaty of friendship and non-aggression with China.

Faced by a communist-led insurrection, British power in Malaya was not so easily relinquished. The British had first imposed their authority on Malacca and Singapore in the 1820s. By the 1880s their control extended to the whole of Malaya. Because of its strategic importance, British Malaya was soon engulfed in the Second World War. In 1942 the Japanese captured Singapore from the north by land. The British defeat meant the loss of its largest naval base in eastern waters, as well as vital supplies of rubber and tin. With the end of the Japanese occupation in 1945 a bitter struggle took place between the British and the communists. Not until 1957 did British arms prevail. In that year the sovereign state of Malaysia was formed and power transferred to the new nation as an independent entity.

The postwar struggle for independence in French Indochina – once the Japanese forces had surrendered – followed an even more violent course. Unlike the British, the French had no intention of abandoning Indochina, which it had ruled for more than a century. Due to the efforts of a great French missionary, Pierre Pigneau de Béhaine, the first treaty between France and the king of Cochin China was signed in 1787. By the middle of the nineteenth century, however, the Christian missionaries had fallen out of favor with the Annamite court (as they had done earlier in Japan and China). In 1858, in retribution for the killing of several Christian priests, the Vietnamese court was shelled. In 1858, on the pretext of upholding Christianity, the French occupied Saigon. By the Treaty of Saigon in 1862 the French were able to establish their rule, and the Catholic religion, in the three eastern provinces of Cochin China. Greater freedom for Western traders was also obtained. Gradually, by the use of "gun-boat diplomacy" common to Western powers in the East, France extended its control from Cochin China to Cambodia, Annam, and Tongking. In 1885, by the Treaty of Tientsin, a defeated China was forced to surrender the province of Tongking. In 1887 all these territories were united under French control as French Indochina. Six years later, in 1893, the French acquired a protectorate over Laos.

Relatively accessible, rich in minerals and rubber, and of vital strategic importance, in 1941 French Indochina became the springboard for Japanese expansion in the Pacific. By the time the French returned there in 1945, Laos, Cambodia, and Vietnam had all developed powerful communist movements demanding independence from France. While the French granted autonomy to Laos and Cambodia after the war, it was withheld from Ho Chi Minh's independent Republic of Vietnam based on Hanoi. Widespread insurrection against the French followed.

French power in Indochina was finally overturned with the decisive defeat of French troops by the North Vietnamese at Dien Bien Phu in 1954. Vietnam was subsequently divided at the 17th parallel into two zones: the northern half led by Ho Chi Minh (1890–1969), and the non-communist South which became an independent republic in 1955. At that point – determined to contain the communist challenge in the East as well as the West – the Americans made what the French leader Charles de Gaulle (1890–1970) predicted would prove to be a disastrous intervention. Henceforth, Vietnam became a pawn in the much wider power struggle between communist

China and Russia on the one hand and the United States on the other. Not until 1973 were the Americans forced to withdraw. On their departure, South Vietnam was quickly conquered by the communist North. Laos and Cambodia were also subsequently overrun by Vietnam. The Vietnamese army withdrew from these areas in 1989.

The fierce struggle for independence which followed the surrender of Japanese forces in Vietnam in 1945 had its parallel in Indonesia. Indonesian nationalists were equally determined to rid themselves of the Dutch who had first appeared in Indonesia at the beginning of the seventeenth century. In 1605, determined to take their share of the profitable spice trade, the Dutch had defeated the Portuguese in the Moluccas; in 1613 they broke the British hold on part of Timor; in 1619 they took Djakarta, which they renamed Batavia; in 1641 they captured Malacca which dominated the straits of that name; in 1666 they triumphed in the Celebes, east of Borneo, and secured a trading post on the eastern coast of Sumatra. Behind all Dutch triumphs was the power they exercised at sea.

Between the 1820s and the 1880s native uprisings forced the Dutch to extend their control to the interior of both Java and Sumatra. In the 1840s they annexed southern Borneo, Bali, and the Celebes. In 1859 they divided Timor and the neighboring islands with the Portuguese. From then, until Indonesia was overrun by the Japanese in 1942, Dutch rule remained unchallenged. As in Burma, the Japanese invaders were welcomed as liberators. Indonesian leaders, such as Sukarno,[241] co-operated with the Japanese throughout the war. The arms which the Indonesians subsequently used in their struggle against the Dutch were provided by the Japanese. In 1945 the Japanese stood by while Sukarno (immediately prior to the return of the Dutch) proclaimed himself President of an independent republic. But the Dutch refused to be so easily dislodged. It was not until 1949 – after much blood had been spilled – that they finally accepted defeat.

In contrast to Burma and Indonesia, the Japanese invasion of the Philippines in December 1941 was met with the greatest resistance. With the Americans, the Filipinos fought the Japanese invaders to the death. Perhaps the Filipino loyalty to the West can best be explained by the long association the Philippines have had with the West. Discovered by Magellan in 1521, and conquered by Spain in 1565, they remained under Spanish control until the United States' victory over Spain in 1898. Perhaps it had something to do with their long-established Catholicism. Perhaps it was because they had already been promised their independence by the Congress of the United States in 1934. Fulfilling that promise, the Republic of the Philippines came into existence on 4 July 1946. Since then the Philippines have remained largely under the protection of the United States.

Japanese imperial ambitions during the 1930s and 1940s also created unrest and turmoil in Asian countries nominally outside the control of the European and American empires. The Japanese invasion of China in 1937 set the stage for the civil war between communists and nationalists which followed the Japanese surrender in 1945. By 1949 the outcome of the struggle for power (except in Taiwan and Tibet) was a communist-led China. The Japanese, having occupied Korea since 1910, were also partly responsible for its division following the Japanese surrender in 1945.

Since the end of World War II, Asian countries outside the area of Japanese conquest and control have also obtained their independence. In south-west Asia the independence movement first took shape in Syria and Lebanon in 1941–1944. Anticipating the French promise of freedom (which had been made in 1936), in 1944 Syria unilaterally declared itself an independent republic. A struggle followed which resulted in the French bombardment of Damascus and the loss of hundreds of Syrian lives. Only by the intervention of the United Nations in 1946 was Syria able to rid itself of French control.

Lebanon gained its independence from the French at the same time. To this day, Syria does not recognize the political division between itself and Lebanon. It still has no ambassador in Beirut. In the "Greater Syria" of the

Turkish Ottoman Empire, which had controlled the area from 1517 to 1918 (an area from the Taurus mountains in the north to the Sinai peninsula in the south, including Palestine and present-day Jordan), the state of Lebanon did not exist. Its origins date only to the various peace treaties which followed the First Great War. In April 1920, after the defeat of the Ottoman Empire, the Allies divided Greater Syria into British and French mandates. Trans-Jordan[242] and Palestine went to the British, the area to the north to the French. In August 1920, partly in an effort to divide and conquer, the French partitioned their mandated territory into the states of Lebanon and modern-day Syria. This division was opposed – as it still is – by Muslims in Lebanon and Syria.

War and discord marked the administration not only of the French but also of the British mandate in the Middle East. Unable to find a solution to the Arab-Jewish conflict in Palestine – the Arabs claimed Palestine by long-term occupation, the Jews by former occupation and now by divine will – unable to satisfy the totally incompatible demands of both Arabs and Jews, the British, on 14 May 1948, voluntarily relinquished their Palestinian mandate to the United Nations. In doing so, the British tried to rid themselves of a problem they had helped to create. In 1917, as an act of political expediency, the British Foreign Secretary, Arthur James Balfour, had promised part of Palestine to the Jews.[243] Balfour's visit to the United States had left him in no doubt about the strength of the American Zionist movement. It was a power that Britain would do well to have on its side in its struggle for survival. Granted the desperate circumstances in which the British found themselves in 1917, their fault lay not in obtaining help wherever they could, but in believing that it was possible to satisfy the totally incompatible demands of both Arabs and Jews. In trying to give the same piece of territory to both Jews and Arabs, the British eventually came to be detested by both sides. On the same day that they relinquished their mandate over Palestine to the United Nations, the Jewish state of Israel was proclaimed.

The problem of creating a Jewish national state in Palestine, although a Zionist ideal since the 1890s,[244] did not become acute until the holocaust of European Jewry resulted in a sharp increase of Jewish refugees. In 1930, out of a total population of one million living in Palestine, three-quarters were Muslim Arabs, the rest were Christians and Jews.[245] Ten years later in 1940, out of a total population of one and a half million, the Jews numbered about half a million or about one-third of Palestine's population. Despite British efforts to resist free immigration of Jews into Palestine, by 1945 the Jewish proportion of the population had become larger still. Today, Israel occupies the whole of Palestine and parts of neighboring Arab states as well.

On 15 May 1948, the day after the state of Israel was created, Egypt, Jordan, and Iraq began the war against the Jews which they had threatened two years before. The outcome was the expansion of Israel's frontiers and the dispersal of the Palestinian Arabs to Jordan, the West Bank, Gaza, Syria, and Lebanon. Henceforth, through war after war (1956, 1967 – which placed the West Bank, Gaza, and Jerusalem under Israeli control – and 1973), Israel has had to fight for its very existence.

Although the United States (under President Wilson) had earlier supported Arab rather than Jewish claims to Palestine,[246] it was instrumental in the creation of the State of Israel in 1948. Since then, in war and peace (except during the Eisenhower Administration), it has unstintingly supported Israel's cause. No other territorial problem since 1945 has taken so much of its time, energy, and wealth. In public aid alone, the United States since 1948 has granted more aid to Israel than it did under Marshall Aid to the whole of western and central Europe. Israel remains the largest recipient of United States aid.

Following United States intervention in the Arab-Israeli War of 1973 on Israel's side, the Arab world responded with an oil embargo under which the Arab nations of the Organization of Petroleum Exporting Countries (OPEC)[247] reduced their production by five per cent; Saudi Arabia cut its production by ten per cent and banned all exports of oil to the United States. Although America and the rest of the world were able to fall back on non-OPEC supplies (chiefly from Mexico, Norway, Britain, and the Soviet Union), the outcome was a serious dislocation of the American and the world economy.

The uprising (the intifada) of Palestinians in the West Bank and Gaza since 1987, with its toll of hundreds of Arab lives, stirred the United States to make new efforts to bring peace to the area. Against the protests of the Israeli government, the United States began direct talks with the Palestine Liberation Organization (PLO) in the spring of 1989.[248] The plea of Secretary of State James Baker, in the summer of 1989, that Israel should abandon the idea of a "Greater Israel" and Jewish settlement of the occupied lands was rebuffed by Prime Minister Yitzhak Shamir. In 1990, following a Palestinian terrorist attack against Israel, talks between the United States government and the PLO were broken off. Charged with emotion, and the suffering undergone by both sides (and despite the Camp David Accords,[249] much of which remain to be implemented) the problem was far from being resolved. On the contrary, for the Palestinians the situation was becoming ever more desperate.

The resurgence of Asia becomes self-evident when one compares the Asia of 1945 with that of the 1980s. British and French possessions have largely disappeared from the map. Except for Macao and Hong Kong, Asia has completely rid itself of European and American tutelage. Japan, China, India and Iran have reappeared as new great powers. India, with a population of 800 million is now second in numbers only to China, and is increasing its population at a faster rate. Its location is of the highest strategic value; its army is the most powerful, most efficient, and most deployable military force between Bangladesh and Turkey. Its swift defeat of East Pakistan in 1971 (which then became Bangladesh) gave notice that India was a major power in Asia. Only India and Japan can seriously affect the moves of China or Russia in the East, and India has the scale which Japan lacks.

India's growing importance since the 1960s is reflected

in the effort made by the Soviet Union to obtain its co-operation. For the Soviets, Indian co-operation was essential if they were to counter Chinese and American influence in the region. India not only possesses 2,000 miles of frontier with China; its cultural impact also rivals that of the Chinese in many parts of south-east Asia. After much diplomatic maneuvering, in 1971 India signed a twenty year Treaty of Peace, Friendship and Co-operation with the Soviet Union – the one exception to India's general policy of non-alignment. For the past twenty-five years the Soviet Union has been the chief supplier of arms and, since 1973, of aid to India. It has consistently supported it against Pakistan (whose nuclear program could involve it in a conflict with India and the USSR), and in its border conflict with China. Soviet relations with Pakistan were transformed when the USSR invaded Afghanistan in December 1979. Aided by the United States, Pakistan's support for the Afghan mujahedeèn (who did much to frustrate Soviet aims) has caused the USSR to further cements its relations with India, Pakistan's major enemy. In 1988 the Soviets took the unprecedented step of leasing a nuclear-powered submarine to the Indian Navy.

In return, India has co-operated with the Soviets on several fronts. It has invariably abstained from condemning Russian conduct in Afghanistan. In trying to gain predominance over this historic crossroads of central Asia, the gateway to Iran, India, and Pakistan, the Russians had hoped to achieve what a hundred years of Czarist effort failed to do. In 1989, however, the Soviets evacuated their troops from Afghanistan. The Soviet Union, with Indian co-operation, has strengthened its forces in the Indian Ocean because that body of water (around which or adjacent to which are the most populous nations of the world) is becoming the most strategically important ocean of all. The West not only needs access to the oil supplies of the Middle East, it also requires unimpeded access to the vital mineral supplies of South Africa.

United States' diplomatic efforts in India have proved less successful. They have been weakened by America's desire to be friendly with Pakistan as well.[250] Relations

between the United States and India were never so warm
as when America was providing arms to help withstand
Chinese aggression in 1962, and never so cool as when,
during 1965 and 1971, Indians fought American-armed
Pakistani troops. The continuing use of Pakistan by the
United States to strike at a Russian-sponsored regime in
Afghanistan has resulted in a further deterioration of
Indian-United States' relations.

Nowhere is Asia's resurgence more visible than in Japan
which by 1990 had become one of the financial and economic titans of the world. Between 1950 and 1973, assisted
by its policy of central-government management of free
market forces, its gross domestic product grew at a rate
(10.5 per cent a year) far in excess of that of any other
industrial nation. In the 1970s its growth rates were often
twice those of its major competitor, the United States.[251]
Throughout the 1980s, in the manufacture of steel,
cement, electronics, autos, and several other leading industrial products, the country held either first or second
place. In the early 1980s it accounted for about half the
world's ship construction. While America's share of the
world economy and world manufacturing has not shrunk,
Japan's annual motor vehicle production in 1990 exceeded
that of the United States by half a million. Its branch
factories had invaded the manufacturing centers of the
world.

From the 1960s onward Japan's success in extending its
influence in world trade and world finance was equally
remarkable. From the 1960s until the mid-1980s it experienced a sustained foreign trade boom. Between 1980 and
1987 the volume of Japanese exports increased more than
40 per cent. The key to its success was an ability to
produce higher quality goods at lower prices. By September 1990 (assisted by its new riches, by the appreciation of
the yen, and by the nation-wide concentration of its banking organization) the world's top seven banks were Japanese owned.[252] Japan's commanding lead in the world's
100 largest business corporations by stock-market value

was equally striking: fifty compared with thirty-five for the United States.[253]

Japan's economic success cannot be disassociated from the large annual surplus (in 1989 about $50 billion) that it has been running in its trade with the United States for many years[254] – a surplus supposedly created by its unwillingness to open its markets to foreign goods. The facts would seem to belie this. Since 1985, encouraged by the rise of the yen, Japan increased its imports considerably. Between 1985 and 1988 the total increase was almost 40 per cent. The increase in the export volume during these years was only five per cent. Almost half of what Japan exported to the United States in 1989 was under compulsory or voluntary restraint. Indeed, it might be argued that Japan has become a more open market while the United States and the European Community (EC) have become more protective.

The American criticisms of supposed Japanese unfair trade practices in the 1980s remind one of the criticism made by the British against the Germans and the Americans at the beginning of the twentieth century. There is the same note of alarm; the same unwillingness either to realize that its monopoly of industrial materials and fuels has been broken, or to apply more efficient methods of production; the same talk of trade wars.[255] Yet the United States cannot wage a trade war against a country upon which it relies for capital, and with which, economically and militarily, it is inextricably bound. One can only be grateful that the Japanese do not settle their trade problems with gunboats, as the western powers did in the nineteenth century.

Whatever trade concessions the Japanese make to the Americans, they are not going to solve America's trade deficits with other nations. (The overall United States $2 billion trade surplus of 1970 had become a deficit of $110 billion by 1989). Even the high-technology goods upon which the United States increasingly relied, fell from the $27 billion surplus of 1980 to $4 billion in 1985, to the first-ever deficit in 1988. Having had things very much its own way since the end of World War II, American industry in the 1980s found it hard to adjust to the demands of a globally interconnected, competitive world in which resource endowment and technology are no longer overwhelmingly in America's favor.

In 1989 there was no bilateral relation in the world as important as that which existed between the United States and Japan. Together they accounted for about thirty per cent of the world's goods and services. The total amount of bilateral trade between them exceeded $110 billion. Almost a quarter of each country's imports came from the other. Japanese direct business investments in the United States during the second half of the 1980s also played an indispensable role in the United States economy. Assisted by a huge trade surplus and the tremendous appreciation of the yen, they grew from $16 billion in 1984 to over $53 billion in 1988. Overall Japanese investments in the United States at the end of 1988 totalled $285 billion.

Although in 1988 the Japanese cumulative total of direct business investments was less than that of other foreign investors in the United States (the British total was $101.9 billion), it was growing more rapidly. In 1989 Japan surpassed the British total and became the world's largest investor in overseas industry and property. As a result, a great deal of United States real estate and industry was transferred to Japanese ownership and control. The fear of many Americans was that United States real estate and productive capacity were being sold to Japanese investors at what the Japanese (taking advantage of the strength of the yen relative to the dollar) considered bargain basement prices.[256]

The first six months of 1990 saw a remarkable reversal of the flow of Japanese investments into the United States. A weak dollar, and an almost stagnant United States economy caused a dramatic decline in Japanese holdings in the United States stock and bond market. American investors have followed suit. In late 1990 both domestic and foreign capital continued to flee the United States.

Fortunate for United States-Japanese relations, the flow of capital across the Pacific has not been all one way. Many

United States businesses operate profitably within Japan. In 1987 the figure was about 1,000. Small as American direct investments were in Japan in 1988 ($17 billion) when compared with the flow from Japan to the United States ($53.4 billion), half of the total foreign direct business investment in Japan came from the United States. Accompanying that investment was American technology.[257]

Japanese funds have also been indispensable in helping to finance the United States' government.[258] Since 1980 Japan has made massive investments in United States Treasury Bonds. Not until August 1990 did Japanese investors show a reluctance to go on doing so. Throughout the 1980s, the difference between what the United States economy and the debt-ridden United States government (America's budget surplus of $22 billion in 1971 had become a deficit of $220 billion by 1990) needed and what could be provided from America's meager savings, was met by foreign lenders. This was especially true of the Japanese who by the late 1980s had begun to subsidize the American standard of living. The United States has not been able to attract these vast funds without paying higher interest rates; which has made the capital costs (the interest and mortgage rates) of running a business in America much greater than in Germany or Japan. Nor has it been able to avoid the serious political, economic, and strategic implications accompanying such foreign indebtedness. Debt on the present scale must ultimately affect America's independence.

While the problem of growing indebtedness was general to American society as a whole,[259] the increasing indebtedness of the United States government to foreigners was the most particularly dangerous long-term problem facing the country. Federal debt held by foreigners rose from $121.7 billion in the fiscal year 1980 to $394 billion in 1989. United States federal debt (domestic and foreign) grew from $709 billion in 1980 to almost $4 trillion in 1991. Interest on the national debt in 1991 reached an all-time high of $286 billion. Foreign ownership of all kinds in the United States – that is federal debt and business investments – in 1989 rose to an unprecedented

$2.076 trillion. In sharp contrast to the situation only a decade ago, when United States foreign holdings were greater than that of any other power, in 1989 United States holdings abroad totalled only $1.4 trillion. The United States' net foreign debt (non-existent as recently as 1984) had by 1989 become $664 billion, more than twenty-five per cent higher than the half trillion dollars of 1988. It is not only the economic costs of running such a deficit that is worrying; it is the loss of leadership that such a deficit entails. Debtors never have led the world. More worrying for a country such as the United States that has been heavily reliant on foreign funds, was the fact that the world capital supply in 1990 – because of the bailout of eastern Europe and the military crisis in the Persian Gulf – was becoming scarcer and more costly.

Japan was not alone in its extraordinary economic upsurge. The vigorous development that took place in China,[260] Korea, Taiwan,[261] Singapore, and Hong Kong during the 1980s was reminiscent of the West's earlier Industrial Revolution. Having doubled their combined gross domestic product since 1960, these countries today make up the world's third major industrial region. In the 1980s some western observers were predicting that China's productive capacity would exceed that of most European powers within a generation. Because of the possibility of political upheaval, perhaps endemic to Chinese society, and its underlying bureaucratic ethos, the long-term development of that country cannot be predicted. (The one outstanding advantage that Japan possesses over both China and Korea is its relative political stability.) Economically speaking, China still has to recover from the ill-conceived land reforms and the "Great Leap Forward" of the 1950s as well as the "Cultural Revolution" of the 1960s.

Curiously enough, the "work ethic", which is associated with the rise of the West, is now more prevalent among the Japanese and their East Asian neighbors (along with Buddhist, Confucian, and Shinto ideals). It always was ingrained in the mass of Chinese, Koreans, and Japanese.

The key to world competition today is not only technology, it is cheap labor; which is what these Asian countries possess. Except for the brief period of Western political and technological predominance in the nineteenth and twentieth centuries, industry always was labor intensive; all the major works of antiquity depended upon labor rather than capital. Under Asian leadership the factor of labor intensity is becoming important again. With the growing co-operation between China, Japan,[262] Korea, Taiwan, Singapore, and Hong Kong, a new and formidable challenge to the West is emerging. During the 1980s, while world rather than inter-Asian trade remained crucial, trade between these countries generally grew faster than trade with the rest of the world.

The resurgence of Asia since the Second World War has had particular significance for the European communities of Australia and New Zealand. Until 1939 they remained largely client states of Britain, their foreign policies were essentially an extension of British imperial policy. So closely tied did the economies of these countries become that changes in one invariably affected the others. The British depression of the late 1920s and early 1930s brought home to Australia and New Zealand how perilously dependent they had become on foreign trade. Worsened conditions in Britain in the early 1930s not only caused major reductions in foreign trade and investment, they almost put an end to British emigration. Not until after the Second World War (which provided a tremendous stimulus to industrialization in Australia, and during which Australia turned for its very survival to the United States) did white immigration to Australia and New Zealand recover. By then it was the continental Europeans – Latins, Dutch, Germans, Poles, Greeks, and Balts – most of them fleeing the chaos of postwar Europe, who predominated. With the cry of "Populate or Perish" in the air, Australia absorbed approximately two million migrants between 1945 and 1963; and four million between 1945 and 1990. In an attempt to accommodate the growing numbers of would-be Asian immigrants, both Australia and New

Zealand have modified their white immigration policies. While European migrants to Australia still predominate, Asians, and other colored people, are no longer excluded on grounds of race.

The Asian presence in Australasia is far more apparent in trade and investment. Before 1945 Australia's and New Zealand's commercial ties had been with Britain and the United States. By 1990 (by which time Australia had become one of the more advanced economies of the world[263]) its trade was virtually dependent on Asia. For Australians, Americans, and Europeans alike, Australia has become a spring-board of economic activity in the Pacific Basin. Since the 1970s Japan has become Australia's leading trader, and, after the United States and Europe, increasingly its largest investor – in 1988 it invested $5.6 billion. In 1976 a Treaty of Co-operation and Friendship was signed between the two countries. Japan is Australia's biggest buyer of minerals, which by far has become Australia's leading export. In 1990 Australia was the world's biggest supplier of coal. It possessed almost one-third of the western world's uranium reserves. It also had enormous reserves of natural gas. In economic orientation Australians were becoming white Asians. They no longer spoke of the Far East but of the Near North.

The New Zealand economy has not been affected so much by Asian as by European developments. Britain's entry into the European Common Market in 1973 ended the protected market in Britain for New Zealand's all-important dairy and meat products.

Ultimately the future of white-settled Australia and New Zealand (with approximate populations of seventeen and four million respectively in 1990) must lie in the political rather than the economic realm. As long as the West dominated the East, Australia and New Zealand's lot as Caucasians was relatively secure. The ANZUS Treaty of 1951, which involved both countries in the Korean and Vietnam wars, remains the formal framework of mutual security for Australia, New Zealand, and the United States. The new volatile order in the Pacific region in which Asia must undoubtedly play an increasing role, has not yet been decided. Like few other countries in the world, both Australia and New Zealand are only too keenly aware of Asia's resurgence, and their growing dependence upon it; both countries have reached a turning point in their relations with East and West.

The spiritual and economic resurgence of the Middle East has been most marked since the Second World War. Since 1945, the world (especially the industrial states of western Europe and Japan) has become critically dependent upon the oil resources of south-west Asia. The Arab oil embargo of 1973 opened a new era in which Asian rather than Western interests prevailed. Dominating all else in south-west Asia is the security of oil supplies and the Arab-Jewish dispute. Helped by the balance of terror, the superpowers have hitherto avoided a general conflagration over Israel. But oil is another matter. An attempt by any power to dominate the oil supply of that region can only end in war. Any extension of Iran or Iraq's influence in the region (Iran's population of more than fifty million is greater than that of all the other Gulf states combined) must be construed as a direct threat to the lives of those conservative Arab regimes (including Saudi Arabia, Oman, Kuwait, Jordan, and Egypt) most closely allied with the United States.[264]

In the summer and fall of 1990, following Iraq's invasion of Kuwait (prompted by Kuwait's refusal to adhere to OPEC quotas and prices, and Iraq's supposed historical claim to Kuwait),[265] the USA, transferred a vast military force to Saudi Arabia. The Middle East once more stood on the brink of war. Marking off this crisis from those that preceded it was the unusual degree of unanimity shown by the world community in its condemnation of Iraq. Also impressive was the manner in which the USA and the USSR were able to agree upon common action. (Several years ago America's movements would have brought a sharp and threatening response from the USSR). Most striking of all, especially for those who believe in the United Nations and the force of international law, is the seemingly new-found, impassioned reliance and advocacy (in contrast to its actions in Nicaragua, Libya, Grenada, and Panama) which the USA placed upon the United

Nations and international law. Going it alone, as the United States did in Vietnam, and the USSR did in Afghanistan, belongs to another period of history.

It is not only conditions in the Middle East that threaten the world; in eastern Asia, vast and hostile armies stand poised on the Russian-Chinese border. The causes of the Sino-Soviet conflict long precede the present border dispute. Much of the Soviet Far East and Soviet Central Asia was, in fact, Chinese territory acquired forcibly by the Russians from the seventeenth century onward. The Russians still occupy the Amur River region and the Maritime Provinces – which make up an area as large as Alaska – that they seized in the 1850s and 1860s. The Chinese (with four times the population of the ex-Soviet Union, but with a deplorable economic base for any country claiming to be a superpower) have never given up hope that they will one day recover these "lost territories". They also claim another million square miles stretching almost to the Caspian Sea. The Chinese are quick to exploit the growing national pride and self-assertion of the non-Russian peoples occupying the Asian part of the ex-Soviet Union (particularly the ethnically alien forty to fifty million Muslims living in those parts of Central Asia which Russia occupied in the nineteenth century). Because of the high birth rates of the Asian regions of the USSR and Russia's own almost zero population growth, in 1989 the Russians accounted for only 54 per cent of total Soviet population. They were rapidly becoming a minority in their own country. The state of Outer Mongolia, about two-thirds of a million square miles, still under Russian influence, is also in question. Prior to 1911 this area was within China's sphere of influence. It is ominous that the border commission appointed by the USSR and China in 1969 – when a border dispute brought them to the brink of war – has still to agree upon an agenda. Whether the resumption of border negotiations in 1987 between the two powers, coupled with Mikhail Gorbachev's calls for better understanding, will relieve tensions in that region remains to be seen.

Asia has also grown in world importance since 1945 because of the revival of Islam. The world's fastest growing religion, Islam has about 900 million adherents. (See Note 149 and Map XV). For the first time since the First World War, it is becoming clear to the Muslim world that its future does not necessarily have to be linked with the abandonment of the Muslim faith (as happened to so many of the faithful in Turkey, Egypt, and Iran) in favor of western modernity.

Nowhere is the danger of a clash between western modernity and the power of Islamic religious fundamentalism more clearly portrayed than in the recent history of Iran. During World War II Iran was occupied by the USSR and the USA. In 1951 the western oil concessions in that country were nationalized by a government headed by Mohammed Mossadegh. With the connivance of the American and British governments, Mossadegh was overthrown and Shah Reza Pahlavi restored to power. The things upon which the Shah subsequently relied most – his race to modernization and his ever-closer relations with the United States (which many Iranians regarded as simply another western imperialist power), as well as his suspected contempt for Islam – proved to be his undoing. Under Ayatollah Khomeini's leadership, the mosque became the symbol of traditional Iranian resistance to westernization.

While not minimizing the importance of Islam's resurgence, one should not ascribe to Islamic unity a strength which, divided by national, tribal, and religious differences, it does not possess. The resurgence of Islam's religious fundamentalism does not seem to have lessened the hostility of Islamic states toward each other, as the war between Iran and Iraq during the 1980s, and Iraq's seizure of Kuwait in 1990 bear out. So politically fragmented is the Islamic world that it is difficult for the present upsurge of religious fundamentalism to make of it a single coherent movement. Islam has possessed a degree of religious unity since the eighth century; political unity, however, especially among the Arabs, has always escaped it. While the vision of Arab unity (Arabism) still grips the Arab imagination, all post-World War I attempts to unite the Arab states, such as the uniting of Egypt and Syria during the 1950s, have failed. In 1990 Arab councils were unable to prevent Iraq from invading Kuwait. Similarly, Saddam Hussein's attempts to arouse the Arab masses against their conservative governments (whom he regards as puppets of the Western powers) have thus far failed.

It is hardly surprising that there has been a resurgence of Asia since 1945. Asia is, after all, the largest and most populous continent. Having suffered a temporary eclipse at western hands, Asia is becoming the center of the world again. In 1988 the United States (which already has an Asian population of twelve million) was drawing more immigrants from Asia (and Latin America) than from any other part of the world.[266] American trade with Asia and the Pacific, which was about half that done with Europe in 1960, in 1989 exceeded Europe's share; four-fifths of California's trade was done with Pacific rim countries; the shipping tonnage handled by United States Pacific ports, such as Los Angeles and Long Beach, exceeded that of New York and the ports of New Jersey. In 1990 every aspect of American economic life was being affected by the Japanese.

One should not exaggerate the resurgence of Asia. It is easy to speak about Asia when no homogeneous Asia exists. It is easy to suggest that Japan and other Asians are dominating the United States when no such threat exists. Total foreign ownership of assets in the United States in 1988 represented only 2.4 per cent of total corporate assets. Given Japan's limitations in resources, area, population (123.4 million in 1988), and productivity (in 1989 Japan's GNP was $2,835 billion compared with $5,234 billion for the United States), its recent tremendous burst of energy might prove to be short-lived. Certainly, the giant gains made by the Japanese in the world economy cannot be disassociated from a new and perilous vulnerability to world forces, especially to conditions in the United States. Its dependence upon the free flow of oil from the Persian Gulf exceeds that of any other power. No major country is more dependent upon the world economy than Japan. Domestically, Japan is faced with a manifestly overvalued yen. Its balance sheets and stock prices have been inflated to unreal levels. Real estate values in the environs of Tokyo and other major cities have reached heights that are unsustainable. Demographically Japan is aging. The cultural situation (the traditional Japanese work and savings ethics are being eroded by demands for a higher standard of living) is also less favorable to Japanese economic growth and development.

It is equally easy to exaggerate the threat to the West of the combined strength of the rapidly growing group-oriented economies of East Asia. While there has been a remarkable increase in trade among the Pacific rim economies, the truth is that these countries still remain highly dependent on the world economy, especially on the United States market. In 1989 almost three-quarters of Japan's trade (imports and exports) was done with countries outside Asia. To a lesser extent the same is true of other East Asian countries. It is fanciful to think of an Asian economy versus a Western economy; at this point West and East are equally dependent upon a world economy.

Despite all the caveats, it cannot be denied that there has been a shift in the center of gravity of world power toward Asia. If the shift from the West to the East continues, it must have far reaching implications for the western world. As a consequence, our children will probably live in a very different world than the one in which we live – one in which they will have to live increasingly on Asia's terms.

13

The Decolonization of Africa

For the non-African Africa is the ambiguous continent. From paleolithic times onward the lower Nile valley has sustained human life. It has seen the coming and going of many great native empires. The first invaders intent on penetrating and colonizing Africa were Arabs whose rule and religion began to spread across the continent from the eighth century onward. From the seventeenth to the twentieth century, Africans fell increasingly under the sway of Europeans. In its long history[267] Africa has fallen prey to the invader, the slave raider, tribal enmity, abject poverty, famine, and disease. Following the Second World War, Africa's dream was to free itself of alien rule and exploitation (see Map XI). Gradually, the dream came true. By 1977 the last colonial European flag had been lowered; for Africa a new age had dawned; a great future was predicted.

Preceding the intrusion of the Europeans by a thousand years, Arab traders had crossed the Sahara in quest of gold, wax, ivory, skins, and slaves; in return for which they gave salt, cloth, iron, and copper goods. They also penetrated the Sudan via the Nile and the Red Sea. Commerce along the east coast of Africa became an Arab preserve. Accompanying the Arab invasion was a language (Arabic) and a faith (Islam) which accepted all men, regardless of color, as brothers. In drought-stricken Africa, the promise of Islam's "wet paradise", with its imagery of fountains and running water, was particularly attractive; also attractive to some was Islam's acceptance of polygamy. Except in those areas where the tsetse fly kept the Arabs' horses and camels out, Islam made far greater inroads than Christianity would do later.

185

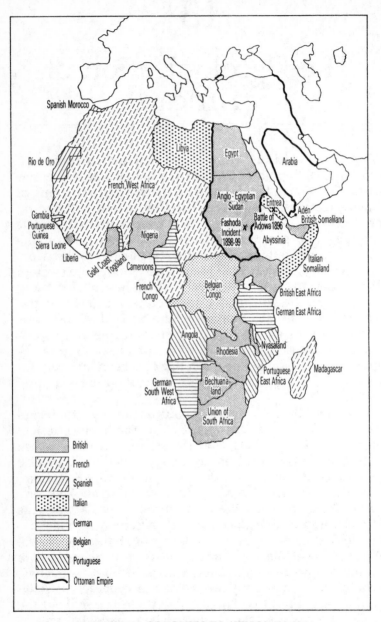

EUROPEAN COLONIES IN AFRICA IN 1914
MAP XI

Yet scattered bands of Christians had found their way to Africa several centuries after the birth of Christ. Christianity was practiced by an isolated group of Ethiopian Copts before the fifth century. In time there grew up in Europe the legend of a Christian kingdom in East Africa. This kingdom of "Prester John" was one of the things the Portuguese went in search of when they began to outflank Islam by sea. By 1484 the Portuguese had reached the estuary of the Congo river (present-day Zaire). A Portuguese diplomat, Pedro de Covilãho, reached Ethiopia in 1487. As the Portuguese pushed down the west coast of Africa, the Gold, Slave, and Ivory Coasts began to appear on European maps. It was in the sixteenth century that the horrendous enslaving of Africans by the Christian West began to take its incalculable toll.

The expansion of the African slave trade by Europeans, Moslem Arabs and Africans (who willingly enslaved their own people), from the fifteenth to the nineteenth century was of epochal importance to Africa and the world. The Europeans did not introduce slavery to Africa (slavery is older than the Pyramids); what they did was to vastly increase its scope. Estimates of the number of slaves shipped to the New World between the sixteenth and the nineteenth centuries range from ten to twenty-five million. Many millions more died en route to the Americas. Not only was the slavery practiced by Christian slave traders much greater, it also lacked compassion; the deliberate breaking up of slave families was more common with Christian than with Muslim slavers. Despite all the rhetoric about Christian love and salvation, the Europeans treated slaves shipped to the New World like cattle.

As a result of the European slave trade, Africa became linked with the other continents as never before. From the eighteenth century African slaves worked in the tropical areas of Brazil, the Caribbean, and later the southern United States. African slaves also turned Caribbean sugar into the "white gold" which helped finance England's Industrial Revolution. In the Americas, African slaves cultivated cotton without which the cotton industry – with its worldwide ramifications – could never have been developed. In the southern United States the plantation industry based on slavery created a society incompatible with that of the North. Together with the question of unity, slavery became the issue over which the American Civil War (1861–1865) was fought. After the Civil War no more slaves were imported.

Slavery brought profound changes to Africa itself. It was the only continent whose population decreased in the nineteenth century. As a result of the introduction of European knick-knacks (colored beads were a favorite), and manufactures, African tribal arts and crafts deteriorated. The weapons, drink, and diseases introduced by the West made the greatest impact of all. Western arms transformed the political organization and power of many tribal states such as Ashanti, Dahomey, and Benin on the west coast. The slave trade also caused a westward shift in the center of gravity of African life – of population, trade, and shipping – from the Indian Ocean to the Atlantic.

Except for European explorers who defined the source and course of Africa's great river systems (Mungo Park the Niger, David Livingstone the Zambezi, Richard Burton and John Speke the Nile, and Henry Stanley the Congo), Europeans showed little inclination to penetrate Africa – especially to settle there – before the closing decades of the nineteenth century. Climate, geography, lack of good harbors on the west coast, health hazards, the few chances to trade, and an inexplicable antipathy of Europeans toward Africa generally discouraged it. For the Europeans, African diseases presented an almost impenetrable barrier. Even as late as the mid-nineteenth century, white intrusion was largely confined to the northern and southern fringes of the continent, as well as to a number of outposts on the west coast.

Because of growing European rivalry, and the introduction of steam railways and improved river boats, this situation changed dramatically in the last third of the nineteenth century. In an effort to bring some kind of order to the Europeans' ever-increasing "Scramble for Africa", the European powers (and a representative from the United States) met at the Berlin West Africa Conference in 1884–1885. No Africans were present, none were consulted. Africa was regarded by the Europeans as a continent with which they could do as they wished. The primitively armed African tribes were in no position to dispute the Europeans' claims for African land and labor. By 1914 there was no part of Africa, except for Liberia[268] and Ethiopia, that was not occupied or controlled by European nations. Great Britain made claim to five of Africa's 11.7 million square miles. Fifty years earlier European control of African territory had extended to no more than one-tenth of the continent.

The scramble by Europeans for African territory in the last third of the nineteenth century brought many changes to African life. Across Africa a network of political boundaries was drawn that had no relation to ethnic or economic reality. Those boundaries still exist and are the cause of wars being fought in several parts of the continent today. Great market-oriented agricultural export industries were established to meet western demands; modern large-scale mining (and the railroads to accompany it) was developed to meet western needs; western economic ideas affecting the use of money, taxation, and labor were imposed. Regardless of native traditions and interests, Africa became dependent upon markets thousands of miles away. Except for missionaries who went to spread the Christian gospel, and certain dedicated government officials, the object was profit and imperialism (however enlightened); the general intention was to serve western ends.

The wonder about the colonization of Africa is that it was done with so little friction between the European powers themselves. Once the cake had been cut at the Berlin Conference in 1884–1885, most Europeans (the Italians had still to make their appearance as colonizers) were satisfied with their share. With the exception of the fight that ensued at the end of the century between the British and the Boers in South Africa – primarily over huge deposits of diamonds (discovered in 1867) and gold (1886) – the European powers were happy to rely upon the pen rather than the sword. Several times they came close to blows, at Fashoda on the Nile in 1898 and at Morocco in

1905 and 1911, but they resolved their differences peacefully. Clashes with the natives were unimportant and invariably piecemeal, until resistance stiffened toward the end of the century. Three major engagements were the Anglo-Zulu War of 1879, the battle between the Ethiopians and the Italians at Adowa in 1896, and the Battle of Omdurman against Sudanese Dervishes in 1898. All three demonstrated the overwhelming superiority of European weapons.

Europe's intrusion into Africa (naked exploitation to some, economic development, as well as political and religious enlightenment to others) continued until the First Great War undermined European prestige. The war gave new life to the African resistance movements that had been fighting European intrusion for fifty years. Even more important, the First World War – and the Russian Revolution that followed it – fructified the seed of nationalism which the Europeans had themselves sown. In time, African nationalism would mean the death of European colonialism.

If the First World War strengthened the native African resistance movements, the Second World War, which saw a renewal of warfare between the imperial powers both in Africa and across the world, provided the opportunity to achieve success. Because of outraged black opinion at Italy's use of poisoned gas in its seizing of Ethiopia in 1935, that year might be considered a turning point in the African independence movement. Italy, the last European power to acquire an African empire, was the first to lose it. In 1941 the British put an end to Italy's empire in Eritrea. In 1942 the Italians were driven out of Ethiopia. Italian Libya was the next to fall.

As the Second World War progressed, and European empires were overrun in Asia as well as Africa, there emerged a new generation of black leaders intent on obtaining self-rule. Among them were Kwame Nkrumah (1909–1972) of the Gold Coast, Léopold Sédar Senghor (born 1906) of Senegal, Jomo Kenyatta (1891–1978) of Kenya, Sékou Touré (1922–1984) of Guinea, and Julius

Nyerere (born 1922) of Tanganyika. Britain's postwar re-linquishing of India (1947), coupled with Dutch and French defeats in Asia (especially France's defeat at Dien Bien Phu in 1954), further strengthened the movement for African independence (see Map XII).

Of critical importance in the spread of African independence was the British, French, and Israeli invasion of Egypt in 1956. The ensuing debacle ensured the victory of Gamal Abdel Nasser (1918–1970) whose rise to power in Egypt gave Arabism and Arab unity a powerful voice. In 1956 he openly challenged western control of the Suez Canal as well as Egypt's oil resources. As a result of the diplomatic pressure asserted by the USA and the USSR against Britain, France, and Israel, the invasion failed. Britain subsequently curtailed its presence east of Suez.

In 1956 France, beleaguered in Algeria, grudgingly granted independence to the protectorates of Tunisia and Morocco. Spain followed suit, peacefully transferring its Moroccan territory. In Algeria, however, the French, who thought in terms of common citizenship for the Algerians rather than independence, refused to yield control. First colonized to compensate psychologically for French humiliation in the Napoleonic Wars, Algeria witnessed a seventeen-year long struggle (1945–1962) in which hundreds of thousands died. Three-quarters of the European population had to flee the country before independence from France was won. By then, following the example set by French Guinea in 1958, all the former colonies of French West and French Equatorial Africa had disavowed French rule. The last African colonial territory to be granted independence by a European power was French Djibouti in 1977.

The independence movement in British colonies in Africa had followed a similar course. The Gold Coast was granted independence in 1957. Renamed Ghana, this was the first European colony south of the Sahara to achieve its freedom. British Nigeria, Cameroon, and Togoland[269] followed in 1960; Sierra Leone in 1961. Also breaking away from European rule were Britain's East African colonies of Somalia (1960), Tanganyika[270] (1961), Uganda (1962), Kenya

(1963), Nyasaland (1964), and Northern Rhodesia (1964). Except for Kenya, where Jomo Kenyatta led a revolt against the British, and Southern Rhodesia, where Robert Mugabe (born 1924) did likewise, power was transferred peacefully. In 1980, with Mugabe as its first President, the state of Zimbabwe was created.

Unable to resist the ground swell for independence, what in 1960 British Prime Minister Macmillan had called "The Winds of Change", the Belgians followed the example set by the other Europeans. Belgian rule in Africa ended in 1960 when the Democratic Republic of the Congo was proclaimed. In 1971 the Congo was renamed Zaïre.

With the exception of French Djibouti, the last colonial powers to yield to native rule in Africa were Spain and Portugal. Portuguese Mozambique and Angola obtained their independence in 1975. Spain's rule in the Spanish Sahara was terminated in 1976. Conflict in Angola between black liberation groups resulted in a 1977 victory for the Marxists (with the help of Cuba). In 1989, after more than a decade of guerilla warfare between the South West Africa People's Organization (SWAPO) and the South Africa backed Democratic Turnhalle Alliance Party (DTA) United Nations supervised elections settled the course of Namibia's independence giving SWAPO a majority and ending South Africa's control. In March 1990 Namibia celebrated its independence after 74 years of South African rule.

The curious thing about African decolonization is that it was accomplished with relatively little violence. By and large, the European nations were as glad to surrender power as the native leaders were to assume it. When one compares the endless struggles for independence in Asia, African independence was won quietly and with relatively little bloodshed; in some instances it was thrust upon those who sought it. For the Europeans, imperialism had fallen into disfavor. Perhaps another reason why the European powers were glad to shed their responsibilities in Africa, is that imperialism had become too costly. While enormous private fortunes were made by some Europeans,[271] it was the Europeans states which met the ever-

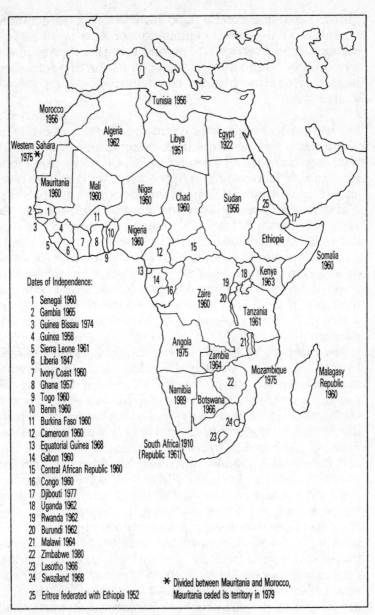

Dates of Independence:

1 Senegal 1960
2 Gambia 1965
3 Guinea Bissau 1974
4 Guinea 1958
5 Sierra Leone 1961
6 Liberia 1847
7 Ivory Coast 1960
8 Ghana 1957
9 Togo 1960
10 Benin 1960
11 Burkina Faso 1960
12 Cameroon 1960
13 Equatorial Guinea 1968
14 Gabon 1960
15 Central African Republic 1960
16 Congo 1960
17 Djibouti 1977
18 Uganda 1962
19 Rwanda 1962
20 Burundi 1962
21 Malawi 1964
22 Zimbabwe 1980
23 Lesotho 1966
24 Swaziland 1968

25 Eritrea federated with Ethiopia 1952

* Divided between Mauritania and Morocco,
Mauritania ceded its territory in 1979

DECOLONIZATION OF AFRICA
MAP XII

growing cost of defending and administering the acquired territories. The overall exploitation of Asia by the West seems to have been a much better business proposition for western governments than the exploitation of Africa. Perhaps that is why western colonialism in Africa was so short-lived.

By 1990 only South Africa remained as an example of white minority rule. Until the coming to power in 1989 of the more conciliatory President F.W. de Klerk, the white elite (firmly convinced that the black and white races should be culturally independent, separate – by apartheid – and distinct) ruled a predominantly black country (in 1985, 4.6 million whites, 21 million Africans, 2.9 million coloreds, 0.8 million Indians). The struggle in South Africa,[272] insofar as it is between black and white Africans, differs from that which has taken place in the rest of colonial Africa. The white Africans' forbears first settled at the Cape in 1652, about thirty years after the "Mayflower" arrived in the New World. They look upon themselves as Africans.

The principle of apartheid, first defined and proclaimed by the Boer leader Dr Daniel F. Malan in 1948 (following the postwar victory of the Boer National Party at the polls), has plagued South African history ever since. It was one of the reasons why South Africa withdrew from the British Commonwealth in 1961. It was the cause of growing divestment by western countries in the 1980s, and the United Nations' sanctions[273] imposed in 1986. All of which – if the elections of May 1987 were any guide – have led not to a weakening but to a strengthening of the Boers' stance. Nevertheless, since the beginning of 1990 hope has been expressed that the attitude shown by President F. W. de Klerk toward the leaders of South Africa's black majority, especially toward the socialist African National Congress led by Nelson Mandela,[274] might bring about the total abolishment of apartheid. More than anything else, it was the policy of apartheid that prevented the white-controlled government of South Africa from re-establishing friendly relations in Africa and abroad. Yet the

Republic of South Africa has a vital role to play in the future economic development of Africa and the world.

South Africa is, after all, the greatest single industrial and military power on the continent. It accounts for half of Africa's productive capacity; it also possesses one of the greatest mineral lodes in the world. Its huge coal (it is the only country in the world presently producing large quantities of oil from coal) and uranium reserves render it independent of outside energy supplies. It produces almost four-fifths of all the gold mined in the non-communist world, and mines more gems, diamonds and platinum than any other country. It is the leading source of antimony, chrome ore, and vanadium. Its supplies of uranium and chrome are essential to the West. It is the leading supplier to the United States of manganese, platinum and industrial diamonds. South Africa is also the only African country with a nuclear capability. Not least important in assessing the geo-political role of white South Africa, is the fact that at least twelve black nations are dependent upon it for trade, access to the oceans, and employment. The oil lifeline between the western industrial nations and the Persian Gulf passes by the Cape route – one of the busiest shipping lanes in the world.

Until the 1980s the United States and South Africa had maintained the strongest and friendliest ties. Investing billions of dollars, hundreds of American companies did profitable business there. American banks have, directly or indirectly, supplied approximately one-third of the money borrowed by government organizations. Although the flight of American commerce and capital during the 1980s from South Africa might be thought to have been unavoidable from a political point of view, it was not achieved without a considerable loss to the American economy. Moreover, America's evacuation from South Africa created a commercial and political vacuum into which the Japanese and other Asians are moving.

Since 1945 the whole of Africa has rid itself of colonial rule. Since then in health services, in education, and in life expectancy, significant progress has been made.[275] Yet progress has fallen far short of expectations. In 1989 many health, education, and social welfare programs were failing. Black-ruled Africa is also suffering from a political malaise that few would have imagined earlier. The western hope that Africa would evolve democratic party politics on the western model has been dashed by regional and tribal rivalry. The Organization of African Unity (OAU)[276] founded in 1963 at Addis Ababa, Ethiopia, remains little more than aspiration. One-party states and military rule are the norm. While military rule is alien to traditional Africa, in 1990 the military was the dynamic element in most African countries. Out of forty-five black African nations, twenty-three were military dictatorships. Few African governments had multiple parties. Most Africans could vote, but only for one man. Only four black African nations – Botswana, Gambia, Mauritius, and Senegal – allowed their people to express themselves freely. Elsewhere in many African countries basic human rights as defined by the West were denied. Scores of African leaders have been assassinated in Africa's ever-recurring purges and coups. In the 1980s massacres of blacks by blacks became commonplace. In 1990 Liberia was torn apart by tribal warfare. In most African countries a free press (as the West would define it) was not tolerated, nor was an independent judiciary. Having thrown off the colonial yoke, Africans now bear a harsher yoke of their own making. Whatever else transpires, Africa is unlikely to develop politically or legally along western lines.

The economic outlook is equally bleak. Instead of fostering the economic development which Africa so badly needs, independence has brought with it a worsening of Africa's economic lot. Despite the Lomé Convention of 1975 between the European Economic Community (EEC) and a number of African countries, which promised reciprocal trade preferences, the foreign trade of many African countries remains either stagnant or sluggish. In 1989 Africa's share of world trade had fallen to 1.5 per cent, half of what it was in 1960. In 1990 twenty-nine of the worlds' forty-two least developed nations were African. Abject poverty grows rather than lessens. Algeria and Nigeria, at one time considered classical examples of indigenous economic progress, are today economically crippled countries. In 1983, to ease its own economic woes, Nigeria expelled two million Ghanians.

Partly due to the advice given by westerners that in developing their countries Africans should follow western practices, independence has been followed by a steady decrease in *per capita* food production. In 1957 nine-tenths of Africa fed itself. Today, while there are some agricultural successes (in recent years countries such as Ghana and Mauritania have increased their grain production considerably), the Republic of South Africa is one of the few states self-sufficient in food. Most major western-induced agribusiness experiments in Africa have failed. Meanwhile the stress placed by the World Bank and the International Monetary Fund (IMF) on mono-cropping and the export of raw materials denies many African countries the broad-based economic growth they so badly need. It has also made Africa particularly vulnerable to volatile commodity prices and unfavorable changes in the terms of trade.

Part of the dramatic change in *per capita* food production must be ascribed to wide-spread drought which has affected the continent for more than a decade. The increase of human and animal pestilence, general mismanagement, and loss of arable land have also reduced the food supply. All of which makes the predicted explosive growth in African numbers more awesome then ever. If present trends continue, the continent's population will double to one billion by the year 2010. Widespread hunger, starvation, and sickness[277] threaten.

Equally alarming is the manner in which the infrastructure of roads, railways, cities and towns built under European rule has deteriorated. When Zaire, then known as the Belgian Congo, gained its independence in 1960, it had 58,000 miles of good roads; now it has 6,200 miles that are passable. The problem extends beyond infrastructure. For want of maintenance, equipment built or financed by westerners has been allowed to fall into disrepair. Steel mills were built that now rust. Dams were constructed that still yield no power. Where small, labor-intensive projects were needed, western-inspired and financed technological "white elephants" have multiplied. One wonders how so many ruinous investments ever came to be made. Any competent economist or geographer could have told those making the loans that these countries did not have the natural resources to pay back the interest on the loans, let alone the capital.

Africa is an example of the difficulties met with in trying to lop off the technology of one culture and fasten it onto another. It is also an object lesson in what happens when the social criteria are allowed to dominate the economic. In the post-1945 era it was thought to be an unquestionably good thing to help the underdeveloped world develop along western lines. It was a period when ignorance of Africa on the part of the western banking community was bliss. Conversely, the indigenous African Development Bank, established twenty-five years ago, has been an impressive success. With an annual lending of more than two billion dollars (the equivalent of the World Bank's assistance to the continent) it provides a striking example of pan-African co-operation and efficiency.

To cap it all, growing poorer by the day, African countries have quadrupled their imports of arms since 1968. If, in spite of its human and material resources, Africa cannot break out of the pattern of setbacks that has plagued it since 1945 then the prospects for the continent, from a western perspective, are dim. The evidence is convincing and frightening. Although it has only one-tenth of the world's population, Africa today accounts for about one third of the world's fourteen million refugees.

It is not difficult to apportion blame for Africa's problems since independence. Most Africans trace their failures to the political and economic distortion caused by the earlier European colonial system. Under western tutelage, Africa was forced to be part of a political and economic organization to which it did not belong. The boundaries which the West arbitrarily imposed on Africa had very little to do with African economic and ethnic realities. In consequence, ethnic differences have brought war to Chad and Nigeria. The Ibo secession in Nigeria in 1967 cost one million lives. Ghana has been troubled for years by a break-away movement from the Ewe tribe, some of whom want to rejoin Togo. Multi-tribal tensions are particularly great in Kenya, Zambia, and Liberia. Since 1962, Ethiopia has fought Somalia over the Ogaden territory to which the Somalians make ethnic claims. Ethnic differences have been the cause of much bloodshed in the Sudan. Only in 1972 did the Sudanese government agree to grant autonomy to the ethnically different South. Notwithstanding this action, the Sudan People's Liberation Army (SPLA) based in the non-Moslem South, continues to fight a wide-spread war against the Sudanese goverment. Such conflicts deny Africa the economic growth and development it so badly needs. Little wonder that the OAU should have laid down the principle at its inception in 1963 that existing frontiers were sacrosanct. In all but a handful of African countries, tribal loyalties still prevail, especially in rural areas where nationalist sentiment never penetrated.

Those Africans who place the blame for their present difficulties on western shoulders have much to support their point of view. The present political despotism and economic malaise is at least to some degree the result of westernization. The disruption of Africa's traditional culture – not least the destruction of spiritual and social values associated with tribal life – is also the fruit of western intrusion. To hear some Africans tell it, it will take a very long time for Africa to recover from centuries of western depredation and cultural shock; and that is assuming that Western colonization has been halted, which present facts belie. Independence has not freed Africa from the threat of foreign domination and meddling; witness the interference of outside powers in Angola and Mozambique. In 1986 the United States bombed Libya. The intervention of outsiders, including the Soviet bloc, the USA, China, and France (whose ex-colonies remain closely tied to the metropolis) continues.

To make the West responsible for Africa's economic and political failures – for its poverty, for its internal wars, and for its mismanagement – is too simple an explanation. It leaves out of account the fact that the Africans have different sets of values and different goals than westerners. African leaders, educated in western universities, have sometimes been just as blind as westerners to the intrinsic values of Africa's cultures. While it is true that Africa was despoiled; while it is equally true that the West did wrong in trying to impose western modernity upon it; Africa cannot hope to escape from its present economic and political dilemmas if it places all blame on others. Only if Africans accept responsibility for their own actions can Africa possibly avoid the threat of increased suffering and privation. If Africa is to play a necessary and constructive role in the world community, it must first rediscover itself. It is African ideas and resolve, rather than foreign leadership and foreign resources that will eventually determine Africa's future.

14
Twentieth Century Latin America

The beginning of the twentieth century marks an important turning-point in Latin America's relations with the rest of the world. In 1900 the dominant outside influence in that region was wielded by France and Britain, whose primary concern was commercial and financial gain rather than political dominance. By 1918, as a result of the First World War, Europe's power over the destiny of Latin American affairs had lessened; that of the United States (whose power on a world scale was now unmatched) had grown. Henceforth, the external relations of the disunited Latin American states would be greatly influenced by the policies of their more united northern neighbor.

North America's myopia and the extraordinary diversity of Latin America have prevented that relationship from being an easy one. Although most of the republics (see Map XIII) share a common colonial and historical background, a common language, religion, legal system, a common political culture, and a common intellectual and educational tradition, it is the enormous variation, the startling contrast, not the common pattern, that prevails. For example, ethnically the Southern Cone nations of Argentina, Uruguay, and Chile are largely homogeneous societies of European stock; Peru, Bolivia, Ecuador, Paraguay, and Mexico are dualistic Indian-Spanish societies; Brazil, Venezuela, and Cuba are blends of Indian, Iberian, and African. Most countries are strongly Iberian in culture. Politically, for most of the twentieth century, the countries have varied from repressive authoritarian regimes (Paraguay until 1989) to liberal and democratic societies (Costa Rica). Economic conditions are equally diverse. Capitalism, socialism, semi-feudalism, and mer-

201

Latin American Republics
with dates of
Independent Statehood

1 Mexico 1821
2 Guatemala 1821
3 El Salvador 1841
4 Costa Rica 1821
5 Belize 1964
6 Honduras 1838
7 Nicaragua 1838
8 Panama 1903
9 Cuba 1898
10 Jamaica 1962
11 Haiti 1804
12 Bahamas 1964
13 Dominican Republic 1844
14 Barbados 1966
15 Trinidad and Tobago 1962
16 Colombia 1886
17 Venezuela 1830
18 Guyana 1966
19 Surinam 1975
20 Ecuador 1830
21 Peru 1821
22 Brazil 1822
23 Bolivia 1825
24 Paraguay 1811
25 Chile 1818
26 Argentina 1816
27 Uruguay 1828

28 French Guiana
29 Puerto Rico (US)

Economic groupings in 1990:

CACM (Central American Common Market)

Andean Group

CARICOM (Caribbean Community)

LAIA (Latin American Integration Association)
formerly LAFTA

LATIN AMERICA IN THE TWENTIETH CENTURY
MAP XIII

cantilist economies exist alongside each other. Argentina, Mexico, and southern Brazil are considered to be industrially developed economies. Ecuador and Paraguay, among others, are essentially agricultural economies. Brazil and the Caribbean nations share a distinct plantation tradition. Socially, the countries vary all the way from virtual feudalism, with rigidly stratified social structures, to increasingly egalitarian conditions. The official languages of Spanish, Portuguese, and French are only three of the many languages spoken. Even military regimes have been intriguingly different: rightist, leftist, nationalist, and a variety of mixed civilian-military regimes exist. Surely, there can be few areas of the world as complex or as rich in paradox. Little wonder if the North Americans sometimes find their diverse southern neighbors perplexing.

The United States seems to have had no inhibitions in fulfilling its destiny as the supreme power of the western hemisphere. Even before the twentieth century began, in 1895, United States Secretary of State, Richard Olney, (in dealing with Britain's boundary dispute between British Guiana and Venezuela) declared his country's supremacy throughout the region. "The United States," he said, "is practically sovereign on this continent, and its fiat is law upon the subjects to which it confines its interposition." It was a conclusion which the British did not contest. In 1901, in the Hay-Pauncefote Treaty, Britain gave the United States a free hand in the Caribbean. Britain had more pressing problems with the Germans in the North Atlantic, the Russians in Manchuria, the Dutch in South Africa, and the French on the Nile. The treaty also renounced an earlier accord stipulating joint Anglo-American construction and operation of a Central American canal.

Also in 1901, as a result of a vacuum of power created by the Spanish American War of 1898, the United States extended its rule to Cuba and Puerto Rico. Under the Platt Amendment to the new Cuban Constitution (1901), the United States assumed the right to intervene in Cuba and to set up a naval base at Guantánamo, which it still occupies. In 1903, by which time Britain had definitely conceded primacy in Latin American affairs to the United

States, President Theodore Roosevelt, who advised his countrymen to "speak softly but carry a big stick", supported a revolution in Colombia's northern province which eventually became the state of Panama, A year later, in 1904, the new nation authorized the United States to build the 51-mile-long Panama Canal joining the Atlantic and the Pacific. Begun in 1904, the canal was completed in 1914. It gave the United States naval forces easy access to either ocean. "I took the Canal Zone," President Roosevelt declared forthrightly, "and . . . while the debate goes on the Canal does also."[278] The sovereignty of Panama and the rights of United States citizens in the Canal Zone have remained a matter of dispute from that day to this.

Under a corollary (announced by Roosevelt in 1904) to the Monroe Doctrine[279] the United States reserved the right of unilateral intervention in the western hemisphere to rectify "chronic cases of wrong doing" or an "impotence which results in the general loosening of the ties of civilized society". Subsequently, under the presidencies of William H. Taft (1909–1913), who became known for his "Dollar Diplomacy", Woodrow Wilson (1913–1921), who, striking a high moral tone, seemed determined to recreate Latin America in the image of the United States, Warren G. Harding (1921–1923), and Calvin Coolidge (1923–1929), the United States assumed the right not only to police Latin America, but to judge it as well.

Nor did the USA fail to match words with deeds. In 1904, 1912, 1916, 1924 and 1965 the United States Army intervened in the Dominican Republic. Similar interventions were made in Nicaragua (between 1909–1910, 1912–1925, and 1926–1933), and Haiti (1915–1934). As an outcome of Mexico's Revolution in 1911, in 1914 the United States Navy bombarded and seized Vera Cruz, Mexico. From 1914 to 1917 the United States continued its military and naval intervention in Mexico. Altogether, between 1898 and 1924, citing threats to the lives and property of its citizens, the United States intervened directly no less than thirty-one times in the internal affairs of Latin America.

Fearful of the growing might of their northern neighbor

(the earlier nineteenth century admiration of the United States had by the end of the century given place to growing distrust), and conscious of the need for common action, the Latin American countries – despite their own deep-rooted divisions[280] – sought to improve relations with each other. Anxious to increase its own commercial, political, and diplomatic influence throughout the hemisphere, the United States fostered such efforts. It hosted the First International Conference of American States in Washington DC in 1889. From this meeting sprang the Washington-based International Union of American Republics, which in 1910 became the Pan American Union.

Yet when war came in 1914 Latin Americans showed a reluctance to follow Washington which favored the Allied cause. They preferred neutrality. Even after 1917, when the United States itself became a belligerent, they held back. The United States had to use considerable pressure before eight of the twenty republics (seven of them tiny Caribbean and Central American nations under the financial control of either Britain or the United States) declared their nominal support of the Allies. Cuba and Brazil, most dependent upon United States markets and money, subsequently offered military aid; five others broke relations with the Central Powers; seven, including Argentina, Chile, Colombia, and Mexico (which openly sympathized with Germany[281]) remained neutral. Important to the Allied cause were the indispensable supplies of primary produce which Latin America provided. The war ended with President Wilson arguing at the Paris Peace Conference in 1919 for national self-determination. To the Latin Americans this seemed ironic, if not hypocritical. At that time five Caribbean nations – Cuba, the Dominican Republic, Haiti, Nicaragua, and Panama – still lay under United States military occupation.

Whereas United States political pressure and direct intervention in Latin America in the period 1900–1918 was felt primarily in the lands around the Caribbean, its economic activity was much more widespread. By 1914 (while Britain still dominated the region's trade and investment, and its pound sterling still provided a kind of international currency), the United States had become the largest trading partner of many Latin American countries. By 1918, by which time the value of Latin America's foreign trade had doubled from $2.2 billion in 1914 to $3.9 billion, the USA was providing about one-third of the imports, and took a little more than one-third of the exports of the entire area. Between 1914 and 1920 United States exports to Latin America tripled. In 1929 the United States provided about 40 per cent of the region's total imports and one-third of its exports. In the countries of the Caribbean and Central America its influence was overwhelming. With little intra-regional trade, and with Europe's share of total trade dwindling in the 1920s, foreign trade with North America had become crucial for many republics.

The shift in Latin American trade from Europe toward the United States during the war did not alter its basic nature. Like colonial trade elsewhere in the world, its raw materials and tropical foods were exchanged for northern manufactures and investment capital. Latin America continued to be dependent on and subservient to the more developed countries of the northern hemisphere. Its economic destiny – whether under European or North American hegemony – relied upon changes in the common western experience to which it was spatially peripheral and over which it had little influence. The wartime policy of import substitution adopted by Argentina, Brazil, Mexico, Chile, Uruguay and others, which led to the region's first industrialization, did little to change this state of affairs.

Latin America's growing reliance upon its northern neighbor for trade during the early decades of the twentieth century was accompanied by a growing dependence upon United States money. Although the USA remained the world's leading debtor nation until the First World War, it had been lending money to its southern neighbors since the 1890s; not least because Latin America offered extraordinary commercial opportunities, and the United States economy had more money than it could profitably absorb. In 1898 United States funds in Mexico, the Caribbean islands, and Central America amounted to more than $300 million. By 1914 the figure stood at $1.7 billion, with Mexico and Cuba accounting for between 30–40 per cent. By then United States investors had acquired 50 per cent of Mexico's oil industry, and 40 per cent of its land (in addition to the Mexican territory seized by the United States in the nineteenth century). Yet United States' holdings (many of them invested in commerce, public utilities, mines, railroads, shipping, and agriculture), were small compared with Europe's ($7 billion). Britain's total investment between 1900 and 1914 had grown from $2.5 billion to $3.7 billion, with Argentina and Brazil receiving 60 per cent of the total, and Chile, Peru, Mexico, and Uruguay taking most of the remainder. In 1914 British investments in the western hemisphere were almost equally divided: 20 per cent of the total was in Latin America, 20 per cent in the United States. French investments, a major source since the 1860s, had grown threefold by 1914 to $1.2 billion. German investments in 1914, principally in Argentina, Brazil, Chile, and Mexico, were about $900 million. Like those of Britain, German funds were equally divided between the northern and southern half of the continent. Until World War I, Europe and North America between them provided much needed development capital to an area rich in natural resources.

The First World War gave the North Americans a tremendous opportunity to increase their financial stake in Latin America. Overall, United States' investments in the war years increased by 50 per cent. In contrast, Germany and France suffered considerable losses. Growing sums of United States direct business investments were used to develop electrical utilities, railroads, and mining. By 1918, 92 per cent of Chilean copper, 50 per cent of Venezuelan, Peruvian, and Colombian oil, 50 per cent of Venezuelan iron, and two-thirds of Cuban sugar were in the hands of United States investors. By then banana monopolies had been established with United States money in Guatemala, Nicaragua, Honduras, and Panama (hence the name the Banana Republics). In 1920 Latin America was receiving almost half of United States direct investments placed abroad.

These sums were not transferred without paying a political as well as a financial price. To safeguard its investments, the United States proceeded to impose control on the fiscal and monetary policies of several states: Nicaragua (1911–1924), the Dominican Republic (1905–1941), Cuba (1920–1923), and Haiti (1915–1941). In Brazil, Venezuela, and Chile, whenever it felt its investments were threatened, the United States also acted (though less belligerently and directly than it had done in the Caribbean and Central America) to extend its financial and political control.

Latin America emerged from the First World War with a new spirit of independence and a new sense of world responsibility. A number of the republics joined the League of Nations – which the United States Congress had rejected – not only to play a greater role on the world stage, but also to provide a counterweight to what they thought were the growing colonizing ambitions of the United States. The German challenge in the Atlantic had died at the Paris Peace Conference of 1919; the possible threats from Britain and Japan had been removed by the Washington Naval Conference of 1921–1922. This left the United States almost invulnerable. Nor did it fear resistance from within the hemisphere. Brazil was large enough to lead an opposition to United States' hegemony in Latin America but its dependence on the coffee market of the United States ruled out any such action. Argentina was antagonistic to the United States but could not obtain support. Except for rare intervention by the League of Nations,[282] there was no counterbalance to United States power in the western hemisphere.

The United States, flushed with its newfound power and fearing no one either inside or outside the region, from 1918 onward intruded in Latin American affairs whenever it thought fit. In January 1926 it landed troops in Nicaragua to overthrow Emiliano Chamorro's government, which it refused to recognize. Resentment against this invasion was given voice at the Inter-American Conference at Havana in January 1928, when the southern republics tabled a motion that " . . . no state has the right to intervene in the internal affairs of another". Only with difficulty did the United States delegation manage to block its passage.

Relations between the northern and southern halves of the American continent worsened until the election of President Herbert C. Hoover (1929–1933). So contentious had relations become that Hoover promptly embarked on a highly successful goodwill tour of eleven Latin American countries. In 1930 he renounced the Roosevelt Corollary to the Monroe Doctrine (which had given the United States the right to intervene in the western hemisphere). In March 1933, in his first inauguration address, President Franklin D. Roosevelt further allayed the region's fear of the United States by declaring his "Good Neighbor Policy". In contrast to its earlier stand, in December that year at the Seventh Conference of American States at Montevideo, Uruguay, the United States reaffirmed that no state in the Pan American Union " . . . had the right to intervene in the internal or external affairs of another". The following year (1934) the Platt Amendment of 1901, which had limited Cuban sovereignty, was abrogated by the United States Senate. The surrender of treaty rights to intervene in the Caribbean basin followed. United States troops were withdrawn from Nicaragua (1933) and Haiti (1934); the financial control which it had exercised in Nicaragua, Haiti, and the Dominican Republic was relinquished. Gradually a sense of growing equality and mutual respect replaced the USA's earlier domineering attitude.

While some Latin American countries met the collapse of the extraordinary wartime boom better than others, by the mid-1920s they had all been hurt by the rapid decline of world trade; some countries were desperate. The value of Chile's and Bolivia's exports, for instance, dropped 80 per cent between 1924 and 1932. Overall, between 1929 and 1932, the value of Latin American exports fell by two-thirds – a perilous situation for a region dependent for its livelihood upon overseas markets.[283] To make matters worse, the price of food and raw materials fluctuated widely. Brazilian coffee which sold at 22.5 cents a pound in 1929, sold at eight cents a pound in 1931. The abandoning of the sterling bill of exchange – the most reliable means of financing foreign trade – and the breakdown of the international gold standard compounded the region's problems. With every country and every part of the world trying to save itself, there was a marked resurgence of economic self-sufficiency.

Efforts made by the United States to halt these trends were unsuccessful. Having agreed at the Geneva Conference on Trade in 1927 that "the time had come to put an end to the increase in tariffs", it then enacted the Smoot-Hawley tariff of 1930, which did the exact opposite. Nor did the bilateral scaling down of its tariff levels with Latin American countries (under the Reciprocal Trade Agreement Act of 1934), because of the use of quotas to control imports, provide much help. So bad did things become that several of the Latin republics were forced to resort to bilateral barter arrangements with European countries.

The end of World War I affected international finance as much as international trade. The complete collapse of the international monetary system in 1929 resulted in widespread default among the Latin American republics. By 1934 four-fifths of United States financial holdings in Latin America were in default. A great deal of the money, especially investments in agriculture and foreign government loans, was as good as lost from the beginning. Indeed, the United States ascendency as the world's leading creditor nation (in 1929 its Latin American investments far exceeded those of all other powers) had in fact been much too rapid for its own good. "I venture to challenge," wrote one authority in 1932 "a denial from any responsible person acquainted with the public borrowings of the years 1926–1928 of the assertion that . . . the bulk of the foreign loans in these years to public authorities in debtor countries would better not have been made."[284] It took a Second World War with its demand for food and raw materials, especially for oil from Venezuela to make good Latin American losses in both trade and investment.

One of the factors changing the outlook of the United States toward Latin America in the 1930s was the fear of communism. Different kinds of socialism had affected Chile, Brazil, Argentina, and Mexico since the depression of the late 1920s. In Brazil in the 1920s and 1930s and in Argentina in the 1930s, there were armed uprisings of communists which caused several governments to outlaw the Communist Party. Yet the only major communist attempt to seize power by force in the interwar years was the unsuccessful 1935 insurrection led by Luís Carlos Prestes in Brazil. By the mid-1930s the menace of communism had been eclipsed by the much greater menace of world war. So great was the threat of war perceived to be that in December 1936, at the Buenos Aires Conference (by which time the Spanish Civil War had begun), President Roosevelt warned those who would carry a war across the Atlantic that they would " . . . find a hemisphere wholly prepared to consult together for our mutual safety and our mutual good". The Eighth Pan American Conference held at Lima two years later in December 1938 – by which time both Europe and Asia were poised for war – not only reiterated its willingness to guarantee the territorial integrity of member states, it also expressed its determination to jointly resist foreign intervention in the American hemisphere. In spite of opposition by Argentina, which preferred to seek hemispheric security through the League of Nations based in Geneva rather than through a collective defense pact based in Washington, the North American outlook prevailed.

When war came in September 1939, the Foreign Ministers of the Pan American states quickly convened at Panama to devise a neutrality zone for the whole western hemisphere. While some countries with close relations to Germany, such as Argentina, Chile, and Uruguay, still feared the North Americans more than the Germans and the Japanese, the majority in due course followed the United States' lead. The collapse of the Low Countries and France during the German invasion of May 1940 brought matters to a head. At a meeting in Havana later that year representatives of Latin America and the United States undertook to oppose the transfer of Dutch and French possessions in the Caribbean and the north-east coast of South America to the victorious Germans. It was further agreed that any foreign attack on any country of the western hemisphere should be considered as an attack upon them all.

Because the Second World War placed Latin America in much greater danger than the First, the need for common action was gradually recognized. In time all the countries joined the Allies; Chile, Argentina, and Uruguay not until 1945. Brazil sent troops to the Mediterranean theater, Mexico (strictly neutral in World War I) sent an air force squadron to the Pacific. As in World War I, the unprecedented quantities of Latin American food and raw materials were much more important to Allied success. By March 1945, when Argentina finally declared war, all the nations of Latin America had broken relations with the Axis Powers. By then the Latin American nations were concerned with laying the political groundwork of the postwar world.

By the time the United Nations' Conference had taken place in San Francisco in 1945, the Latin American republics had already met with the United States in Chapultepec in Mexico City to work out a common position toward postwar development. The Latin Americans were not prepared to sacrifice their independence of action to the United Nations, which was then dominated by European and United States interests. Instead they insisted upon a regional organization within the global network. This was a reversal of their attitude in 1919 when, unlike the United States which had repudiated the League of Nations, they had insisted upon a global rather than a regional organization.

Fortunately, President Harry Truman (1945–1953) took the Latin Americans' point of view. To this end, Article 51 was inserted by the United States government into the United Nations Charter, sanctioning the right of member states to establish regional organizations with powers of enforcement outside the United Nations' authority. The outcome was the Treaty of Reciprocal Assistance, signed by the United States and 21 American republics at Rio de Janeiro in September 1947, which provided a defence alliance from aggression from outside and inside the hemisphere. The treaty confirmed the idea of regional defense first expressed at the Buenos Aires meetings in 1936.

As a sequel to the Mexico and Rio meetings, the Ninth International Conference of American States held at Bogotá, Colombia, in 1948, adopted the United States-sponsored Charter of the Organization of American States (OAS).[285] This was meant to replace the much more loosely organized Pan American Union. The aims remained the same: to establish peace and justice throughout the hemisphere, to ensure collective security, safeguard the territorial integrity and independence of the Latin American republics, and to facilitate their economic, social, and political co-operation.

While the United States' primary concern in helping to found the OAS was hemispheric security, at that time challenged once more by international communism, the main concern of the Latin American nations was to safeguard their sovereign rights. With the onset of the Cold War in 1948, the United States began to look upon the OAS as a military alliance in its fight against communism – an attitude which the Latin republics found difficult to accept. When the United States called upon the republics, at meetings in Caracas, Venezuela, in March 1954, to condemn the domination by any member state by "the international communist movement", its opinion was accepted only reluctantly and only then under the threat of United States economic reprisals.

The reluctance of the Latin American nations to support the United States in its Cold War against the Soviet Union did not deter Washington from acting alone. The fall of the agrarian reformist, left-wing government of President Jacobo Arbenz Guzmán of Guatemala in June 1954 (Arbenz had antagonized the foreign landowners, investors, and the military) was widely attributed to the covert actions of the United States, which used armed Guatemalan exiles to topple Arbenz. Arbenz was followed by Carlos

Castillo Armas who revoked the land reforms, suppressed the leftwing political parties, and concluded a mutual defense pact with the United States. The Guatemalan affair only added to the smoldering fires of resentment against the United States in the hemisphere. When Vice-President Richard Nixon made his 1958 goodwill tour of eight of the republics he was met with extreme hostility.

None of which prevented the United States from using the same tactics against Fidel Castro's Marxist-Leninist regime in Cuba[286] in 1961. In April of that year President John F. Kennedy launched the abortive Bay of Pigs invasion by Cuban exiles, mobilized and trained in the United States. Castro's request to the Kremlin for military protection led directly to the missile crisis of October 1962. By putting missiles in Cuba, the USSR had challenged the hegemony of the United States in its own hemisphere. It had sought to shatter a pattern of United States policy that had been in place since the Monroe Doctrine.

The threat of nuclear war, and a possible communist takeover, quickly changed the attitude of many Latin Americans to Castro (who had been seen as a David taking on a Goliath). Nor did relations with Castro improve once the missile crisis was over. Two years later, in 1964, when Venezuela and others charged Cuba with providing arms to guerilla movements in Latin America, the OAS willingly broke off relations with Cuba entirely. With the exception of Mexico and Jamaica, economic sanctions were upheld by the OAS until 1975. Castro's earlier hopes that Cuba would become the center of Latin American revolt probably ended with the expedition of the Cuban guerilla leader Ché Guevara to Bolivia, and his death there in 1967. Since then Castro has been little more than a pawn in world-wide superpower rivalry.

While President Kennedy's handling of the Cuban missile crisis undoubtedly raised United States prestige in Latin America, his death in November 1963 led to a worsening of hemispheric relations. In 1964 the Johnson Administration (1963–1969) used strong-arm tactics against rioters in Panama. In 1965, claiming " . . . to save the lives of our citizens and all people", as well as "to prevent another communist state in this hemisphere", President Johnson – in violation of the OAS charter – mounted a unilateral militarily intervention against the Dominican Republic.

Johnson's counter-insurgency policy was continued by President Nixon (1969–1974) who quickly abandoned the social and humanistic Kennedy goals. In 1973 Nixon helped to topple Chile's government led by Salvador Allende, the first democratically elected Marxist president of a Latin American nation. While indigenous forces – not least rampant inflation, government deficits, and social tension – were paramount in Allende's fall, his support of the ongoing nationalization of copper and other foreign corporate assets, held by firms such as Anaconda, Kennecott, and ITT, was a factor in sealing his fate. The repressive military junta, led by General Augusto Pinochet which overthrew and succeeded Allende, at once initiated a process of privatization of the holdings of the Chilean state.

With President Jimmy Carter's election in 1976, the Johnson and Nixon counter-insurgency strategy was abandoned. In an effort to exclude military governments within the hemisphere, Carter terminated military assistance to several right wing dictatorships; a new stress was placed upon human rights. In 1977 Carter endeared himself to the Latin republics by obtaining recognition of Panamanian authority over the Canal Zone.[287] What he was unable to do was to bring peace to Central America.

With President Ronald Reagan's election (1980–1988) the United States' policy once more returned to unabashed, unilateral military intervention. Reagan promptly lifted restrictions on military assistance to Latin American governments which the Carter Administration had found to have been in violation of human rights. Twice – in the Caribbean island of Grenada in 1983 (to prevent the establishment of a Cuban-dominated regime), and in Panama in the fall of 1989 (with the declared intention of stemming the flow of narcotics by capturing General Noriega, whom the OAS refused to condemn, as well as to maintain the security of the Canal Zone) – the

United States intervened militarily. American actions in Grenada and Panama were clear violations of the Charter of the OAS, a document which the United States had helped to draft. In Nicaragua[288] the United States gave military aid to armed exiles until there was no alternative for most Nicaraguans (other than more war) but to accept a United States-sponsored president. In El Salvador, where 60,000 people have died in war since 1980, the United States has also provided military aid to right-wing governments. In 1982, during the Malvinas (Falkland Islands) War, in contrast to most Latin American leaders who overwhelmingly came out in support of Argentina, it unilaterally assisted its NATO ally Britain. Whereupon the United States was accused of practicing a double standard: while Soviet armed intrusion into the western hemisphere had been resisted, British armed intrusion in the defense of the Falkland Islands was being tolerated, even assisted. To the traditional charges against the United States of subversion and intervention was added the charge of betrayal. Political reality in 1990 was that the United States was still the superpower in the area and that, despite the OAS Charter and international law, it would resort to unilateral intervention wherever it felt its interests, or the interests of its European allies, were threatened.

The United States' apparent disregard for the OAS stems partly from the fact that the Latin American republics have rarely spoken with one voice. The political and economic turmoil of the region has never made for concensus; impermanence and uncertainty rather than firmness of resolve have dominated the political scene. This is as true of the relations within Latin American countries as it is between them. Between the 1930s and 1980s well over a hundred heads of state had been replaced by other than constitutional means. Bolivia has experienced almost two hundred coups since its independence in 1825. Even Brazil, which has been spared the worst abuses of caudillism (and which in 1989 returned once more to popularly elected civilian rule) experienced Getulio Vargas' seizing of dictatorial power in 1937. His overthrow in the bloodless revolution of October 1945, and the military coup that once more ousted him from office in 1954 led to his suicide. With United States assistance Brazil's Joào Goulart was likewise ousted by the military in 1964. Since 1960 Argentina has had almost a score of military coups. In 1973 Uruguay and (with United States support) Chile became military dictatorships. In 1990 Chile returned to its long democratic tradition. Ecuador's return to civilian control in 1979 was heartening until one realized that it was the nineteenth time in 149 years. The history of the area suggests that the surge of democracies in the 1980s in Chile, Uruguay, Argentina, Brazil, Bolivia, Nicaragua, Paraguay, and Panama may prove to be still one more swing of the political pendulum. "Democracy," said Ms. Altolaguirre, a professor at the Francisco Maroquin University in Guatemala City, "has not become a process by which men govern, but a licence to do whatever they want once they're in office.[289]" Disunity, instability, and discontinuity remain the scourge of Latin American political life.[290]

The end of the Second World War, which reinforced the long-term trend toward absolute United States political and economic dominance within the hemisphere, witnessed the usual postwar decline in world demand for primary produce and raw materials. With a smaller share of a shrinking world market, Latin America remained a precariously dependent economy, especially for those countries which relied on one or two major products, such as Bolivia (tin), Chile (copper), Mexico and Peru (cotton and oil), Uruguay (wool), Venezuela (oil), and Colombia (coffee and cocaine). Furthermore, until the early 1970s, the fluctuating price of primary produce was consistently tilted (as it has been on and off since the 1880s) in favor of the manufacturing countries of the northern hemisphere. Imports averaged about ten per cent more than exports.

Because of these less favorable circumstances, in the ten years ending in 1959 the external expenditures of primary producing countries, such as those of Latin America, exceeded their annual income from abroad by $30 to $40 billion. Thereafter, until the oil price rises in the 1970s[291] (which brought temporary prosperity to oil-producing countries such as Venezuela and Mexico, and increased costs for fuel for those countries without oil), the divergence in favor of manufactures became greater. In due course, the postwar world economy experienced a remarkable economic expansion, but it was an expansion in which the industrialized countries gained most.

While the influx of petro-dollars in the 1970s gave some relief to Latin American countries in their eternal struggle to make ends meet, overall, from 1945 to 1990, the outflow of funds (as flight capital, profits, interest, and royalties) has exceeded the inflow. Brazil's total capital receipt for the period 1947–1960 was $1.8 billion; its total outgoings were $3.5 billion. Between 1960 and 1966, the flow of direct investment from United States to Latin America amounted to $2.8 billion. Repatriation of profits and income was $8.3 billion.

Great hopes were held out in the 1960s that Latin America's disadvantages in world trade and investment could be offset by industrialization and import substitution. In 1990 such hopes remained unfulfilled. What industrialization there has been in Mexico, Argentina, Chile, Uruguay, and Brazil has not provided economic independence. Industrialization in the southern hemisphere has never been the dynamic element it was in the north. Conditions are so dissimilar that it is almost pointless to try to draw a parallel between the two. There never was the same tendency in Latin America for the technology of the more developed sectors of the economy to spread spontaneously nation-wide. Instead, the dynamic element for economic change remains not the independent profit-seeking, risk-taking entrepreneur, but what it has always been: the state.

The greatest outside effort to promote economic development in the southern half of the western hemisphere these past thirty years was President Kennedy's comprehensive Alliance for Progress[292] launched in 1961. The target set was an annual overall increase in *per capita* income of 2.5 per cent. The total cost was estimated at $100 billion over the next decade, of which the United States undertook to pay $20 billion.

Though progress was made in some quarters, the Alliance, like all the efforts at Latin American integration, sadly disappointed its high hopes. By 1970 Latin America's annual *per capita* economic growth rate was nearer 1.5 per cent than the 2.5 per cent proposed by the Alliance. The proposed political, social, and economic changes, agrarian reform, and more equitable tax structures were never realized. With the assassination of President Kennedy in 1963 expectations receded, the momentum of reform was lost. Gradually the earlier view under President Kennedy that the United States would "carry any burden, pay any price . . ." to become the protector and benefactor of the non-communist world, gave way to a more critical attitude – not least because of the growing arms race and the war in Vietnam.

The Alliance failed primarily because it was unrealistic. The idea that a grandiose scheme and $100 billion could change the nature of Latin American life was visionary. The proposed agrarian[293] and financial reforms – which some Latin American leaders suspected would bring revolution to the region – received little more than lip service. The first goal of the Alliance, democracy, was similarly ignored. Indeed, the opposite was achieved. Brazil under Goulart moved in the direction of a Marxist rather than a democratic government. The democratic regimes in Brazil, Argentina, Peru, Ecuador, the Dominican Republic, Honduras, Panama, and Bolivia were all deposed during the 1960s by the military.

The collapse of the Alliance not only caused growing dissatisfaction with United States policy within the hemisphere, it encouraged the leaders of Latin American countries to cultivate their economic relations with areas other than North America. While in 1990 the United States remained the dominant trading nation in Latin America,[294] since the 1970s West Germany[295] (Latin America's second most important trading and investment partner after the United States), Canada, and Japan have all grown in importance. By 1970 Japan took about seven per cent of the region's total exports as compared to about three per cent in 1956–1958. Because of the growing activity in Pacific rim countries, that figure has risen to about ten per cent. After the United States, Japan has become a major customer of Mexico, Peru, and Brazil. With the exception of its relations with Cuba, the contribution of the Soviet Union to Latin American trade since the 1960s has been minimal.

Since the 1970s there has been a similar increase in the flow of money from the EEC, Canada, and Japan. Yet the United States still retained a commanding position in private and public investments throughout the region.[296] By 1968 the United States share of all private foreign investment in Latin America was still about 70 per cent. Four-tenths of the United States total of $17 billion was invested in petroleum mining; 70 per cent of it was in Venezuela, Brazil, Mexico, and Argentina. Because of the influx of money from Europe, Canada, and Japan, the United States share of private foreign investment in 1990 stood at a lower level.

Nothing has changed the financial picture of the region since the 1970s as much as the inundation of Latin America (by way of the United States and Europe) of a surfeit of Arab petro-dollars. In comparison with past totals, the scale of Latin American foreign debt has become gigantic. Whereas total indebtedness of the region in 1969 (before the oil price rises of the early 1970s) was about $20 billion, by 1982 outstanding loans to Latin America's five largest debtors: Mexico, Brazil, Argentina, Venezuela, and Chile were larger than the total capital of the United States banking system. By 1990 Latin American foreign debt had risen to approximately $500 billion. Borrowing on this scale would not have mattered if it had been used to create sufficient funds to service the debt. Instead, much of it (some say half) was used to re-equip and enlarge the military, conceal budget deficits, increase imports, offset flight capital, and assuage political allies. To a considerable extent, the money borrowed from international agencies such as the Inter-American Development Bank, the IMF, and the World Bank was used to finance huge but largely barren "white elephant" projects, such as dams, steel mills, and petrochemical plants.

The end of Latin America's borrowing spree came with

the second oil price shock of 1979. Floating interest rates soared; the economies of North America and Western Europe went into recession; the United States experienced double digit inflation. Because of steeply rising interest rates, between 1978 and 1981 Brazil's net interest payments on its foreign debt more than tripled (from $2.7 billion to $9.2 billion). During the 1970s and 1980s, for countries such as Brazil, Argentina, Peru, Ecuador, and even oil exporting countries such as Venezuela and Mexico, debt service payments as a percentage of exports rose sharply until by 1984 it was consuming almost half of their foreign earnings.[297] In 1990 the possibility of widespread default still threatened hemispheric finance.

Defaulting on foreign debt is not unprecedented. In the nineteenth century nine states of the United States defaulted. Britain and France defaulted on loans to the United States in the 1930s. They did so on grounds similar to those used by the leaders of Brazil, Peru, and Mexico during the 1980s. Their obligations, they said, "to meet the needs of the people were greater than legal obligations to creditors". Nor is there anything unusual about imprudent loans, or a state's ability to squander whatever domestic or foreign sums it receives. Twice in recent decades (in the 1920s and again in the 1970s) the United States made loans to Latin American countries that on any sound banking principle would be difficult to service, impossible to repay. The one thing that is new about Latin American indebtedness is its scale.

Even before the present debt crisis compounded an already difficult trade situation, Latin American countries had made several combined attempts to grapple with the trade problems of the region. During the 1960s and 1970s they sought relief by joining with other parts of the developing world to control the drastic price fluctuations in some of the region's principal exports: oil, copper, bauxite, tin, fruit, coffee, cocoa, iron ore, phosphates, and mercury. Most of these efforts proved unsuccessful. They also tried to increase the economic integration of the region through the Latin American Free Trade Association

(LAFTA),[298] 1960, the Central American Common Market, (CACM)[299] 1960; the Andean Group,[300] 1969; the La Plata Basin Group,[301] 1969; and the Caribbean Community (CARICOM),[302] including the Caribbean Common Market, 1973.

Between 1960 and 1965 LAFTA achieved considerable trade liberalization. Since then, largely because of historical rivalries, topography, national sovereignty, population pressure, dissimilar size and power, and the endemic disunity of the entire region, the movement has come to a standstill. The needed political will to make LAFTA a success is still lacking. Hence the resort made to sub-regional groups, such as the CACM or the Andean Group where dissimilarities were not so great. While the Central American Common Market has proved more successful than LAFTA (between 1960 and 1965 regional trade increased seven-fold), the goal of full integration by 1966 has proved equally unrealistic;[303] not least because of the wars fought by El Salvador, Honduras, and Nicaragua.

One should not allow the seeming intractability of Latin America's political and economic problems to obscure the enormous richness and potential of the region. Until the sharp fall in the world demand for raw materials in the 1980s, many countries in Latin America, including Mexico, Brazil, and Venezuela had experienced remarkable rates of growth and development. Rates of industrial growth in Mexico and Brazil in the early 1980s were in fact greater than those of several North Atlantic countries. Brazil (always "the giant of tomorrow"), despite its desperate financial troubles, is still the eighth largest economy in the world. In 1989 it had a foreign trade surplus. Mexico's economic performance in the opening months of 1990 was especially encouraging. Helped by trade liberalization, by a strengthening of oil prices, by the return of flight capital and other new investment inflows, as well as by increased agricultural exports to the United States, for the first time in ten years Mexico's economic growth exceeds population growth. In 1990 Chile presented a heartening example of a successful transition to democracy. Since 1986 there has been improvement in growth rates, investment, exports, and debt reduction. Ultimately, what matters is not how well or badly these countries are doing relative to the richer nations of the world, but how well or badly they are doing by their own absolute standards.

Yet one should not minimize the problems that face the countries of Latin America. The region shares with sub-Saharan Africa and the Middle East the highest levels of population growth in the world. It is plagued by corruption, mass urbanization, poverty, grim unemployment, labor unrest,[304] and hyperinflation. In 1990 Latin America was printing money to the point where inflation rates had become incredible. Peru's inflation rate in 1988 was 1,720 per cent; in 1989 it was 2,775 per cent. In early 1990 Argentina had an inflation rate of about 3,000 per cent. Carlos Saul Menem, who was elected President in December 1989, called "fighting inflation" his first priority. Latin America is an area where for the masses the standard of living is falling. In a continent of over 350 million people, the bottom 40 per cent take home only seven per cent of GNP. Real *per capita* income in 1989 was nine per cent lower than it was in 1980. In Brazil, Venezuela, Peru, and Argentina, it is less than it was in 1970. Foreign debt is growing and with debt, dependence. For many countries international trade opportunities lessen; the terms of trade worsen. Of central importance, in 1990 the land-owning, commercial, financial, and industrial oligarchies, in allegiance with the hierarchy of the church and the military, still resisted changes that threatened their power. Indeed, one might say that most violence in Latin America has been exercised not to change the *status quo* but to uphold it. While it is true that the Church has generally resisted change, in Brazil, Chile, and El Salvador segments of the church have been progressive.[305] While new values must eventually replace old beliefs, and new forms of communication must break down Latin America's traditional power structure and isolation, in 1990 most countries of the region were still committed to the past.

One lesson that emerges from Latin America's experience in recent decades is the difficulty of trying to help that area from the outside. As in Africa and the other poorer parts of the world, the economic development of Latin America appears to have been much too vast, much too complex and paradoxical for the outside world to be able to introduce fundamental change. No amount of outside money, no refined economic prescription, it seems, has been able to recreate in this area the much more favorable circumstances for development that Western Europe and North America knew at an earlier stage of their unique passage of history. Another lesson is the extent to which the interests of the countries of both the southern and the northern halves of the American continent have become intertwined and interdependent. Latin American immigrants have given the United States the fourth-largest Spanish-speaking population in the western hemisphere. Between 1965 and 1990 fourteen million legal immigrants entered the United States – eighty per cent were Hispanics and Asians. One to two million illegal immigrants enter the United States every year. In 1990 Latin American debt, illegal immigrants, and narcotics threatened the stability of the United States. The war on narcotics has given a new twist to the relations between the United States and the other countries of the hemisphere. It has also made military intervention more probable. Meanwhile, oblivious of the fact that Latin America might well become their Achilles heel, the people of the United States in 1990 were preoccupied with eastern Europe and the Middle East.

15

Epilogue: The Threat of World Anarchy

Five hundred years ago the center of world power lay in Asia. Four centuries later Europe had gained dominion over the earth. Inspired by the messianism and dynamism of Christianity, by the rationalism and sense of curiosity and progress which emerged from the Renaissance, as well as by the new stress placed upon individualism by the Protestant Reformation, the Europeans laid claim not only to the lands but the seas and the oceans of the earth. Supporting those claims was their will to power, their sense of racial superiority, and their superior naval technology and weaponry. Except for China and Japan, which soon shut their doors to the West, European interests and European values gradually became paramount.

By 1914 almost the whole world had become an appendage to the West. Only Japan in Asia,[306] and Liberia and Ethiopia in Africa, had remained free of European control. Western resolution, Western confidence, Western economics, Western values and laws, Western systems of transport and communications, Western science and technology, Western industries and finance, Western sicknesses and medicines, and especially Western armaments, had combined to change the world. Its superiority matched only by its moral outlook, the West felt it had a duty to organize, govern, and develop the whole world. It is Europe's unparalleled influence that some parts of the world are presently trying to unlive.

But then came the First Great War, dwarfing in horror all the wars that had preceded it. The Europeans having created wealth on an unparalleled scale proceeded to use it to destroy each other. Because Europe was the fulcrum of world political and economic power, the war eventually became world-wide. Never before had so much suffering been inflicted upon Europe. At Verdun and Passchendaele, on the Somme, and at Ypres – in a tragedy that could have been avoided – Europe's hopes were buried. The economic stability upon which the Euro-centric world economy depended was undermined. Out of the ensuing chaos emerged Lenin and communism, Mussolini and fascism, Hitler and nazism. It was as a result of untold slaughter and suffering that Marxism-Leninism first took hold in Russia and then in the world.

In 1939 – demonstrating the height of human folly – a second, and even greater war broke out. Nothing has had greater influence in shaping the world in which we live than the two world wars. Faced by the dictators' determination to use brute force, the Western democracies had little choice but to fight. Six years of savagery followed. By 1945 Europe lay in ruins. The only countries powerful enough to think of controlling the world were the United States and the Soviet Union. With the collapse of German power in central Europe, the United States and the Soviet Union, for the first time in their history, found themselves facing each other across the barricades. So great were the capitalist and communist powers that they deceived themselves into believing that they could unilaterally impose their will on the entire world. Only gradually did they realize that there were parts of the world that would not be dictated to by Moscow or Washington.

This was especially true of the group of new and old nations which appeared in the 1950s under the designation of the Third (or developing) World. The Third World, including China, India, Indonesia, and parts of Africa and Latin America – much of it the imperial world of the Europeans which two world wars had washed away – accounted for most of the world's population. In the eighteenth century countries like China and India were known for their wealth. As a result of the Industrial Revolution of the eighteenth and nineteenth centuries, by 1914 the previously rich nations had become relatively poor. Because of the lopsided concentration of productive power and wealth in the industrial areas of the world (in particular in Europe, North America, and Japan), as well as what were for some countries the debilitating effects of Western imperialism, the Third World became relatively poor and almost entirely anti-Western. "Our nation will never again be an insulted nation," said Mao in 1949, "We have stood up." Mao was expressing the hope of so many of the poorer people of the world that they could break the economic and political ties with the West which had kept them subservient and humiliated for so long. Thanks to him and other Third World leaders, in the poorer parts of the world a new pride was born, a new hope was expressed for material improvement. The hope still lives; the actual material improvement remains unrealized.

Since the late 1940s the maldistribution of wealth has become a central issue in world politics. For the people of the Third World the issue no longer is capitalism versus communism, or the Western versus the Eastern bloc, but affluence versus poverty. Between 1945 and 1965, a period of unparalleled increase of wealth in the world, the gap between the rich and the poor nations – between the so-called developed and the least developed countries – doubled until one-sixth of the world's population was obtaining 70 per cent of the world's real income. By the mid-1970s the gap had widened still more and the trend has continued. In 1989 the forty-two poorest countries (twelve per cent of world population) were becoming relatively poorer with growth rates lagging behind the increase in population (average annual growth of the countries' gross domestic product was 2.3 per cent during 1980–1988, compared with a 7.2 per cent target set by a United Nations conference in 1981). The poorest countries' share of world exports was equally disturbing. Faced by the declining trend in world prices for primary commodities and domestic policies that have restricted their export development, exports declined to 0.3 per cent in 1988, compared with 1.4 per cent in 1960.[307]

In the 1980s the problem of the rich and the poor of the world was exacerbated by the world debt problem which not only made the poor poorer, but threatened to destabilize the world economy. The present phenomenal indebted-ness[308] of the Third World to the West (being matched since 1985 by the United States' indebtedness to Japan and Europe) carries with it the danger of financial collapse on a world scale. In 1989 the relation between the poorer and richer nations of the world had reached a paradox. While the repayment of loans by the poorer to the richer nations was being made only by impoverishing the poorer nations still more, the richer parts of the world continued to absorb the capital of both the developed and the under-developed world. As much of the money loaned to the Third World was subsequently channelled to the United States and Europe as debt service and flight capital, the Third World, the developing world, was receiving little financial assist-ance. Even where massive transfers of capital have taken place, money alone seems to have done little good to the poorer parts of the world (see Chapter 14).

Economically, the world has also been at risk since the 1940s from the inordinate capacity of the world's defense industries to consume an ever-greater proportion of wealth. Defense spending has become one of the indis-pensable economic pillars of the modern state. So much so that in many nations military expenditures during these years exceeded public outlays for education and health combined. By 1990 much of the scientific manpower and capital formation of the Western world was being used by defense industries. For the United States the price of increased defense spending during the 1980s has been unprecedented indebtedness, wide-spread profligacy, and a loss of competitive ability in world markets.[309] By 1990 the military-industrial complex against which President Eisenhower had warned in his 1961 Farewell Address[310] had become a reality.

The extent of defense spending since the late 1940s was no better in the Soviet Union, and was much worse in the impoverished Third World. Between 1977 and 1987 the Third World spent forty per cent of the $580 billion they borrowed on arms. Military spending has always followed an upward course, but the upward spiral has never been as rapid or as alarming as during the past decade. Indeed the sale of arms has become a major item of international trade. In 1982, for the first time, world imports of arms exceeded world imports of grain. Nor can sharp changes be made to these huge military outlays overnight. While the defense budgets of both the developed and the developing world must be looked upon as a grievous loss of economic resources, a significant and sudden curtailing of arms production has always carried with it a serious risk of economic recession.[311]

No less a threat to the world community has been the growth in recent decades of religious fanaticism, particularly in the Middle East (see Map XIV). Even though Israel, Syria, Iraq, Jordan and the PLO, all major players in the Middle East drama, are secular-oriented, the militant versions of Judaism and Islam are becoming explosive.[312] The Semites (both Arabs and Jews) now influence world affairs, especially since the creation of Israel in 1948 and the OPEC oil embargo of 1973, as they have not done for centuries. In particular, Islam has now returned to the center of the stage of world politics. In the countries of North Africa and the Middle East, as well as in the Sudan, Islamic fundamentalists are intent on obtaining political power. Iran has been transformed by the ongoing Islamic revolution initiated by Khomeini. Egyptian President Anwar Sadat was assassinated by Sunni fundamentalists. Kuwait, Bahrain, and Saudi Arabia have all been attacked by Shi'ite fanatics who believe that any regime not under the rule of the prophet's true heirs may be justifiably overthrown. The Shi'ites of southern Lebanon, following Israel's invasion of Lebanon in 1982, have usurped the traditional role of the PLO in trying to drive Israel out of occupied territory. In the countries of North Africa and the Middle East, Islamic political fervor is growing.

If Islam reserves its sharpest criticism for the United States, it is because America's influence has grown at a time when the other colonial powers have been in retreat. The United States is seen as the last of the Western colonial powers, the successor to Britain and France. America is now identified with secular, materialistic, Western modernization

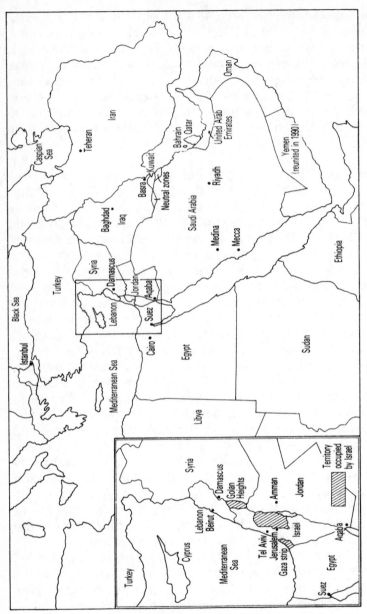

THE MIDDLE EAST IN 1990
MAP XIV

to a greater extent than other Westerners. Paramount in arousing the hostility of the Muslim world is what is perceived as America's unqualified support of Israel. Every victory of United States power in the Middle East increases the underlying friction between the Muslim world and the West.

With the resurgence of Judaism and Islam and the new vigor which Pope John Paul II is giving to Christianity, especially in Africa and Latin America, theism is on the rise again (see Map XV). There is a new search for meaning, for consolation, for refuge, for a total perspective, which some people do not find in communism, or nationalism, or Western modernism. There can be no more striking example of this than the freeing of religious worship in the Soviet Union in 1990. The power of the spiritual word, whether voiced by Jerusalem, Mecca or Rome (and now perhaps Moscow) is once more in the ascendancy.

The extraordinary resurgence of theism during the past decade should make us chary of ascribing the power of a nation to any one factor. In the last resort, it is not the power of religion, or the military, or economics that make up the power of a nation; nor is it impersonal "dynamics". It is people. On the evidence of the past half millenium, it is people that are the greatest resource that any nation possesses. The world power struggle must surely take account of productive economic forces, but it must also allow for what people feel, think, and do. The limits to the possible have been set in the past more by human imagination, than by material resources.[313] It is here that the intangible forces, including spiritual, religious, ethnic, and cultural, must play an important role.

There are few such intangible forces at work in the world today that carry with them a greater threat to world peace than revolutionary nationalism. The idea of nationalism which first emerged in the Western world has now been taken up across the globe. While it is true that there are more sovereign nation states than there have ever been – in 1989 there were 171 – it is equally true that there are more stateless nations seeking nationhood.

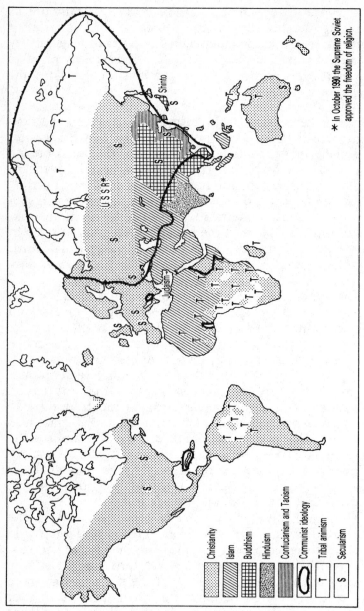

* In October 1990 the Supreme Soviet approved the freedom of religion.

Christianity
Islam
Buddhism
Hinduism
Confucianism and Taoism
Communist ideology
T   Tribal animism
S   Secularism

WORLD RELIGIONS IN THE 1980s
Map XV

National aspirations, as well as religious fanaticism, are at the heart of the struggle since 1948 between the Palestinians and the Israelis in the Middle East. In 1990 Iraq's Saddam Hussein was appealing to the ideal, and perhaps illusion, of Arab nationalism. Age-old national aspirations lie at the heart of the discord between the British and the Catholic Irish in Northern Ireland, between Flemings and Walloons in Belgium, between Catalonian separatists and Spain, between the Baltic states and the Soviet Union, and between English- and French-speaking Canadians. National conflicts are growing in Soviet-controlled Central Asia, including Islamic Azerbaijan, Tadzhikistan, Kirghizia, and Kazakhstan. As a result of the growing demands for national independence the USSR was replaced by a Commonwealth in December 1991. Similar problems face the former Yugoslavia; Serbia and Croatia continue to dispute the territory of Bosnia and Herzegovina. Hungary and Romania dispute the territory of Transylvania. Following the Yalta Settlement in 1945, German Pommerania, Silesia, and part of East Prussia were transferred to Poland (see Map VIII), thereby sowing the seeds of future border disputes between Poland and Germany (reunified on 3 October 1990). Since 1974 an armed truce has existed between Turkey and Greece in Cyprus. In Turkey, Syria, Iran, Iraq, Afghanistan and the Soviet Union, dissenting Kurds, Baluchis, and Pathans also seek national independence. India is plagued with the national aspirations of (among others) the Sikhs, the Hindu Bengalis, the Kashmiris, and the Tamils of Sri Lanka. China is faced with the growing demands for autonomy being made by the Tibetans and by its Islamic minority living mostly in the Xingiang Province. The Ibo's failure to form an independent state of Biafra in 1966–1970 is only one of many unsuccessful attempts made since 1945 by groups of Africans to achieve self-determination (see Chapter 13). Elsewhere the threat of militant, exaggerated nationalism grows. The threat to world peace continues.

This threat – whether it springs from an economic, a spiritual, or a political source – is no less strong today than it was in 1500. Crude power, strategy, and interest remain the language of international relations. It was not moral criteria, or love and voluntary co-operation, or international law that determined the outcome of world affairs these past five hundred years; nor was it the supposed death throes of capitalism or communism; rather it was conflicting interests and ever-changing levels of force.

What has entered a new phase is the destructive power of mankind. One American stategic submarine in 1990 possessed more firepower than all the cannons that have fired in history. In devising weapons that can destroy the world we have neutralized power. The world has been at bay since 1945 not because – as in 1939 – a group of evil men sought world dominion, but because of the almost incomprehensible damage that man can now inflict upon the world. If there is any correlation between the growing number of nuclear warheads available to small as well as great powers (about 57,000 at the end of 1989, the equivalent of 3.5 tons of TNT for every human being on this planet[314]) and the security of the human race we must reluctantly conclude – despite the Geneva talks and the INF Treaty of 1988[315] – that the world is still a very dangerous place. Somewhere down the road, perhaps because of the on-going proliferation of weapons, perhaps out of desperation, impulse, or weariness, or madness, or terrorism, some group will use nuclear, or biological, or chemical weapons (as the Iraqis did recently against the Kurds). If, at this stage in history, we cannot abolish war, we can and should make a beginning by abolishing weapons of mass destruction.[316] One cannot harbor illusions about the difficulties of this task. But then one cannot harbor illusions about the possibility of a world conflagration, either. On the evidence of the past, if it is war we prepare for, it is war we will get.

Ironically, because of the threat of annihilation, the optimist who looked at the world at the beginning of 1991 might have concluded that in terms of war and peace the world was more stable than it had been since the beginning of the twentieth century. The retreat of communism in eastern Europe and the world, coupled with the strenuous efforts made by the Soviet and American leaders to improve their relations, had helped to strengthen the belief that the threat of world war had been banished. There was a feeling of euphoria because the Cold War was ended; peace had broken out; the Berlin Wall had fallen; there was talk of sharing a peace dividend. On 19 November 1990, in Paris, the twenty-two nations making up the North Atlantic Treaty Organization and the Warsaw Pact signed an arms-control treaty which provided for a massive reduction of conventional weapons. Two days later, in the Charter of Paris, thirty-four European and North American states proclaimed the end of the "era of confrontation and division". A Permanent Conference on Security and Cooperation in Europe was established. Our sophisticated, technocratic internationalism was thought to have brought the world to the end of history.

While the threat of world war is only one of the threats that face mankind, it is no mean thing to have reduced that threat. (In economics, health care, politics, ecology, the pollution of the biosphere, widespread drought, the wasting of the world's non-renewable resources, and especially in the present explosion of world population,[317] mankind is still at risk). The threat of world anarchy arising out of nuclear conflict between the superpowers has certainly lessened. The specter of Russian invasion which had haunted Europe since the 1940s has vanished; the Brezhnev Doctrine, enunciated in 1968 to justify the Warsaw Pact countries' invasion of Czechoslovakia, has been abandoned. More than any other leading statesman, Gorbachev grasped the point that world politics needed an entirely new configuration; one in which the idea of a bipolar world ruled by two superpowers, or even by one superpower has become outdated. The collapse of communist power in eastern Europe has caused a radical change in the geopolitical equation. The Iraqi crisis has suddenly thrust the United Nations to the center of the world stage, providing it with new powers and new opportunites. In 1990 an unusual emphasis was being placed by both the Soviets and the Americans on the need for international law and international government.

The optimist might also point to the fact that since 1945, among the leading powers, problems have never been allowed to get completely out of hand. Regional wars have never been allowed to become world-wide. In Berlin, in Korea, in Vietnam, in Afghanistan, in Angola, in Israel, in Syria, and in Egypt, the superpowers have had a dozen excuses for going to war, but have always drawn back. Except for minor skirmishes along the border between China and the USSR, words were always substituted for blows. Because there can be no victory in an all-out third world war, the world's leaders have avoided a general conflagration. Time and again, the balance of terror has saved the world from utter destruction or total anarchy. Indeed, one might conclude that military power (having become concentrated largely in the hands of the now cooperative United States and the ex-Soviet Union) ought to be easier to control. Even allowing for the diffusion of power that has taken place since the 1950s – allowing, that is, for the resurgence of Beijing, Tokyo, and Bonn, and the rise of Riyadh and Rio – it is evident that the USA and Russia are still major actors in the world power struggle.

In continuing to strike an optimistic note, on the evidence of the past forty years, there are further grounds for hope for an alternative to warfare in the growing voluntary economic and political cooperation between nations. With the receding of bipolarism, future emphasis would seem to lie not in world-wide military alliances but in coalitions of nations based upon regional, religious, cultural, economic, and political ties and interests. The EEC, founded in 1957 by the Treaty of Rome, has brought more peace to Europe than crude force ever did. Other examples are the Association of South East Asian Nations[318], the Arab League[319], the Organization of African Unity[320] and the Organization of American States.[321]

The multi-national EEC, founded with the object of gradually integrating the European economies and eventually obtaining political union,[322] has become the world's leading trading community with 40 per cent of world exports. In 1985 faced by growing United States and Japanese competition, the European Community (EC) set 31 December 1992 as the date when money, goods, people, and services would move freely throughout Europe. Political unity has presented greater difficulties.[323] Only the future knows whether by 1992 Europe will have resolved problems concerning immigration, tax, trade, and monetary policy in order to transcend nationalism and become a new world power. (See Map XVI)

Relief from national militancy might also come from the ever-growing number of international corporations, as well as from internationally recognized financial organizations such as the World Bank and the International Monetary Fund. Indeed, there are aspects of the world economy today which the nation-state is powerless to control; globalism in business – which demands a world rather than a national outlook – is limiting the economic and military powers of the nation-state. A new economic order far from Adam Smith's stress on the nation is emerging, in which a new emphasis is being placed on the weal as well as the wealth of nations. The older concepts of *homo economicus*, value-free economics, and a faceless self-regulating market are being disputed. Capitalism having triumphed over communism is now challenged by ecology.

Economic power – whether conscious of social obligations or not, whether expressed by a nation, or a regional grouping of nations, or by an international organization – is on the rise. World trade,[324] which in the past six years, 1984–1990, has expanded at a rate exceeding anything experienced since 1945, might become an alternative to Great Power military rivalry. Of growing relevance to the world are geoeconomics as well as geopolitics. The economic power held by some countries – Japan, for example – has come to outweigh the military power held by others. Before the onset of the Iraq-Kuwait crisis in the Middle East, the trend in 1990 was for military superiority to be temporarily eclipsed by economic superiority.

A study of the world during the past half millennium suggests that such optimism is incautious, not least because it is too reasonable. In human affairs there is always the element of the incalculable. Action based on emotion rather than reason has always had a fatal attraction. In world politics a bland trust in reason as a sovereign standard of truth applicable at every level of human activity is very recent and very fragile. The leaders of the French Revolution of 1789 took pure reason as the basis of their formidable work of destruction. The West errs in assuming that its own exceptional "Age of Reason" is normal and universal. To this day, countries like China, or those of the Middle East, are incapable of basing a world outlook on rationality alone. With them, because of the deep religious and cultural differences, the West holds a dialogue of the deaf. Reason, we are discovering, is not a universal attribute. On the contrary, it is a tiny island threatened by a sea of primeval emotions, passions, prejudices, and vitality. The same can be said for Western forms of democracy. In 1990 there were remarkably few examples of a working democracy either in the whole of Africa or in the Middle East. Setbacks in the communist world during the late 1980s and the new democratic states that have appeared in eastern Europe and Latin America, coupled with the growing cooperation shown by members of the United Nations – however heartening – should not lead us to believe that a new age of reason has arrived. Nor should we minimize the threat which the disintegration of communism entails. Viewed geopolitically, the decline of Soviet power might well introduce a new and more dangerous era. The Cold War did at least provide a balance, one power offsetting the other; there was a common basis of understanding; a degree of reason prevailed. Unless it lies with the United Nations, there is no such balance today. Instead, there is one superpower, the United States, which cannot understand why it no longer enjoys the overwhelming economic power that it had in 1945.

Economically and politically, the Great Powers must adapt to an entirely changed world where the rules of the Cold War no longer apply. Because of the fear of a communist or capitalist threat, the common commitment of the NATO and the Warsaw Pact nations was upheld. With the Cold War ended and the Warsaw Pact dissolved, divergent political, economic and commercial interests are emerging, especially in eastern and western Europe and Japan.

As for the euphoria that accompanied the ending of the Cold War, one cannot help recalling the nationalist euphoria that swept across Europe during the 1830s and 1840s, out of which only Greece and Belgium achieved independence. Elsewhere – in Poland (1830), Germany (1848), Italy (1848), and Hungary (1849) – after much bloodshed, nationalist aspirations were crushed. Euphorias have a habit of fading. Stability in human affairs is a myth, as the war which broke out in the Middle East in January 1991 confirms.

The optimist's proposition that military power concentrated in the hands of the United States and the ex-Soviet Union should make the world a safer place also needs to be questioned; not least because the superpowers represent only eleven per cent of the world's population. Arms control without the agreement of the other eighty-nine per cent of the world is a meaningless exercise. It was ignorance that permitted the two superpowers to see the threat to world peace purely in terms of what the other was doing or not doing – sometimes as if the rest of the world did not exist.

Far from another general conflagration being unlikely, some problems seem to invite war. The most we can hope for at this point is not to banish war – as long as people are people conflict will remain – but to limit it.[325] The seemingly insoluble Arab–Jewish problem in the Middle East, central to the politics of that region, certainly threatens ongoing conflict. Iraq's invasion of Kuwait brought war to the Middle East. No less a threat to world peace are the tensions that exist (despite Gorbachev's visit to Beijing in 1989) between the Soviet Union and China.[326] The most fortified and perhaps the most dangerous frontier in the world is that separating the USSR from China. In 1945 Moscow was in a position to dictate to Beijing. In the 1990s with the Mongol and Tatar hoof beats of a much earlier age still echoing in their ears, Russians look to eastern Asia with growing fear. In 1988 the Russians had fifty-seven of their best divisions protecting their eastern Asian

1 *Netherlands
2 *Belgium
3 *Luxembourg
4 ° Switzerland
5 Czechoslovakia
6 Albania
+ Germany reunited in 1990

* Members of the European Community
   Members of NATO
° Members of EFTA
   (European Free Trade Area)

EUROPE IN 1990
Map XVI

possessions.[327] In Brezhnev's time the number was about seventeen. In 1987, Gorbachev expressed the Soviets' willingness to remove Russian nuclear missiles from Europe but he was reluctant to remove them from eastern Asia. In recent years India has drawn closer to Moscow because it too has frontier problems with China. China still has the territory it seized from India in 1962.

Since the recognition by America of the People's Republic of China, Beijing has sought a coalition with the United States against the Soviet Union. While economic, social, and geographic reasons leave the United States no option but to go on playing the role of a major power in Asia and the Pacific, such a coalition, while doing nothing to cement the relations between China and the United States, would add considerably to the risk of a major confrontation. China's attempt to rid itself of its rigid communist orthodoxy and become more pluralistic ended on 4 June 1989 with the massacre of Chinese students in Tiananmen Square. In 1990, hoping to improve its trade relations, the American government extended most favored nation status to China. Power politics are as much alive in the East as they are in the West.

While recognizing the central role of power in any society, we must surely work for something better. We cannot be satisfied with the moral poverty of present-day Machiavellism. What must strike anyone who studies world history since 1500 is the relativism in morals. To protect the state, it seems that anything was permissible.[328] Sometimes the difference between one country's outlook and that of another strikes one as hypocritical. It seems possible for the greatest powers (democratic or totalitarian) to uphold the sanctity of law on the one hand, while espousing lawlessness on the other. Violation of human rights in one country is deplored; equal or worse violations elsewhere, despite the Helsinki Accords of 1975, are ignored. There can be no true justice in world affairs as long as double standards prevail. International courts and tribunals might decide what is legally and morally right or wrong, but they cannot enforce their decision. At this point in history only a nation-state can do that.[329] Against the backcloth of the past half millennium, it too often did so, not because of legal or moral principle, but because of national interest and expediency. Political expediency of nations these past five hundred years, rather than law and morals, seems to have carried the day.[330]

Yet unless we can effectively ensure international law and order – and that means meeting acts of aggression with superior force – we run the risk of world anarchy. But to ensure international law and order is easier said than done. While a body of international law exists and is generally accepted, its details are still very much disputed.[331] Law by itself, national or international, without the will to enforce it, is not going to take us very far. It is not new titles or a new set of laws that are needed; above all, it is a new resolve to apply the laws we already possess. It also entails the formulation of new moral criteria.[332]

With the passing of the Western empires and the end of the Cold War old problems are reemerging, and must be re-negotiated. We are now poised between the geopolitics of the Western Age and the geopolitics of a new world order in which regional ethnic, religious and national aims are re-asserting themselves. The new powers that are appearing on the world scene – most of whom did not count during the Western era – will not respect the map that the West has drawn. As in the 1500s, we have reached a period of trans-ition in world history in which the balance among civilizations must change dramatically. The overwhelming power of the West is now under increasing challenge.

Whatever the basis of future rivalry and accord between human kind, ultimately, in the building of a better, safer world, we shall have to live and let live. We shall make little progress as long as we refuse to accept the fact that truth is shared; that no nation, no continent, no race has a monopoly of truth; that all societies, all human institutions have rela-tive strengths and weaknesses. The world is going to have to tolerate different concepts of God, man, nature, morality, economics, government, and society. It is going to have to decide what the focus of its efforts should be: man or matter. In the rise and expansion of the West, man was elevated to a dominant place in nature; today there is a danger of the opposite occurring. Yet, unless our efforts are directed to enhancing the value and significance of human life, life itself will have been in vain. The choice is ours to make. For myself, I turn from this study of the past five hundred years strengthened in the belief that the human spirit will prevail.

Select Bibliography

Listed below are works of a general nature. They exclude the references given elsewhere in this volume. Except as noted, the dates given are for first editions.

For more comprehensive bibliographies see my trilogy:

Impact of Western Man, A Study of Europe's Role in the World Economy 1750–1960, rev. ed., Washington DC, 1982.

America's Impact on the World, A Study of the Role of the United States in the World Economy, 1750–1970, London, 1975.

The Struggle for World Power, 1500–1980, London, 1981.

Acheson, D., *Power and Diplomacy*, Cambridge, Mass., 1958.

Adamthwaite, A.P., *The Lost Peace: International Relations in Europe 1918–1939*, London, 1980.

Addington, L.H., *The Patterns of War Since the Eighteenth Century*, Bloomington, Ind., 1984.

Albrecht-Carrié, R., *The Meaning of the First World War*, Englewood Cliffs, N.J., 1965.

Ambrose, S., *Rise to Globalism: American Foreign Policy Since 1938*, 4th ed., New York, 1985.

Andrews, K.R., *Trade, Plunder and Settlement*, Cambridge, 1983.

Aroian, L. and R.P. Mitchell, *The Modern Middle East and North Africa*, London, 1984.

Ashton, T.S., *The Industrial Revolution*, Oxford, 1948.

Ashworth, W., *A Short History of the International Economy*. London, 1962.

Barnet, R., *Global Reach*, New York, 1974.

Barnett, A.D., *China's Economy in Global Perspective*, Washington, DC, 1981.

Barraclough, G., *An Introduction to Contemporary History*, London, 1964.

Barraclough, G., ed., *The Times Atlas of World History*, London, 1978.

Bartlett, C.J., *The Global Conflict, 1880–1970: The International Rivalry of the Great Powers*, London, 1984.

Baumont, M., *The Origins of the Second World War*, New Haven, 1978.

Bianco, L., *Origins of the Chinese Revolution 1915–1949*, Stanford, Cal., 1971.

Blakemore, H., *Latin America*, London, 1966.

Boorstin, D.J., *The Discoverers*, New York, 1983.

Boxer, C.R., *Four Centuries of Portuguese Expansion*, Berkeley, Cal., 1969.

Braudel, F., *The Mediterranean and the Mediterranean World in the Age of Philip II*, 2 vols., New York, 1972.

Brierly, J.L., *The Law of Nations: An Introduction to the International Law of Peace*, Oxford, 1955.

Bull, H., *The Anarchical Society: A Study of Order in World Politics*, New York, 1977.

Bushnell, D. and N. Macaulay, *The Emergence of Latin America in the Nineteenth Century*, New York, 1988.

Butterfield, H., *The Origins of Modern Science*, New York, 1956.

Carr, E.H., *The Bolshevik Revolution 1917–1923*, 3 vols., London, 1953.

Carr, R., *Spain 1808–1975*, 2nd. ed., Oxford, 1982.

Carr, W., *Poland to Pearl Harbor*, London, 1985.

Cipolla, C.M., *The Economic History of World Population*, Baltimore, 1962.

Clark, G.N., *Early Modern Europe from about 1450 to about 1750*, London, 1957.

Claude, I.L., *Power and International Relations*, New York, 1962.

Clissold, S., *Latin America: New World, Third World*, New York, 1972.

Craig, G.A., *Force and Statecraft: Diplomatic Problems of our Time*, New York, 1983.

Curtin, P., *The Atlantic Slave Trade*, Madison, Wisconsin, 1969.

Daniels, R.V., *Russia, the Roots of Confrontation*, Cambridge, Mass., 1985.

Davidson, B., *Africa in History*, London, 1968.

Davis, D.B., *Slavery and Human Progress*, New York, 1984.

Dawson, C., *The Dynamics of World History*, New York, 1956.

Deane, P., *The First Industrial Revolution*, Cambridge, 1965.

Dehio, L., *The Precarious Balance*, New York, 1962.

Divine, R.A., *Causes and Consequences of World War II*, Chicago, 1969.

Draper, T., *Israel and World Politics*, New York, 1968.

Easton, S.C., *The Rise and Fall of Western Colonialism*, New York, 1964.

Edwardes, M., *Asia in the European Age*, London, 1961.

Elliot, J.H., *Imperial Spain, 1469–1716*, London, 1963.

Emerson, R., *From Empire to Nation: The Rise to Self-Assertion of Asian and African Peoples*, Cambridge, Mass., 1960.

Fairbank, J.K. and Teng Ssu-yu, *China's Response to the West*, Cambridge, Mass., 1954.

Fairbank, J.K. ed., *The Chinese World Order*, Cambridge, Mass., 1968.

Fieldhouse, D.K., *The Colonial Empires: A Comparative Study from the Eighteenth Century*, London, 1966.

Fisher, C.A., *South-East Asia*, London, 1964.

Foreman-Peck, J.A., *A History of the World Economy: International Economic Relations Since 1850*, Brighton, Sussex, 1983.

Fulbright, J.W., *The Arrogance of Power*, New York, 1966.

Fussel, P., *The Great War and Modern Memory*, New York, 1975.

Gann, L.H. and Duignan, P., *Africa and the World*, San Francisco, 1972.

Gansler, J.S., *The Defense Industry*, Cambridge, Mass., 1980.

Gillard, D., *The Struggle for Asia 1828–1961*, London, 1977.

Gilpin, R., *War and Change in World Politics*, Cambridge, 1981.

Graebner, N.A., *America as a World Power*, Wilmington, Del., 1984.

Hall, D.G.E., *A History of South-East Asia*, New York, 1955.

Halle, L.J., *The Cold War as History*, London, 1967.

Halperin Donghi, T., *The Aftermath of Revolution in Latin America*, New York, 1973.

Hanke, L., *Modern Latin America*, Princeton, 1959.

Harrison, J.A., *The Chinese Empire*, New York, 1972.

Heilbroner, R.L., *Marxism: For and Against*, New York, 1980.

Herring, G., *America's Longest War: The United States and Vietnam 1950–1975*, New York, 1979.

Herring, H.C. and H.B., *A History of Latin America*, New York, 1955.

Hillerbrand, H.J., *The World of the Reformation*, New York, 1973.

Hobsbawm, E.J., *The Age of Revolution 1789–1848*, London, 1962.

Hsü, I., *The Rise of Modern China*, New York, 1975.

Johnson, P., *Modern Times: The World from the Twenties to the Eighties*, New York, 1983.

Jones, F.C., *Japan's New Order in East Asia: Its Rise and Fall 1937–1945*, London, 1954.

Kann, R.A., *A History of the Habsburg Empire 1526–1918*, Berkeley, Cal., 1974.

Kedourie, E., *England and the Middle East*, London, 1956.

Keegan, J., *The Second World War*, London, 1989.

Keen, B. and M. Wasserman, *A Short History of Latin America*, Boston, 1980.

Kennan, G.F., *Russia and the West under Lenin and Stalin*, Boston, 1961.

Keylor, W.R., *The Twentieth-Century World: An International History*, Oxford, 1984.

Khouri, F.J., *The Arab-Israeli Dilemma*, Syracuse, New York, 1968.

Kindleberger, C.P., *The World in Depression: 1929–1939*, Berkeley, Cal., 1973.

Knorr, K.E., *The Power of Nations*, New York, 1975.

Koch, H.W., ed., *The Origins of the First World War*, New York, 1972.

Kohn, H., *The Age of Nationalism: The First Era of Global History*, New York, 1962.

Lach, D.F., *Asia in the Making of Europe*, Chicago, 1965.

Lamb, D., *The Arabs: Journeys Beyond the Mirage*, New York, 1987.

Landes, D.S., *The Unbound Prometheus: Technological Change and Industrial Development in Western Europe from 1750 to the Present*, Cambridge, 1969.

Langer, W.L., *An Encyclopedia of World History*, Boston, 1972.

Laserson, M., *Russia and the Western World*, New York, 1945.

Levin, N., *The Holocaust: The Destruction of European Jewry, 1933–1945*, New York, 1968.

Lewis, B., *The Arabs in History*, London, 1950.

Linder, S.B., *The Pacific Century*, Stanford, Cal., 1986.

Marriss, S., *Deficits and the Dollar: The World Economy at Risk*, Washington DC, 1985.

Mayer, A.J., *Politics and Diplomacy of Peacemaking*, New York, 1967.

McEvedy, C., *The Penguin Atlas of Recent History*, Harmondsworth, Mddsx., 1982.

McNeill, W.H., *The Pursuit of Power*, Chicago, 1982.

Mead, R.O., *Atlantic Legacy*, New York, 1969.

Minogue, K.R., *Nationalism*, New York, 1967.

Morgenthau, H.J., *Politics among Nations*, New York, 1948.

Mortimer, R.A., *The Third World Coalition in International Politics*, New York, 1980.

Moulder, F.V., *Japan, China, and the Modern World Economy*, Cambridge, 1977.

Myrdal, G., *The Challenge of World Poverty*, New York, 1970.

Needham, J., *Science and Civilization in China*, vols. 1–5, Cambridge, 1954–1962.

New, J.F., *The Renaissance and the Reformation: A Short History*, New York, 1969.

Nogueira, A.F., *The Third World*, London, 1967.

Oliver, R. and A. Atmore, *Africa since 1800*, London, 1969.

Panikkar, K.M., *Asia and Western Dominance*, London, 1953.

Parry, J.H., *The Age of Reconnaissance*, London, 1963.

Paxton, R.O., *Europe in the Twentieth Century*, New York, 1975.

Pipes, R., *The Russian Revolution*, New York, 1990.

Polanyi, K., *The Great Transformation: The Political and Economic Origins of Our Time*, New York, 1944.

Price, A.G., *The Western Invasions of the Pacific and its Continents*, Oxford, 1963.

Reischauer, E.O., J.K. Fairbank, and A.M. Craig, *East Asia*, rev. ed., Boston, 1989.

Reischauer, E.O., *Japan: The Story of a Nation*, New York, 1974.

Reynolds, R.L., *Europe Emerges: Transition Toward an Industrial World-Wide Society*, Madison, Wisconsin, 1961.

Riasanovsky, N.V., *A History of Russia*, New York, 1963.

Robertson, E.M., *The Origins of the Second World War*, London, 1971.

Robertson, J., *Future Wealth*, London, 1989.

Romein, J., *The Asian Century*, Berkeley, California, 1962.

Rosenberg, N. and L.E. Birdzell, *How the West Grew Rich*, New York, 1986.

Rostow, W.W., *The World Economy*, Austin, 1978.

Schell, J., *The Fate of the Earth*, New York, 1982.

Shafer, R.J., *A History of Latin America*, Lexington, Mass., 1978.

Skidmore, T.E. and P.H. Smith, *Modern Latin America*, New York, 1984.

Smith, W.C., *Islam in Modern History*, Princeton, 1957.

Snyder, L.L., *The New Nationalism*, Ithaca, New York, 1968.

Spear, T.G.P., *India: A Modern History*, Ann Arbor, Michigan, 1961.

Spence, J., *The Gate of Heavenly Peace*, New York, 1981.

Stavrianos, L.S., *Global Rift: The Third World Comes of Age*, New York, 1981.

Stein, S.J. and B.H., *The Colonial Heritage of Latin America*, New York, 1970.

Taylor, A.J.P., *The Origins of the Second World War*, New York, 1962.

Taylor, R., *The Sino-Japanese Axis*, New York, 1985.

Taylor, T., *Munich: The Price of Peace*, Garden City, N.Y., 1979
Toland, J., *The Rising Sun: The Decline and Fall of the Japanese Empire*, New York, 1970.
Toynbee, A.J., *Mankind and Mother Earth: A Narrative History of the World*, New York, 1976.
Treadgold, D.W., *The Great Siberian Migration*, Princeton, 1957.
Trevor-Roper, H.R., *The Rise of Christian Europe*, New York, 1965.
Troeltsch, E., *Protestantism and Progress*, Boston, 1958.
Van Alstyne, R.W., *The Rising American Empire*, New York, 1960.
Van Leeuwen, A.T., *Christianity in World History*, London, 1964.
Viljoen, S., *Economic Systems in World History*, London, 1974.
Wallerstein, I.M., *Africa: The Politics of Independence*, New York, 1961.
Wang, G., *China and the World Since 1949*, London, 1977.
Webb, W.P., *The Great Frontier*, Boston, 1952.
Wight, M., *Power Politics*, London, 1978.
Wilson, C.H., *The Transformation of Europe 1558–1648*, London, 1976.
Wolpert, S., *A New History of India*, rev. ed., Oxford, 1989.
Wrigley, E.A., *Population and History*, New York, 1969.

Notes

1. The historian-philosophers Ernst Troeltsch (1865–1923), Benedetto Croce (1866–1952), and R.G. Collingwood (1889–1943) considered the comprehension of the present as the final goal of all historical study. Understanding the present is not the only legitimate goal of history, but it is a very important one.
2. Published in Leipzig in nine volumes, 1883–1888.
3. A.O. Hirschmann, *National Power and the Structure of Foreign Trade*, 1945, examines the relation between economic and political power.
4. Contrary to the western Greco-Roman tradition, which is mental and intellectual, Gandhi epitomized India's spiritual traditions. Gandhi was fortunate in that he was not opposed by out-and-out tyrants either in South Africa or India. Had he been opposed by someone like Hitler or Stalin, not much would have been heard of his "soul force".
5. Consider the examples of regional co-operation (such as the EEC) that have taken place in every continent since 1945.
6. A point emphasized by the philosopher Karl Jaspers (1883–1969): "All the crucial problems are world problems". See his *The Origin and Goal of History*, London, 1953, the first part of which deals with "World History".
7. See J. Huizinga (1872–1945), "Fundamentals of Culture", *In the Shadow of Tomorrow*, 1936.
8. The French astronomer and mathematician, Pierre Simon Laplace (1749–1827), the father of present-day futurists, thought differently: "Give me full knowledge and I will predict the future precisely," he said.
9. The line that had been drawn along arbitrarily chosen meridians of longitude was moved 270 leagues to the west in 1494. The new line brought Brazil within the Portuguese half of the world.
10. The German philologist and philosopher, Friedrich W. Nietzsche (1844–1900) expressed in his *Der Wille zur Macht* the will to power and the cult of force.
11. The years 1300–1450 were a virtual *Götterdämmerung* of feudal Europe.
12. Caesar and the Christian God had unified Europe; nationalism was to diversify it. One of the strongest root causes of the First Great War, 1914–1918, was an excess of nationalism.
13. Prior to the mid-nineteenth century, the term "Christian nations" was used regularly in western diplomatic exchanges. After Muslim Turkey was invited to join the Concert of Europe in the mid-nineteenth century, the term "civilized nations" was substituted for "Christian nations".

14. In the early sixteenth century they were thought to number about fourteen million as against Spain's five and England's two-and-a-half million.

15. The Islamic religion began with Mohammed's flight from Mecca to Medina on 16 July, AD 622 (the *hajira*). The basic statement of Muslim belief is contained in the *shahada*, which holds that "There is no God but Allah, and Mohammed is His prophet." The whole of Mohammed's revelation is written down in *The Koran*. Like Judaism and Christianity (but unlike other Asian religions, such as Hinduism or Buddhism), Islam claims to be the most perfect revelation of God's will. In their monotheism (the worship of a single god) Islam and Christianity are the two branches of the Judaic tree. Islam differs from Judaism and Christianity in that it has no ten commandments. Instead it has a definite set of laws – the *Shari'a*, or straight path – which provides guidance to every aspect of a Muslim's life. The god of Islam, unlike the Christian god of love, is a god of power who tempers his justice with mercy.

16. It continues to do so. See chapter 8, note 149.

17. Europe had responded to the growing Islamic threat by closing its ranks under the papacy and the renewed Roman (later the Holy Roman) Empire. Charlemagne was crowned as emperor in AD 800. Its counter-attack took the form of eight major crusades launched between 1096 and 1270.

18. Between 1512 and 1520 the Ottomans also conquered Syria, Palestine, and Egypt.

19. Blocked in Europe, the Arabs extended their rule in Africa. Hundreds of years later the western Christians would make similar inroads into the "Dark Continent". The success of Islam – one-third of the present African population is Muslim – far exceeded the gains of Christianity. Islam imparted a sense of time (five times a day the faithful must worship) and direction (in praying they must turn to Mecca).

20. When the Prophet Mohammed died in AD 632, Ali, his son-in-law was denied his right to become Islam's leader. But Ali persisted in his claim and in AD 656 was installed as the rightful successor (caliph) to Mohammed. Five years later he was assassinated by religious rivals. His son Hussein, who now fought to establish his own claim as Islam's leader, was subsequently tortured and killed at Karbala in Iraq. Karbala, the place of Hussein's martyrdom, was used by the Shi'ite Iranians as a rallying cry in their recent war against the Iraqi.

21. Persian for Mongol.

22. The development by the British of a deeper sense of responsibility toward the Indians had, in fact, preceded the Mutiny, and is reflected in the emancipation of slaves, the abolition of female infanticide, and the suppression of Suttee (the burning of Hindu widows). Other changes took place in education, administration, and the dispensing of justice. The growing use of the English

language after 1833 encouraged the study of western science and political ideas.

23. Its population in the fifteenth century, 100–130 million, is thought to have been twice that of the whole of Europe.

24. The conquest of China by the nomadic Mongol horsemen and their more numerous Turkish allies in the fourteenth century is an example of a more civilized, cultured people being overwhelmed by a less refined, more aggressive foe. However primitive the Mongols may have appeared, they founded the largest contiguous empire there has ever been. Marco Polo, carrying a Mongol "passport" in the form of a seal, made an unhindered journey from the Mediterranean to the Yellow Sea in the late thirteenth century. Only the Egyptians in the West (in 1260 at Ain Jalut, Palestine), and the Japanese in the East (1274 and 1281), were able to withstand the Mongol tide.

25. Confucius, known originally as Kung Chui (551–479 BC) was a public administrator and teacher who profoundly influenced Chinese philosophy and ethos.

26. As President Theodore Roosevelt did with his "Great White Fleet" almost half a millennium later.

27. See Philip F. Riley and Others (eds.), "Cheng Ho: Ming Maritime Expeditions," in *The Global Experience, Readings in World History since 1500*, Englewood Cliffs, New Jersey, 1987, Vol. II, pp. 3–5.

28. Much earlier, at the naval battle of Lepanto in 1571, Venice and her allies had destroyed Islam's hold on the eastern Mediterranean, with the result that Venice became the most powerful state south of the Alps.

29. Jacob Burckhardt's *The Civilization of the Renaissance in Italy*, 1860, provided the first rounded synthesis of Italy's contribution. On the contributions of Arab Spain, Byzantium, and Northern Germany, see Wallace K. Ferguson, *The Renaissance in Historical Thought: Five Centuries of Interpretation*, New York, 1948. Despite all the work that has been done: in character, causes, and geographical and chronological limits, the Renaissance remains one of the most intractable problems of historiography.

30. Copernicus studied at Padua and Bologna. In 1503 he obtained his doctorate of canon law at Ferrara. Galileo was professor of mathematics at Padua.

31. See J.B. Bury, *The Idea of Progress*, New York, 1955.

32. The stress upon personal salvation is reflected in the works of St Augustine (AD 354–430) *The Confessions*, AD 400; Thomas Hobbes (1588–1679) *The Leviathan*, 1651; and Martin Luther (1483–1546).

33. Christianity combined a material with a spiritual role. It is not only concerned with the resurrection of the spirit, but of the body as well.

34. Christianity's certainty is sometimes ascribed to the fact that like Judaism and Islam, it is monotheistic, that is, it knows only one God.

35. Spain's contending material and spiritual elements eventually culminated in the Spanish Civil War (1936–1939).
36. One of the principal aims of the order of the Jesuits, founded in 1534 by the Spaniard Ignatius of Loyola (1491–1556), was to counteract the Protestant Reformation.
37. Contrast this with the English novelist, Tobias George Smollett (1721–1771), who wrote at a time when England's respect for money and commerce grew by the hour: "Without money, there is no respect, honour, or convenience to be acquired in life."
38. Spain's population in 1500 was about nine million; by 1700, because of war and empire-building, it had fallen to approximately six million. Especially significant were the terrible losses Spain sustained in Germany and the Netherlands during the Thirty Years War, 1618–1648.
39. See Werner Sombart, *Der Moderne Kapitalismus*, 1928.
40. The Spanish Inquisition, established in 1478, had much more popular support than we are sometimes led to believe. Contrasted to the greater horrors that have been committed in our own age, its victims were relatively few, and strictly accounted for.
41. See Max Weber, *The Protestant Ethic and the Spirit of Capitalism*, London, 1930. See also Hisao Otsuka, translation by Masaomi Kondo, *The Spirit of Capitalism, The Max Weber Thesis in an Economic Historical Perspective*, Iwanami Shoten, Tokyo, 1982.
42. See R.H. Tawney, *Religion and the Rise of Capitalism*, London, 1936.
43. With the shift of trade from the Mediterranean to the Atlantic, Antwerp (before Spain sacked it in 1576) had become an international port rivalling Genoa and Venice.
44. Said Spain's Don Francisco de Quevedo y Villegas (1580–1645): "As poor men we conquered the riches of others; as rich men these same riches are conquering us."
45. Even though a Spanish state did not yet exist in 1492. The *Reconquista* was chiefly the work of Castile.
46. Although we tend to link Dutch fortunes with the sea (in 1670, Dutch tonnage equalled that of England, France, Portugal, Spain, and the German states combined), agricultural improvements were also important. See Jan De Vries, *The Dutch Rural Economy in the Golden Age, 1500–1700*, Yale, New Haven, 1974.
47. Europeans reached the Americas long before Columbus. See Tim Severin, *The Brendan Voyage*, New York, 1978. Also Alfred W. Crosby, *Ecological Imperialism*, Cambridge University Press, 1986, chapter 3, "The Norse and the Crusaders". Artifacts found off the coast of Brazil suggest that the Romans may have discovered the New World before the birth of Christ.
48. Portuguese power in the Indian Ocean in the sixteenth century rested upon its superior naval artillery. The capture by the Portuguese of Goa (1510), and the Strait of Hormuz (1515), made their control of the Indian Ocean possible. The Muslim fleets, though superior in numbers, were no match for them.

49. See Geoffrey Parker, *The Military Revolution*, Cambridge University Press, New York 1989.
50. Sea power was all-important during the past half millennium.
51. Broken by da Gama, who returned in 1499 from the East with pepper, cinnamon, and cloves. He had sailed in a single, unbroken voyage from Southern India to Lisbon (bypassing Venice, the *entrepot* for the European spice trade). It took about twenty years for the Muslim merchants who controlled the shorter route to Europe through the Red Sea to partly reassert their control of the eastern trade.
52. In 2540 years of recorded Chinese history the Yellow River has flooded 1590 times.
53. See E.L. Jones, *The European Miracle*, Cambridge University Press, 1981 and W.H. McNeill, *Rise of the West: A History of the Human Community*, Englewood Cliffs, N.J., 1970.
54. Johann Wolfgang von Goethe (1749–1832), *Faust*. In contrast the genius of Greek culture was its capacity to be diverted from action to the study of action.
55. Lao-tzu, its founder, was born c.600 BC.
56. Even allowing for the Persian and Mogul miniatures.
57. Daoism aims at individual salvation, but it is mystical rather than rational.
58. A student in Tokyo does not say his father is an attorney or a mechanic. He says his father is an attorney with Mitsubishi or a mechanic with Toyota.
59. After the French philosopher René Descartes, c.f. Chapter 5.
60. See William Woodruff, *Impact of Western Man, A Study of Europe's Role in the World Economy 1750–1960*, rev. ed., Washington DC, 1982.
61. And the same is true of Vasco da Gama's rounding of Africa in 1497, and Ferdinand Magellan's attempt to circumnavigate the globe in 1519.
62. So much so that in 1707, England and Scotland began to call themselves the United Kingdom of Great Britain. The song *Rule Britannia, Britannia rules the waves* dates from 1740.
63. Coupled with British victories at Wandewash (1760), Pondicherry (1761), and Buxar (1764).
64. Little more than a century after Waterloo, British supremacy was undermined by the far greater strain imposed by the First Great War. Conditions in the post-1918 years were to prove much less favorable to Britain than they had been after 1815.
65. See Chapter 8.
66. See Alfred W. Crosby cited above, Chapter 9, "Ills".
67. In the Ottoman Empire all railroads were operated by European companies; in China most of the railroads belonged to Europeans by 1911. The same was true of Africa and South America.
68. Its introduction to Africa is said to have altered the course of African history. According to some writers, maize helped to offset

the loss of lives caused by the slave trade. Statistically, very little is known.

69. Karl Jaspers, in his *Origin and Goal of History*, p. 76, quotes the German philosopher Hegel: "The Europeans have sailed around the world and for them it is a sphere. Whatever has not yet fallen under their sway is either not worth the trouble, or it is destined to fall under it."

70. Though the Czars of Moscow would rule over the Ukraine only after the mid-seventeenth century.

71. In 1700, Russia (with about 17.5 million people) was the most populous state in Europe next to France (19.0 million). Britain's population at this time was about 9.0 million; the Habsburg Empire 8.0 million; Prussia 2.0 million; Spain 6.0 million.

72. See J.V. Stalin, *Works*, Vol. XIII.

73. The 1908 poem "On the Field of Kulikovo" by the Russian poet Alexander Blok is a brilliant distillation of the Russian view of war and the nature of power.

74. In 1849 Russia had helped put down a rebellion against the Austrian throne. In 1866, when Prussia threatened Austria, Russia left Austria to her fate.

75. Although the Treaty of Berlin of 1878 had granted Serbia its independence, the coveted territories of Bosnia and Herzegovina remained under Austrian occupation.

76. England's Richard the Lionhearted, whom English schoolboys are taught to respect, could sit unmoved at Acre (during the Crusades) while 2,700 infidel Muslims were beheaded before him. Alas, when compared with history's other dark figures, such as the Mongol Timur (Tamerlane), Richard emerges as relatively unimportant in the history of carnage.

77. See W. Bruce Lincoln, *Red Victory*, New York, 1990.

78. See Robert Conquest, *The Harvest of Sorrow*, Oxford, 1986.

79. Stalin's mother had hoped that her son might become a priest. She attached little importance to his appointment as General Secretary of the Communist Party. "Had he remained in the Church," she lamented, "he could have become a bishop."

80. Russia was the last European country to free its serfs. Abolished in 1861, serfdom has provided the legacy of what Yevtushenko calls *poiterpelost*, Russia's servile patience.

81. The word science comes from the Latin word *scientia* which means knowledge. Until quite modern times "knowledge" also meant "magic." The Sanscrit word "Vidya" has this double meaning.

82. Made possible by Johannes Gutenberg's (1400?–1468?) discovery of moveable type.

83. The Greek astronomer Aristarch had put forward a sun-centered theory in the third century BC, but the time was not ripe and his ideas were rejected. See Hans Blumenberg, translation by Robert Wallace, *The Genesis of the Copernican World*, Cambridge, Mass., 1987.

84. Gerardus Mercator (1512–1594), a Flemish cartographer, was the first to draw a map of the globe based on his scientific Mercator projection.
85. History being paradoxical, it took a conservative scholar like Copernicus to cause a revolution by looking at the universe in an entirely unconventional way.
86. Darwin's "law of organic nature" and Marx's "economic law of motion," as well as the work in psychology of Ivan Pavlov (1849–1936), and Sigmund Freud (1856–1939) strengthened the deterministic, mechanistic trend of western society.
87. To the faithful, the major religions of the world offer a greater degree of certainty than western science. Unlike so-called "scientific truths", the absolute truths of religion are unchanging. Religion is not "the opium of the people", as Marx held, but a necessary antidote to the uncertainties of life. Man may never know the absolute, may never find the true meaning of life, but he cannot help seeking it.
88. Technology is derived from the Greek word "techne" meaning art or skill.
89. Arnold Toynbee, who popularized the term, dates the Industrial Revolution to the reign of George III (1760–1820). See E.A. Wrigley, *Continuity, Chance, and Change: the Character of the Industrial Revolution*, Cambridge University Press, New York, 1988.
90. Watt made Newcomen's engine more economical in fuel. He also developed the rotary motion to drive other kinds of machinery. The first known Newcomen engine was erected in 1712.
91. Though it is not until 1957 that world trade in manufactured goods exceeded the trade in primary produce.
92. At the time of the arrival of the Spaniards, Mayan, Aztec, and Inca populations were in the region of 0.5, 12, and 8–10 million respectively.
93. Ecuador, Colombia, and Venezuela.
94. See note 66.
95. It has been estimated that the native population of North America numbered approximately one million.
96. Estimates are twenty-one million native Americans, twelve million blacks, and, among the European casualties, eight million Spaniards.
97. See Alfred W. Crosby cited above.
98. Imports of gold at Seville between 1503 and 1560 totalled hundreds of millions of grams. Silver production of the Spanish Indies in 1570 was about five times Europe's and Africa's combined production thirty years earlier.
99. Friedrich von Gentz, "On the Influence of the Discovery of America on the Prosperity and Culture of the Human Race." translated and quoted in H.S. Commager and Elmo Giordanetti, *Was America a Mistake?; An Eighteenth Century Controversy*, New York, 1967, p. 219.

100. One of the heroes of the American Revolution, the French Marquis de Lafayette, said: "Humanity has won its battle. Liberty now has a country."
101. "And God . . . said . . . replenish the earth and subdue it; and have dominion over . . . every living thing that moveth upon the earth . . ." *Genesis*, I, 28.
102. One of the few battles of any consequence between native Indians and United States Army units.
103. See Daniel Cosio Villegas, *American Extremes*, University of Texas Press, Austin, 1964. pp. 37–38, who speaks of Mexico as a miracle of survival; in contrast he describes the United States as a miracle of fecundity.
104. See William Woodruff, *America's Impact on the World: A Study of the United States in the World Economy, 1750–1970*, London and New York, 1975, p. 39. The quotation is from W.W. Howard, "The Rush to Oklahoma," *Harpers* (18 May 1889) pp. 391–2.
105. Western Europe experienced a fall in agricultural prices, land rents, and land values.
106. Then as now, the countries most attracted by a gold standard were those that stood to gain from it. Because of its access through its ally Portugal to Brazilian, and later Australian and South African gold deposits, Britain led the way. The countries that would gain most from a return to the gold standard are South Africa and the Soviet Union – the leading producers and possessors of gold. If Japan, the United States and Britain seem reluctant to return to the gold standard it is because they stand to gain least. Yet the world economy needs an international monetary standard. Yesteryear it was the British pound tied to gold. Today, in contrast, it is the American dollar, the currency of the world's leading debtor nation.
107. Recognition of America's changing place in the world was made by the European powers in 1892 when their diplomatic representatives in Washington DC were upgraded from minister to ambassador.
108. Comparative figures, per capita, were US $377; Britain $244; Germany $184; France $153; Italy $108; Austria-Hungary $57; Russia $41; Japan $36. Similarly its national income of $37 billion far exceeded that of Germany $12 billion; Britain $11 billion; Russia $7 billion; France $6 billion; Italy $4 billion; Austria-Hungary $3 billion; and Japan $2 billion.
109. See Chapter 4. In 1910, realizing how close to war they had been, Russia and Austria pledged their support of the *status quo*.
110. Helmuth von Moltke, chief of the German Staff at the outbreak of war, is thought to have exaggerated the importance of railways in general mobilization. Nevertheless, strategy (even by 1870) depended less on soldiers' legs and more on railway wheels.
111. In the 1880s Britain had built about four-fifths of world shipping.
112. See Michael Balfour, *The Kaiser and his Times*, Boston, 1964, p. 425.

113. "Were Germany united," said the English writer David Hume in 1748, "it would be the greatest power that ever was in the world."
114. The United Kingdom's share of world manufacturing output declined from 22.9 per cent in 1880 to 13.6 per cent in 1913. A similar downward trend is reflected in Britain's share of world trade which fell from 23.2 per cent in 1880 to 14.1 per cent in 1911–1913.
115. In 1913 France's GNP, its share of world manufacturing production, and its national income were all about half of those of Germany. On the eve of war it planned to mobilize 80 divisions, the Germans 100.
116. Ominously, in the Treaty of 1871 between Germany and France, mention of soldiers' graves (foreshadowing the carnage to come) is made for the first time.
117. See Richard Hough, *The Great War at Sea*, Oxford, 1983. Hough maintains that the unrelenting pressure of the Royal Navy was the prime factor which led to the defeat of the Central Powers on land by 1918.
118. Although the machine-gun had had devastating effect in the Russian-Japanese War of 1904–1905, the war plans of the continental powers left it out of account.
119. At that time France was conscripting 89 per cent of its eligible young males; Germany 53 per cent. Germany's army budget grew from $204 million in 1910 to $442 million in 1914. Similar figures for France were $188 and $197 million.
120. The First International was established in London in 1864. Karl Marx drafted its constitution. The Second International was formed in London in 1889. The Third International resulted from meetings held at Bern in 1919. Since then there have been two separate international organizations of labor: the Third Communist International in Moscow, based on revolutionary principles, and the non-revolutionary Labour and Socialist International in Zürich. When war came, despite all rhetoric, the labor movement shed its internationalism.
121. Before the war ended the 4 per cent (on average) of the national incomes being spent by the combatants before 1914 on armaments had risen to something in the region of 25 to 30 per cent.
122. Rupert Brooke, "The Dead," *The Complete Poems*, New York, 1977, p. 148.
123. In 1900 western Europe accounted for ninety per cent of world industrial production.
124. There was even controversy how dead German airship crew should be buried in England – as soldiers (with military honors), or as pirates.
125. The decision, said the German Chancellor Bethmann Hollweg, who had resolutely opposed the move, meant *"finis Germaniae."*
126. For the sharp divergence between official and non-official accounts of this tragedy – which turned the United States public

against Germany – see Colin Simpson, *The Truth about the Lusitania*, Boston, Mass., 1972.

127. Rupert Brooke, "Peace," cited above, p. 146.
128. Wilfred Owen, "Dulce Et Decorum Est," *The Complete Poems and Fragments*, Vol. I: *The Poems*, New York, London, 1984, p. 140.
129. Published in English in New York in 1926. Spengler jolted people out of their unreasoning faith in the providential nature of progress.
130. Poland had been divided in 1772, 1793, 1795, and 1815 because Britain and France would not risk war. It regained its freedom in 1918, not because of President Wilson, but because Austria-Hungary, Russia, and Germany were convulsed and defeated.
131. In 1929 the Serbo-Croat-Slovene state became Yugoslavia.
132. Under the leadership of Eamon de Valera (1882–1975) Ireland (except Northern Ireland) eventually obtained independence under the Republic of Ireland Act which came into operation in April 1949.
133. During 1915 and 1916, Sir Henry McMahon, British High Commissioner in Egypt, exchanged ten letters with Hussein ibn Ali, Sharif of Mecca. The purpose: to enlist Arab support against the Turks. The promise behind the correspondence, however ambiguously worded, was Arab independence. See *British Parliamentary Papers*, 1939, Misc. No. 3, Cmd. 5957.
134. The Balfour Declaration was contained in a letter dated 2 November 1917, addressed to Lord Rothschild, a British Zionist leader (who had, along with President Wilson's legal aide, Louis Brandeis, an American Zionist, already helped in its drafting). It was signed by Britain's Foreign Secretary, Arthur James Balfour, and appeared in the London *Times*, 9 November 1917.
135. The Dawes and Young Plans were terminated by the Lausanne Conference in 1932.
136. The Revolution of 1905 had forced Nicholas II (who had come to the throne in 1894) to accept an elected Duma (parliament), but its power was limited.
137. In 1903 the Russian Socialist Democratic Party had split into two groups: the Bolsheviks, who wanted party leadership to be restricted to a select number of revolutionaries, and the Mensheviks, who wanted a wider membership and a more democratic leadership.
138. See Leon Trotsky, *A History of the Russian Revolution*, vols. 1–3, New York, 1932.
139. 25 October by the old Julian calendar then used in Russia.
140. The election returns, made known in November 1918, showed the Bolsheviks with 225 out of the 707 delegates.
141. The separate peace treaty between Germany and Russia is only one of the milestones in a long and often co-operative relationship. Following the Treaty of Rapallo in 1922, Russia secretly assisted Germany to rearm.

142. See W. Bruce Lincoln, cited above.
143. See J. Bradley, *Allied Intervention in Russia 1917–1920*, New York, 1968.
144. Contrary to the commonly held opinion that pre-revolutionary Russia was a country of economic stagnation, Russia's growth rate between 1908 and 1914 was 8.8 per cent. In overall production it lagged behind the Western powers.
145. See Chapter 12.
146. Marx's determination to seek redemption *in* this life rather than *from* this life was really a return to the Judaic past; for ancient Jewish theology saw virtue as being rewarded not in the hereafter, but here on earth.
147. It was the socialist theoretician Eduard Bernstein (1850–1932) who said that Marxism is Calvinism without God. Marxism has the comfort of faith and religion without belief in a supreme being.
148. See Max Weber cited above.
149. See David B. Barrett *World Christian Encylopedia*, Oxford University Press, 1982, from which the following figures (and estimates) concerning the major faiths are taken.

Adherents of the world's religions in millions and as a percentage of world population

	1900	%	1980	%	2000	%
Christian	558	34.4	1,433	32.8	2,020	32.3
Atheist	3	.2	911	20.8	1,334	21.3
Muslim	200	12.4	723	16.5	1,201	19.2
Hindu	203	12.5	583	13.3	859	13.7
Buddhist	127	7.8	274	6.3	359	5.7
Jewish	12	.8	17	.4	20	.3
Other	516	31.9	433	9.9	467	7.5

Although the center of Christian missionary work is now in the Americas rather than the Far East, large Roman Catholic populations persist in the Philippines (about 40 million, 79.7 per cent of the population), Vietnam (about 2 million, 3.9 per cent), South Korea (about 1.5 million, 3.9 per cent), Indonesia (about 4 million, 2.7 per cent), Taiwan (about 1/2 million, 2.7 per cent), Papua New Guinea (about 3/4 million, 27 per cent). Islam has also expanded. (See Map XV)
150. Mikhail Gorbachev, *Perestroika*, New York, 1987.
151. Members of the Society of Jesus, founded by the Spaniard Ignatius of Loyola in 1534, and given Papal authorization in 1540, played a leading role in all early East-West relations. The Treaty of Nerchinsk (1689), the first treaty concluded between China and the West, was their doing. In providing a bridge between East and West, they also introduced Confucius to Europe, and the Bible, Copernicus, and Euclid to China.

152. See Philip F. Riley and Others (eds), *The Global Experience*, Vol. II, cited above, pp. 26–27.

153. Certain Jesuits remained behind in Peking to care for the dynastic calendar. Almost two centuries later in 1939 the pope decreed that ancestor worship and Confucian rites were not incompatible with the dogma of the church.

154. For centuries now the Japanese have been living in more concentrated masses than the westerners – which helps to account for the inclination of the Japanese towards group action and group organization.

155. See Philip F. Riley and Others, cited above, pp. 31–32.

156. On the inequity of British importation of opium into China, see J.K. Fairbank and Ssu-yu Teng, *China's Response to the West: A Documentary Survey, 1839–1923*, Camb., Mass., 1954, pp. 24–27.

157. In 1836 British sales of opium in China totalled $18 million; Chinese sales of tea and silk to the British amounted to $17 million.

158. Four new ports – in addition to Canton (Ghangzhou) – were opened up for western trade; trade was regulated to benefit western interests; under the principle of extra-territoriality, British subjects in China could only be tried by British laws. Hong Kong was leased to Britain.

159. The famine of 1877–1879 in northern China left ten million dead.

160. Gun production was restricted as a safeguard against insurrection under the long peace of the Tokugawas; more importantly, in comparison with the much more widely used sword, a gun was culturally unacceptable. See Noel Perrin, *Giving Up the Gun*, Boston, Mass., 1979.

161. During the First World War Japan had made demands upon China that threatened China's independence. In 1915 Japan established its rule in Shantung, Manchuria, and Inner Mongolia.

162. In 1921 Outer Mongolia declared its independence. In 1924 it became the Mongolian People's Republic and was recognized as such by China in 1946; its independence was guaranteed by China and the Soviet Union in February 1950. Tibet's experience was much more ill-starred. Following the establishment of the People's Republic of China in 1949, Communist China proceeded to enforce its will in Tibet. Since the revolt of 1959, when the Dalai Lama fled to India, any aspirations for Tibetan independence have been brutally suppressed.

163. Sun Yat-sen founded the Republic of South China in 1911. See H.Z. Schifferin, *Sun Yat-sen and the Origins of the 1911 Revolution*, University of California Press, 1969.

164. See E. Hahn, *Chiang Kai-shek: An Unauthorized Biography*, New York, 1955.

165. For a first-hand view see the autobiography of Han Suyin, Book Three, *Birdless Summer*, London, 1968.

166. The Chinese Exclusion Act of 1882 made the Chinese the first nationality specifically banned from immigration into the United

States. United States hostility to Japan and the Japanese grew only after its victory over Russia in 1904–1905. The most conspicuous example was President Roosevelt's World War II order to intern Japanese Americans.

167. See David Kaiser, *Economic Diplomacy and the Origins of the Second World War*, Princeton, N.J., 1980.

168. See Alan Bullock, *Hitler: A Study in Tyranny*, New York, 1952.

169. See J.M. Keynes, *The Economic Consequences of the Peace*, New York, 1920, which did much to create the legend of the "Carthaginian Peace" imposed on the Germans at Versailles. An economist of unusual brilliance, Keynes later attained fame as the architect of national economic policies. His unorthodox *General Theory of Economy, Interest and Money* (London, 1936), which among other things introduced the idea of deficit spending by states in recession, aroused controversy among economists throughout the world.

170. See D.M. Smith, *Mussolini: A Biography*, New York, 1982.

171. Most historians attribute the nine-fold increase in Nazi votes to the deepening of the economic crisis. Yet the communal elections of 1929 – a relatively prosperous year – show that the appeal of the Nazis had already begun to grow.

172. History says otherwise. Since ancient Greece and Rome, the demagogue has always been the strangler of civilization.

173. Tacitus tells us that the Roman Republic succumbed to the Caesars because people became sick of disorder.

174. The onset of the Great Depression began with the commercial collapse of the United States in 1929. By 1932 Germany's output and trade had fallen to about half their 1928 figures.

175. See "Great Men in History", Chapter 7, Morris R. Cohen, *The Meaning of Human History*, New York, 1947.

176. His racist laws, his insistence upon Aryan superiority, and his intended colonization of the Slav lands separate Hitler from the German statesmen who preceded him.

177. The League's failure to halt Mussolini in Abyssinia convinced Hitler that the democracies lacked the will to uphold the Covenant of the League.

178. Czechoslovakia was one of a number of nation-states (others were Austria, Hungary, Poland, Yugoslavia, Finland, Estonia, Latvia, and Lithuania) which came into existence as a result of the First Great War. Finland, Estonia, Latvia, and Lithuania gained their independence as a result of the breakdown of Russian rule in 1917–1918. Except for Finland, they were repossessed by the Soviet Union under the secret protocol of the Soviet-German frontier treaty of 1939.

179. For my generation, the word appeasement had a pejorative connotation. However, before 1938 the term was commonly understood to mean a necessary and desirable relation between nations. See Andrew J. Crozier, *Appeasement and Germany's Last Bid for Colonies*, London, 1988.

180. See Anthony Read and David Fisher, *The Deadly Embrace: Hitler,*

Stalin, and the Nazi-Soviet Pact 1939–1941, London, 1988. In 1940 the USSR forcibly annexed Estonia, Latvia, and Lithuania. Finland, attacked in the winter of 1939, offered heroic resistance, but by March 1940 was forced to accept Russia's terms. Because it had violated the Covenant, the USSR was expelled from the League of Nations on 14 December 1939.

181. In the First Great War the Germans had invaded Belgium not knowing what the British would do. This time they knew that an attack upon Poland would bring Britain (and France) into the war. Earlier, on 31 March, sixteen days before Hitler entered Prague, Chamberlain had announced in Parliament that if Poland were to be attacked. "His Majesty's Government would feel themselves bound at once to lend the Polish Government all support in their power." Having declared war, Britain and France found themselves virtually unable to help Poland.

182. Influential in helping to form American policy was J.P. Kennedy (United States ambassador in London). Like many other ardent American isolationists, he supported the powerful America First Movement led by the famous aviator Charles Lindbergh. The America First Movement, which at one time appeared to represent the majority opinion in the United States, died within hours after Japan's attack on Pearl Harbor in December 1941.

183. Well might Winston Churchill write: "I slept that night with the peace of one who knows he has been saved."

184. Including Edouard Daladier, Georges Bonnet, Pierre Laval, Stanley Baldwin, Samuel Hoare, Ramsay MacDonald, John Simon, Edward Halifax, and Neville Chamberlain.

185. In 1938 Germany devoted to war preparation seventeen per cent of its GNP, an amount exceeding that of Britain, France, and the United States combined.

186. See Lieutenant Commander P.K. Kemp, RN (Ret.), *Key to Victory*, Boston, 1958, p. 26.

187. Only Portugal, Switzerland, Sweden, Eire, and Turkey succeeded in remaining neutral.

188. At this point United States' naval protection against German warships was advanced to the mid-Atlantic; economic and military aid was given to Britain.

189. "The hand that held the dagger," said President Roosevelt in a speech made at the University of Virginia on the same day, "has struck it into the back of its neighbor."

190. In an effort to keep France in the war, Churchill offered France what Cromwell had earlier offered the Dutch: common citizenship.

191. Churchill refused to compromise.

192. See H.G. Dahms, *Die Geschichte des zweiten Weltkrieges*, Munich, 1983, p. 211, note 64. German civilian deaths from Allied bombing were in the region of 570,000, p. 621, note 15.

193. See W.H. Baldwin, *Battles Lost and Won*, New York, 1966, pp. 112–113.

194. Emulating Hitler's annexation of Czechoslovakia in 1939, Mussolini annexed Albania. With disastrous results, he went on to attack Greece in October 1940.
195. These efforts were frustrated by communist resistance led by Marshall Tito (Josip Broz, 1892–1980) who later became head of the Socialist Federal Republic of Yugoslavia.
196. See John Toland, *Infamy, Pearl Harbor and its Aftermath*, New York, 1982. Toland argues that Roosevelt and his top advisors knew about the planned attack but remained silent in order to draw the United States into the war.
197. For three years, from June 1941 until June 1944, the Red Army inflicted over 90 per cent of German Army battle losses.
198. At the outset of the battle, in October 1942, the British had overwhelming superiority in the air, three times the number of soldiers, and six times as many tanks as the Germans and the Italians.
199. Being an ally rather than an enemy was to make a very great difference to Italy once the war was done.
200. The odds against the Germans on the eastern front were formidable: in manpower, in armor, in aircraft, they had a fifth, or less than a fifth (especially in the air) of Russia's strength. Yet in the course of the Russian campaign, more than five million officers and men surrendered to the Germans.
201. The Allies had an almost inexhaustible supply of troops, a 20 to 1 advantage in armor, and a 25 to 1 advantage in aircraft. In addition they had complete command of the waters separating Britain from the continent.
202. Although none of the Japanese victories had a crippling effect on overall allied strategy.
203. Although Truman thought the bomb would save half-a-million Allied lives, a worst-case scenario of the time envisioned 20,000 deaths.
204. The Japanese had 600,000 troops in the area.
205. *World War II Deaths*

	Military	Civilian	Jewish victims°
Austria	380,000	145,000	(60,000)
Belgium	9,600	75,000	(25,000)
Britain	271,300	60,000°°	–
British Commonwealth	133,000	–	–
Bulgaria	18,500	n.a.	14,000
China	1,324,500	10,000,000*	–
Czechoslovakia	6,700	310,000	(250,000)
Denmark	4,300	n.a.	–

(*continued on p. 264*)

	Military	Civilian	Jewish victims°
Estonia	–	140,000	**
Finland	79,000	n.a.	–
France	205,700	173,300	(65,000)
Germany°°	4,000,000	3,100,000	188,000
Greece	16,400	155,300	(60,000)
Hungary	147,400	280,000	(200,000)
Italy	262,400	93,000	(8,000)
Japan	1,140,400	953,000	–
Latvia	–	120,000	**
Lithuania	–	170,000	**
Netherlands	13,700	236,300	(104,000)
Norway	4,800	5,400	900
Poland	320,000	6,028,000	(3,200,000)
Romania	519,800	465,000	(425,000)
USA	292,100	–	–
USSR	13,600,000	7,720,000	(1,252,000)
Yugoslavia	305,000	1,355,000	(55,000)
Total	23,054,600	31,584,300	5,906,900

° Figures in parentheses are also included as civilian casualties.
°° Figures taken from H.G. Dahms cited above p. 616. * Estimate.
** Baltic States (228,000).
Source: Robert Goralski (ed.), *World War II Almanac*, New York, 1981.

206. See Arno J. Mayer, *Why did the Heavens Not Darken? The Final Solution in History*, New York, 1989. Also Charles S. Maier, *The Unmasterable Past: History, Holocaust and German Identity*, Cambridge Mass., 1989. Also Lucy S. Dawidowicz, "Perversions of the Holocaust," *Commentary*, October 1989.
207. Not Italy, which avoided indictments by changing sides in 1944.
208. Said Jackson: "The wrongs which we seek to condemn and punish have been so calculated, so malignant and so devastating, that civilization cannot tolerate their being ignored because it cannot survive their being repeated". Robert H. Jackson, "Opening Address" in *Trial of German War Criminals*, Senate Doc. no. 129, 79th Cong., 1st sess., Washington DC, Government Printing Office, 1946, p. 1.
209. See H.G. Dahms cited above, p. 618.
210. Those on trial at Nuremberg and Tokyo used the same defense as Shakespeare's soldiers accused of crime in *Henry V*: "We know enough if we know we are the king's men. Our obedience to the king wipes the crime of it out of us."
211. See Ann and John Tusa, *The Nuremberg Trial*, New York, 1984, also, R.H. Minear, *Victor's Justice: The Tokyo War Crimes Trial*, Princeton, 1971.

212. At the Cairo Conference in 1943 Roosevelt had insisted on treating China as the fifth power. Churchill had demurred.
213. About one-third of present-day Poland was German territory. The Yalta settlement not only laid the groundwork for future discord between Poland and Germany, it also made Poland a hostage to Russia.
214. Because the Russians were now feared more than the Germans, and the weakening of Germany would have meant the strengthening of Soviet Communism, some Americans and Britons (particularly Churchill) prevented Secretary of the Treasury Henry Morgenthau from reducing Germany to a pastoral state. The Russians were the strongest supporters of the Morgenthau Plan.
215. A communist-led attempt to seize power in Greece in 1944 was thwarted by British intervention. Further communist attempts to seize power (1946–1949) were foiled by United States intervention.
216. In current dollars, its GNP had risen from approximately $80 billion (1939) to $220 billion (1945). America came out of the war with two-thirds of the gold reserves, half the world's manufacturing output, half the world's exports, half the world's income, and half the world's shipping.
217. See Thomas B. Cochran, *The Nuclear Arms Industry*, Natural Resources Defense Council, Washington DC, 1987.
218. See Jonathan R. Adelman, *Prelude to the Cold War*, London, 1988.
219. Roosevelt's ideas reflected the same grand design for world peace put forward by Metternich, the Austrian foreign secretary, in the Holy Alliance of 1815. It is chiefly due to Roosevelt that the idea of a United Nations came to fruition. President Wilson had had a similar aim in helping to form the League of Nations in 1919.
220. See Nicholas Bethell, *The Last Secret: The Delivery to Stalin of Over Two Million Russians by Britain and the United States*, New York, 1974.
221. In October 1947 the Cominform (successor to the Comintern – the Third Communist International – which was dissolved by Stalin in 1943) was reestablished to coordinate communist action throughout the world.
222. In numbers of dead (292,131), it was the costliest war they had fought since the Civil War (214,938).
223. Proposed in 1947 by United States Secretary of State, General George Marshall (1880–1959), it provided western European countries (the aid was rejected by the Soviet bloc) with $13 billion of economic and financial assistance. Introduced in 1948, Marshall Aid was discontinued in 1952. See Michael J. Hogan, *The Marshall Plan*, Cambridge, 1987.
224. See Ann and John Tusa, *The Berlin Blockade*, London, 1988.
225. Member states in 1990 were: Belgium, Canada, Denmark, Federal Republic of Germany, France (nominal membership since 1966), Greece, Iceland, Italy, Luxembourg, Netherlands, Portugal, Spain, Turkey, United Kingdom, and the United States.
226. The death of the Portuguese dictator António de Oliveira Salazar

in 1968 prompted a struggle between the militarists and the communists.

227. Born the son of a farmer, Mao Zedong helped found the Chinese Communist Party in 1921. After 1935 he dominated it. After 1949, having defeated the Nationalist forces, he became the first Chairman of the People's Republic of China, a position he held until his death. Contrary to Marxist doctrine, he was the first communist leader to express the view that revolution must come from the peasantry rather than the urban proletariat. See Stuart Schram, *Mao Tse-Tung*, New York, 1966.

228. It included Australia, France, New Zealand, Pakistan, the Philippines, Thailand, the United Kingdom, and the United States.

229. It was meant to guard against possible Russian aggression. It included Iran, Iraq, Pakistan, Turkey, and the United Kingdom. Although the United States had sponsored the defense agreement, it refused to become a full member. Iraq withdrew in 1959.

230. See Robert Conquest cited above.

231. The year that hostilities between the Soviet Union and Japan were officially terminated. With Russian opposition withdrawn, Japan took its place as a member of the United Nations.

232. See P.F. Riley cited above, pp. 257–262.

233. On 20 May 1989 India became the first Third World nation to admit developing an intermediate-range ballistic missile.

234. See Chapter 12. Eighteenth-century revolutionary France and twentieth-century Czarist Russia are historical warnings of the dangers involved in reckless borrowing.

235. Although the composition of output and different relative prices make any comparison of GNP's hazardous, ranked by 1988 real gross national product in trillions of 1988 US dollars, the general magnitudes are as follows: United States $4.86, USSR $2.54, Japan $1.76, Germany $0.87, France $0.76, Britain $0.76, Italy $0.75.

236. The Indian National Congress Party, which eventually succeeded in its struggle for independence, was greatly assisted at its outset by Englishmen.

237. See M.K. Gandhi, *An Autobiography*, Boston, Mass., 1957.

238. See H. Belitho, *Jinnah*, London, 1954.

239. He was the first Prime Minister of independent India (1947–1964); and was four times President of the Indian National Congress Party (1929–1930, 1936–1937, 1946, and 1951–1954). See *The Autobiography of Jawaharlal Nehru*, New York, 1941.

240. The military dictator of Burma, Ne Win (born 1911), who has influenced the course of events in Burma more than any other man since 1945, received his military training from the Japanese in Formosa (Taiwan) in 1941.

241. Achmed Sukarno (1901–1970) helped to found the Indonesian National Party in 1928. In 1955 he hosted the Bandung Conference of non-aligned African and Asian nations. In 1959 he assumed

dictatorial powers. In 1967, following a military coup, he was deposed.

242. Part of the old Ottoman province of Damascus (most of which is now Israel) came under the British mandate for Palestine in 1921. In 1946 it was renamed Jordan.

243. Approved at the San Remo Conference in 1920, the Balfour Declaration was incorporated into the mandate for Palestine granted to Britain by the League of Nations in 1922. In the Palestine National Charter adopted by the Fourth Palestine National Assembly, Cairo, 17 July 1968, the Balfour Declaration was declared "null and void."

244. The publication in 1896 of Theodor Herzl's *Judenstaat* precipitated Zionism as an active Jewish world movement.

245. Even earlier than the figures given above, a 1893–1894 census by the Ottoman Empire, which controlled Palestine until the end of the First World War, showed a total of 9,817 Jews in Palestine and 371,969 Muslims.

246. The report of the King-Crane Commission of 1919 was considered pro-Arab and anti-imperialist. The Commissioners recommended that a greatly reduced Zionist program be attempted by the Paris Peace Conference. "This would have to mean . . . that the project for making Palestine distinctly a Jewish commonwealth should be given up."

247. OPEC was founded in 1960. Members in 1989 were Algeria, Ecuador, Gabon, Indonesia, Iran, Iraq, Kuwait, Libya, Nigeria, Qatar, Saudi Arabia, United Arab Emirates, and Venezuela. Saudi Arabia, Iran, and Iraq lead both in oil quotas and reserves.

248. Israel has always refused to negotiate with the PLO because it denied Israel's right to exist. In 1985, King Hussein of Jordan and Yasser Arafat of the PLO declared their willingness to make peace with Israel provided Israel withdrew from the territories occupied in 1967. Also in 1985 Arafat undertook to accept United Nations Resolution 242 guaranteeing Israel's right to exist if the United States explicitly endorsed the right of Palestinians to self-determination. On 13 November 1988 the PLO accepted U.N. Resolution 242.

249. In September 1978 meetings took place between President Jimmy Carter, Egyptian President Anwar Sadat, and Israeli Prime Minister Menachem Begin to formulate a 'peace plan' to lessen the growing tensions in the Middle East between Arabs (including Palestinians) and Jews. Although a Peace Treaty between Israel and Egypt was signed in 1979, whereby the Sinai was returned to Egypt, in 1990 the basic problems – the future of the occupied territories, the question of Palestinian autonomy, and the international status of Jerusalem – remained unaddressed.

250. See Tariq Ali, *Can Pakistan Survive? The Death of a State*, New York, 1984.

251. See Michio Morishima, *Why has Japan 'succeeded?'*, Cambridge, England, 1982.
252. The eighth and ninth were both French; US Citicorp ranked tenth. Twenty-eight of the world's largest banks were owned by Japan. The next in line were the United States with thirteen, West Germany and France both with ten. In 1990 Japan had the world's leading financial institutions; its stock market capitalization was more than half of the world total; its Postal Savings Bureau was the largest savings institution in the world. The Japanese not only save money, they save everything. They are just as psychologically impelled to save as Americans are to spend. See Akio Morita, *Made in Japan*, Tokyo, 1987.
253. See *Annual Survey of World Business*, Wall Street Journal, 21 September 1990.
254. Although West Germany's trade surplus with the rest of the world in 1989 exceeded that of Japan ($30 billion a month compared with Japan's surplus of $20 billion) one heard few complaints against it. One reason why there is less criticism is that Germany's trade surplus is more evenly distributed in the world.
255. See *Japan's Economic Challenge*, Joint Economic Committee, Congress of the United States, October 1990, Section VII.
256. See Martin and Susan Tolchin, *Buying into America*, New York, 1988. For a more sanguine view see Edward M. Graham and Paul R. Krugman, *Foreign Direct Investment in the United States*, Washington DC, 1990.
257. According to a 1987 study by the American Chamber of Commerce in Japan (A.C.C.J.), "foreign companies have invested more in Japan in the last five years than they had in the previous thirty years combined."
258. Compounding America's overwhelming reliance on Japanese funds has been the gradual shift in the United States from saving to spending. Compared to Japan (fifteen per cent) and West Germany (thirteen per cent), the United States personal savings rate had fallen from nine per cent of GNP in the mid-1970s to three per cent in 1989.
259. Public and private United States debt in 1988 totalled about $9 trillion – more than twice the country's GNP. Of this sum, private consumer debt (which had grown 40 per cent over the previous three years) accounted for $2.2 trillion. In mid-1987 consumer installment debt stood at a record $591 billion; Americans were buying on credit about 18–20 per cent more than they were earning.
260. In 1987 the increase in China's GNP equalled South Korea's total GNP.
261. Taiwan's effect upon the world economy still exceeds that of the People's Republic of China. As Taiwan's currency is tied to the US dollar (the same is true of South Korea, Singapore, and Hong Kong), depreciation of the dollar helps to boost Taiwan's competitiveness.

262. In 1978 Japan signed a Treaty of Peace and Friendship with China.
263. In 1988–1989 exports of Australian manufactured goods were valued at almost $23 billion.
264. But since 1985 being increasingly wooed by the Soviets. The USSR has improved its ties with Egypt, Oman, the United Arab Emirates, Kuwait, Saudi Arabia, and Jordan. With its increased naval presence in the Persian Gulf, the United States is trying to offset the advance of Soviet influence.
265. Prior to Britain's nineteenth century intervention, Kuwait was an Ottoman province controlled from Basra. In 1922, to protect its interests, Britain drew borders which denied Iraq access to the sea.
266. The percentage of Asian migrants entering the United States multiplied more than four times between 1960 and 1980: from roughly nine to 42 per cent of total immigration. Immigrants from Latin America almost doubled: from about 20 to 40 per cent. Europe, at one time the chief source of United States immigrants, provided only ten per cent of the total in 1988.
267. In addition to the wonders of ancient Egypt, the sub-Saharan empires and kingdoms of Ghana (eighth to eleventh century), Mali (twelfth to fourteenth century), and Songhai (fourteenth to sixteenth century) were known for their cultural richness.
268. Founded as a colony for freed American slaves, it gained its independence in 1847. The slave trade was outlawed by the leading European powers (and the United States) in the first half of the nineteenth century, but continued to flourish between East Africa and the Middle East.
269. Following the Berlin Conference of 1884, Germany took possession of Togoland and Cameroon. It also obtained a block of coastal land which became German South West Africa. Germany lost these territories to Britain in 1919.
270. Proclaimed the protectorate of German East Africa in 1890. In return for a German promise to keep out of Uganda, the British gave up German Heligoland, which they had obtained from Denmark in 1815. German East Africa, later called Tanganyika, with all other German possessions in Africa were seized by the British during World War I.
271. See Lance E. Davies and A. Huttenback, *Mammon and the Pursuit of Empire*, Cambridge, 1988.
272. See T.R.H. Davenport, *South Africa: A Modern History*, 2nd ed., 1978.
273. Despite the almost uniformly discouraging history of such measures in the present century, in the 1980s the United Nations tried to strengthen its hand against South Africa by imposing sanctions. American sanctions have been lifted against Poland, but in 1989 they remained in force against Cuba, Libya, Nicaragua, and South Africa. In 1990 the United Nations imposed sanctions against Iraq. See Robin Renwick, *Economic Sanctions*, Harvard University Center for International Affairs, Cambridge Mass., 1982.

274. On 12 February 1990 Nelson Mandela was released after 27 years in prison.
275. On African accomplishments see "Whose Dream Was It Anyway? Twenty-Five Years Of African Independence", Michael Crowder, *African Affairs*, January, 1987.
276. The OAU sought the furtherance of African unity, the coordination of the political, economic, cultural, health, scientific, and defense policies, and the elimination of colonialism in Africa.
277. AIDS, which is spreading at an alarming rate in some parts of Africa, might be a crucial factor determining future demographic trends.
278. In 1921, after seven years of dispute, the USA paid Colombia $25 million for the loss of its Panama territory.
279. Proclaimed by President James Monroe on 2 December 1823, it forbad further colonization of the western hemisphere by Europeans. However, until well into the twentieth century, it was the British not the American navy that guarded the Latin American republics from outside political interference and military intimidation.
280. In the nineteenth century national rivalries and boundary disputes caused the republics to fight at least five wars among themselves. Between 1825–1828 Brazil fought Argentina. Between 1842–1852 Argentina fought Uruguay and then Brazil. Between 1864–1870 Paraguay fought Brazil, Uruguay, and Argentina. Between 1836–1839 and 1879–1883 Chile fought Peru and Bolivia.
281. On 19 January 1917 the German Foreign Secretary Alfred Zimmermann sent a coded message to von Eckhardt, German Minister in Mexico, trying to enlist Mexico's support in the event the United States entered the war. The Germans undertook to restore Mexico's lost territories in New Mexico, Texas, and Arizona. The message was intercepted and released to the USA press on 1 March 1917.
282. The League intervened twice during the 1930s: in efforts to halt warfare between Bolivia and Paraguay (1928–1938), and Peru and Colombia (1932–1935).
283. The value of a country's exports varied all the way from 20 to 40 per cent of its GNP.
284. Arthur Salter quoted in *The Problem of International Investment*, R.I.I.A., 1937, reprinted ed., New York, 1965, p. 11.
285. Based in Washington, membership included: Argentina, Bolivia, Brazil, Chile, Colombia, Costa Rica, Dominican Republic, Ecuador, El Salvador, Guatemala, Haiti, Honduras, Mexico, Nicaragua, Panama, Paraguay, Peru, USA, Uruguay, Venezuela. (Trinidad and Tobago, Barbados, Jamaica, Grenada, and Surinam were added later). The OAS was effective in settling regional conflicts between Nicaragua and Costa-Rica in the 1940s and 1950s, a boundary dispute between Nicaragua and Honduras in 1957, and the war between El Salvador and Honduras in 1969.
286. Castro, having overthrown Fulgencio Batista in 1959, expropriated the landholdings and refineries of the United States sugar

companies in June 1960. In October that year he went on to nationalize many United States-owned financial, commercial, and industrial undertakings. The United States responded by reducing its Cuban sugar quota by 95 per cent, by imposing a trade embargo, and by breaking off diplomatic relations in January 1961. In February 1962, at a meeting of the OAS at Punta del Este, Uruguay, the United States succeeded in excluding socialist Cuba from the OAS.

287. Carter reaffirmed the United States' commitment to "honor national sovereignty and the principle of non-intervention." Under the treaty ratified in 1978 the Panama Canal will pass into complete Panamanian control by the end of the century.

288. Rebel leader Augusto Sandino, having been assassinated in 1934 by the Nicaraguan National Guard, became a national hero. Led by Daniel Ortega, in 1979 the Sandinistas were successful in ending the forty-year US-backed dictatorial regime of Anastasio Somoza Debayle. See Neill Macaulay, *The Sandino Affair*, Durham, N.C., 1984.

289. Quoted by the *Wall Street Journal*, p. 11. 10 August 1990. A military coup in Suriname in December 1990 offers evidence of a swing in the opposite direction.

290. Yet it is worth remembering that for all its political instability, Latin America has had only four social revolutions: Mexico (1910–1917), Argentina (1942), Cuba (1959), and Nicaragua (1979–1990). The will to change the social structure (the basis of any revolution) of Latin American countries is absent.

291. Oil prices quadrupled from $2.70 per barrel in 1972 to $9.76 in 1976. The second round of oil price increases in 1979 raised the price per barrel to $33.47 in 1982.

292. The Alliance for Progress was formally brought into existence at the Inter-American Economic and Social Conference at Punta del Este, Uruguay, in August 1961.

293. Several countries began agrarian reform; one of the larger and most successful was Chile's, launched in 1965. From 1973 on, the government of General Pinochet undermined these efforts.

294. By the mid-1960s once-dominant Britain was taking only about nine per cent of Latin America's exports and supplying a little more than five per cent of its imports. Similar figures for imports and exports of the United States were about 40 per cent. By 1970 half of United States imports came from the western hemisphere (including Canada); almost half the total exports of United States manufactures went to Central and South America.

295. In 1970 West Germany replaced the United States as the world's leading exporter of manufactured goods. The USA recovered its leadership in 1989.

296. In 1989 Japan supplanted the United States as the largest donor of foreign aid.

297. Brazil's external debt-repayment in 1989 (on a principal of $115 billion) was 4.5 per cent of its GNP which in 1989 increased 0.5 per

cent. To make matters worse, the world dollar price for its primary produce continued to decline.

298. LAFTA was established under the Treaty of Montevideo, Uruguay, in June 1960. Members were Argentina, Brazil, Chile, Mexico, Paraguay, Peru, and Uruguay. Colombia and Ecuador joined in 1961, Venezuela and Bolivia in 1966 and 1967 respectively.

299. The groundwork was laid by the Treaty of Central American Economic Integration, December 1960; it included El Salvador, Guatemala, Honduras (withdrew in 1969), and Nicaragua; Costa Rica joined in 1962. It was also called the Organization of Central American States or ODECA (Organización de Estados Centroamericanos).

300. Members were Bolivia, Chile (withdrew 1976) Colombia, Ecuador, and Peru.

301. Members were Argentina, Bolivia, Brazil, Uruguay, and Paraguay.

302. Members were Barbados, Guyana, Jamaica, Trinidad and Tobago. They were joined in 1974 by Antigua, Belize, Dominica, Grenada, St Lucia, St Vincent, Monserrat, and St Kitts-Nevis-Anguilla. It was also called CARIFTA (Caribbean Free Trade Association) founded early in 1968.

303. Perhaps it is a reflection of declining United States influence in the region, as well as a loss of belief in grandiose schemes, that the Caribbean Basin Initiative (CBI), a joint effort in 1982 by the United States, Canada, Mexico, and Venezuela to promote trade, investment, and aid, should have such a small budget ($350 million).

304. In protest to the austerity programs imposed by the World Bank and the IMF, in March 1989 Brazil experienced the largest general strike in its history.

305. In Chile the church initiated agrarian reform; in El Salvador it has championed human rights. It is no accident that a Theology of Liberation flourishes in this continent. Currently the "communidades de base" (church sponsored grass roots groups) are a most important dynamic element in Latin American life.

306. Thailand, nominally free, was divided into British and French spheres of influence.

307. Figures drawn from *United Nations Conference on Trade and Development Report 1989*, Part II, The Least Developed Countries. U. N., New York, 1990.

308. The World Bank in its assessment of developing-country debt for 1990 gave a total of $1.341 trillion, up six per cent from $1.261 trillion in 1989. For developing countries the Persian Gulf crisis has compounded an already difficult situation.

309. On the face of it, the peak share of United States GNP allocated to defense, 6.5 per cent in 1986–1987, is small compared with the 39 per cent allocated in 1944–1945, the 14.9 per cent allocated in 1953 during the Korean War, or the ten per cent allocated in 1968

during the Vietnam War. In March 1990 the United States still held a dominating position (both in manufacturing output and employment) among the Organization for Economic Co-operation and Development (OECD) nations.

310. "This conjunction of an immense military establishment and a large arms industry is new in the American experience. We must guard against the acquisition of unwarranted influence, whether sought or unsought by the military-industrial complex. The potential for the disastrous rise of misplaced power exists and will persist."

311. See William Hartung *et al*, *The Economic Consequences of a Nuclear Freeze*, New York: Council on Economic Priorities, 1984.

312. The Middle East is not the only part of the world where religious wars are under way. Fighting is endemic between Protestants and Catholics in Northern Ireland; between Hindus, Muslims, and Sikhs in India; and between Buddhists and Hindus in Sri Lanka.

313. The easily computed numerical measures of power used by recent authors writing about the decline of nations place too great a reliance on our present cult of numbers. The rise and fall of the powers is much more problematical than tidy columns of figures suggest. No figure can explain the all-important human element. See my review of Paul Kennedy's *The Rise and Fall of the Great Powers*, New York, 1987, in *The American Historical Review*, Vol. 94. No. 3. June 1989, pp. 719–721.

314. Figures drawn from *World Military and Social Expenditures*, 13th edition, edited by Ruth Leger Sivard, World Priorities, Washington DC 1989.

315. While the treaty undoubtedly creates a more constructive climate for arms control, it deals with fewer than four per cent of the nuclear warheads in existence. The two major obstacles to the reduction of overall strategic arsenals in 1990 were the Soviets' 308 heavy land-based missiles presently aimed at the United States, and the American "Star Wars" program.

316. Dilatory attempts to establish international control of chemical and biological weapons have been made since 1969.

317. Nineteenth-century world population was thought to have expanded more rapidly than in any other period of history. Twentieth-century population has grown approximately four times faster.

318. Formed in August 1967 ASEAN members are Indonesia, Malaysia, the Philippines, Singapore, and Thailand.

319. Inspired by Jamal ad-Din al-Afghani (1838–1897) and the Arab awakening of the nineteenth century, and in response to increased Jewish immigration into Palestine, the Arab League was formed in Cairo, Egypt in 1945. Original members were Egypt, Iraq, Saudi Arabia, Syria, Lebanon, Jordan, and Yemen. Membership in 1989 also included Algeria, Bahrain, Kuwait, Libya, Mauritania, Morocco, Oman, Qatar, Somalia, Sudan, Tunisia, the United Arab Emirates, and the Yemen Peoples Democratic Republic.

320. See Chapter 13.
321. See Chapter 14.
322. A need foreseen by Winston Churchill, Jean Monnet (1888–1979), and Robert Schuman (1886–1963). The original six member states were: Belgium, France, Federal Republic of Germany, Luxembourg, Italy, and the Netherlands. The United Kingdom, the Irish Republic and Denmark became members in 1973; Greece, Spain, and Portugal were added in 1985. By 1990 the EC comprised 320 million people in twelve countries, speaking nine different languages.
323. The European Parliamentary Assembly dates back to the signing of the Statute of the Council of Europe in May 1949. Founding members were Belgiun, Denmark, France, the Irish Republic, Italy, Luxembourg, the Netherlands, Norway, Sweden, and the United Kingdom. Many other European states subsequently joined the Assembly.
324. The General Agreement on Tariffs and Trade (GATT) was signed by the United States and twenty-two other nations in 1947. While the Reagan Administration tended to reverse the trend, since 1945 America has fostered the freedom and expansion of world trade before meetings of GATT. GATT, however, could be undone if the changes going on in Europe (EC) and North America (a proposed free trade area between the US, Canada, and Mexico) were to lead to world trade being divided among protective regional trading blocs.
325. The Kellog-Briand Pact of 1928 foolishly outlawed war while taking no steps to prevent it.
326. From the Chinese point of view, three things have hitherto prevented the normalization of relations with Russia: the Soviet's support for Vietnam in Cambodia, Russia's intervention in Afghanistan, and the Sino-Soviet frontier dispute. The frontier dispute remains. Following Gorbachev's visit to Beijing in May 1989, the first of its kind in thirty years, the Chinese (in the statement of rapprochement) expressed caution at renewing the relations with their Soviet neighbor.
327. See *Soviet Military Power, 1988*, Department of Defence, Washington DC, 1988.
328. It was Frederick II, the Great, of Prussia (1740–1786) who wrote *Testament Politique* (1752 and 1768) which embodied the belief that Reason of State (*raison d'etat*) should overrule law and international obligation. The Venetians, arguing that reasons of state justified the end (and in so doing removed politics from morals) had spoken of "Ragione di Stato". See G.P. Gooch, *Frederick the Great*, New York, 1947.
329. In a 1986 ruling of the International Court of Justice concerning the illegal mining by the United States of Nicaragua's harbors, the United States was found in violation of international law. Before the ruling it had already withdrawn from the compulsory jurisdic-

tion of the court. Since then it has again accepted the court's jurisdiction.
330. Of the four kinds of lies – lies, damned lies, statistics, and government statements – the official lie in our age has become the biggest. Perhaps George Orwell said it all: "Political language is designed to make lies sound truthful and murder respectable."
331. See D.P. Moynihan, *On the Law of Nations*, Cambridge, Mass., 1990.
332. Eighteenth century philosopher Immanuel Kant argued that war would only cease when there was nothing left to fight about, or when new moral insights were obtained. See his *Plan for Perpetual Peace*, 1795.

Index

Index